The South:
Old and New Frontiers

The South: Old and New Frontiers

Selected Essays of Frank Lawrence Owsley

Edited by Harriet Chappell Owsley

Published by
The University of Georgia Press
Athens 30601

Acknowledgements

Grateful acknowledgement is made to the following who have granted permission for the reprinting of the copyrighted material from the periodicals and books here shown:

University of Chicago Press. For "Local Defense and the Downfall of the Confederacy: A Study in State Rights" from *State Rights in the Confederacy* (Chicago, 1925), "America and the Freedom of the Seas, 1860–1865" from *Essays in Honor of William E. Dodd,* ed. Avery Craven (Chicago, 1935), and "Why Europe Did Not Intervene" from *King Cotton Diplomacy,* rev. ed. (Chicago, 1959).

The Georgia Review. For "A Southerner's View of Abraham Lincoln," XII (Spring 1958), and "Democracy Unlimited," XV (Summer 1961).

The Journal of Southern History. For "The Fundamental Cause of the Civil War: Egocentric Sectionalism," VII (February 1941), and "The Pattern of Migration and Settlement on the Southern Frontier," XI (May 1945). Copyright 1941, 1945, by the Southern Historical Association.

Louisiana State University Press. For "A Rebel War Clerk and His Diary" from *The Southern Review,* o. s., I (Winter 1936), and "Plain Folk and Their Role in Southern History" from *Plain Folk of the Old South* (Baton Rouge, 1949).

North Carolina Historical Review. For "Defeatism in the Confederacy," III (July 1926).

Harriet Chappell Owsley, literary executrix of the late Frank Lawrence Owsley. For "The Making of Andrew Jackson," "The Pillars of Agrarianism," "The Soldier Who Walked With God," and "Lucius Quintus Cincinnatus Lamar" from *The American Review,* I (May 1933), IV (February and April 1935), and V (September 1935).

Vanderbilt University Press. For the quotation from *Fugitives' Reunion: Conversations at Vanderbilt, May 3–5, 1956,* ed. Rob Roy Purdy (Nashville, 1959).

Frank Lawrence Owsley: A Chronology

1890	Born in Montgomery County, Alabama, January 20.
1906–1909	Attended Fifth District Agricultural School, Wetumpka, Alabama. (The curriculum included two years of college.)
1909–1911	Attended Alabama Polytechnic Institute at Auburn and was graduated as valedictorian.
1912	Awarded the master of science degree in history with honors by Alabama Polytechnic Institute.
1912–1914	Taught at Fifth District Agricultural School.
1914–1915	Instructor in history at Alabama Polytechnic Institute.
1915–1916	Farmed and studied law.
1916–1917	Attended graduate school at the University of Chicago, receiving the master of arts in June.
1917–1919	Served briefly in the armed forces and returned to graduate school.
1919–1920	Professor of History, Birmingham-Southern College.
1920	Married Harriet Chappell in Birmingham.
1920–1924	Assistant Professor of History, Vanderbilt University.
1924	Awarded doctor of philosophy degree, *magna cum laude,* by University of Chicago.
1924–1927	Associate Professor, Vanderbilt University.
1927–1928	Guggenheim Fellow in England and France.
1928–1949	Professor, Vanderbilt University.
1948	Walter Lynwood Fleming Lecturer, Louisiana State University.
1949–1956	Friedman Professor of American History, University of Alabama.
1952–1955	Chairman, Department of History, University of Alabama.
1955	Blazer Lecturer, University of Kentucky.
1956	Fulbright Lecturer, St. Johns College, Cambridge University.
1956	Died, October 21, at Winchester, England.

Contents

Foreword

Frank Owsley has written the three crucial books on the Civil War, crucial in the sense that, without them, we could not understand the true nature of that revolution, nor its outcome. The first book, *State Rights in the Confederacy*, has for subject a common mind made inflexible by an abstract political principle and so incapable before the changing flow of circumstance. The actuality was this: there would be no Confederacy until it had established itself by military victory. The curious mind which took the rhetorical statement of withdrawal from the old Union as a fait accompli, not the provisional act it was, is presented in all its disastrous consequences in "Local Defense and the Downfall of the Confederacy," one of the most radical essays in the collection.

Local defense is one kind of evidence. The book must be read to comprehend how total was the effect of this attitude upon the fortunes of war and the original concept of the Federal Union. In the Southern mind the rights of the states came to pre-empt the full meaning of the federal system. Under the long sectional struggle against the partisan pressure from the Northeast this mind took one part of the system and forgot the balanced whole. It is understandable, but as a principle it has the same limitation as the divine right of kings. In Christendom the office of kingship represented the profane branch of a divine order, only God being sovereign. The person holding the office had no divine right nor ever had. He had responsibilities and prerogatives. The king represented God's sovereign power, not his own. The misunderstanding about this allowed the Stuarts to extend the divinity of the office to themselves as persons. The office was immortal; but as persons they were mortal, as history so brutally showed. In the same kind of way the principle of State Rights extended limited and specific powers to unlimited and selfish ends on the part of the states, and more narrowly, to the private wills of governors and various politicians. The limits of the divided powers was not only ignored but in the Confederacy itself gave rise to an internecine controversy which impaired the common defense. It makes no difference that other sections had already violated the fact and spirit of the Union. The folly arising from this state of mind exposed itself when, towards the end of the war, certain states (with the sympathy of most) forgot that the common war had to be fought both legally and sensibly from Richmond, and rebelled against the central government—that is against themselves as states and people. The absurdity and vanity of this attitude displays itself in Governor Brown of Georgia, who ordered the Georgia troops home just before the battle of the first Bull Run, because they had taken Georgia rifles out of that state.

In *King Cotton Diplomacy,* his greatest and most lasting contribution to the subject, Mr. Owsley exposes further this state of mind. The book is primarily about the Confederacy's foreign policy. With an innocence which today would be appalling, the Southern farmers, not the state, acted politically on what they took to be an economic law, that cotton was king. These men took for truth what England had been telling them for years, that the English economy depended upon Southern cotton and so that country must be compelled to side actively with the Confederacy. So widespread was this belief among the Southern farmers and planters that most of the 1861 crop remained on the farms, some thirteen thousand bales only going down the river to New Orleans. Of course the economic coercion did not work. Mr. Owsley, with an argument based on exhaustive research, shows the reasons why in great detail. "Why Europe did not Intervene," as summary to the book, makes a fine introduction and indicates the extent and brilliance of the scholarship involved.

A valuable discussion about a subject too little known must be included here, as it is related to the failure of the blockade of the Southern coastline—"America and the Freedom of the Seas." Lincoln's government, through either ignorance or necessity, reversed its policy concerning search at sea and the blockade of neutral ports. Since England's ships were the chief sufferers, at first it seems strange how this proud and mighty power could accept such invasions, but Mr. Owsley makes this clear. England was looking to the future and its empire, when it could resume its old right of entry and search. As a corollary New England lost its mercantile fleet, the only great rival England had in the carrying trade. Of course the Confederate privateers had something to do with this. The essay itself is long and circumstantial, since it is making a case and must present the evidence.

Part one of the *Selected Essays,* although historically first, was actually the last of the author's research and writing. The two studies here and his book as a whole, *Plain Folk of the Old South,* go far to establish the cultural pattern of Southern society in all its variety, including the migration and settlement of individuals, families, and even communities. Until his systematic collection and interpretation of the material, very little had been known about the pastoral areas of the South, especially the high lands, or about the importance of hogs, cattle, and sheep to the whole economy. The misinterpretation of observation by such writers as Frederick Law Olmsted, who was trying to show the blight of slavery, is corrected by Mr. Owsley. Olmsted mistook the temporary abodes of the wandering shepherds for evidence of what the Slavocracy had done to the poor whites. This Slavocracy is the Northern myth that the South (there was not a unified South with one mind until after the Civil War) was composed of big plantations, slaves, and poor whites perforce hanging to the fringe, left out on the poorer lands. The author conclusively disposes of this misconception. By county records, unpublished census reports, diaries and wills, and also private correspondence—in other words by the only kind of evidence that is relatively complete —an entirely different kind of economy shows itself as clearly as a blueprint can. Most particularly Mr. Owsley examines the ownership of land and slaves in the Black Belt, a terrain by its richness and level surface most suitable for large plantations. But he found little to support the false myth. There were large plantations, but alongside them stood medium-sized farms, small farms, all intermingled; ownership of slaves without land, and lands, sometimes as large as two thousand acres, without slaves. There was the greatest diversity, but it had a thing in common: a society set upon a wide distribution of ownership of all kinds of property—a land of stable independent men in communities made up of families able largely to live without much outside trade. What the trade brought was luxury, not necessity. The tables of statistics—and Mrs. Owsley must be given credit for her part in this—deal with the same kind of distribution of slaves. There were some large holdings, but the numbers of slaves followed the holdings in lands. There was little to distinguish the ownership among the moderate-sized farmers and small planters. The procedure of investigation followed the censustaker, who went down the pike, stopping first on one side, then on the other. There can be no doubt as to where the farms lay, touching one another as they did at the boundaries. In spite of this research, curiously enough, in progressive minds today the old false myth is still with us. The Progressive is a Puritan who has lost his belief in God and so, of necessity, is a sentimentalist. Sentimentalists as historians are not to be trusted.

One of Mr. Owsley's best essays deals with egocentric sectionalism as the fundamental cause of the Civil War. His understanding is this: the dominant section of the country assumed its sectional views and interests to be the national interests. First it was New England; then the Virginia dynasty. With some humor and sharp historic perspective he discusses the commercialism of the one and the agrarian ideas of the other. Certainly Jefferson intended his university, for example, to be a national institution, until the Missouri Compromise and the vituperation released against the Southern states after that. This kind of attack changed his opinion. He protested that young Virginians and Southerners should not be sent North, to be corrupted and turned against their raising. Cassius Marcellus Clay of Kentucky, having fallen under the influence of William Lloyd Garrison at Yale, is a dramatic instance of Jefferson's fear. Being a young man who acted out his beliefs, Clay came home and freed his slaves and became the head of the abolition movement in his part of the world.

It must be said that, when Mr. Owsley is writing history, he writes as a historian looking for fact and truth. When he writes as a man of ideas, his knowledge of history informs him. He does not confuse the two approaches; but, since man is not God, it is well to know your own prejudices before you explore the facts which will establish what you think you are looking for. Mr. Owsley has the kind of courage and discipline which makes him as objective as a historian can be. As a man of opinion and political being, he can expound his belief in all kinds of matters, knowing full well that he is taking the risk of judgment. This book of essays comprises both kinds of attitudes, but they are never confused. He proposes remedies for what he considers disastrous policies ("The Pillars of Agrarianism" and "Democracy Unlimited"). If the "Pillars" seem extreme and a desperate remedy, I can only say that during the great depression I saw good people skulking around cornfields not their own stealing ears in broad daylight, while the government acting on an abstract economic and fiscal law was destroying food, plowing under a man's labor, and killing livestock—the most heinous and stupid acts ever to be perpetrated by any government.

"Democracy Unlimited" is perhaps the best and may be the last summary of what was expected of constitutional government and the ways in which it has been and continues to be betrayed, with the ultimate betrayal of human dignity and the final confusion of what is public and what is private. The argument follows how the mass has usurped the limits set out in the Constitution to protect the individuals who compose this mass. This is the old tune, betrayal in the name of the thing or person betrayed. There is always the emergency to appeal to. Once established, this emergency perpetuates itself. Betrayal is as old as Christendom. The Supreme Court is responsible to no one for its actions; yet it "has taken upon itself the character of a permanent constitutional convention with powers to add to, subtract from, and repeal whole sections of the constitutions of the United States and the states," thus entering "on a broad front the field of social legislation." Ignoring language and thereby confusing offices cannot be charged merely to the sentimental rebels of this country. The confusion derives from that historic moment when the profane arm of God's kingdom became the only arm. The separation of Church and State separated nothing; it obliterated the Church as a necessary spiritual discipline by multiplying sects—and any man can start one—as religious institutions. When princes learned they could rule by private will and not as interpreters of the divine will, the old order was disrupted and the modern world begun. The world was taken as the end in itself, not as the stage for the drama of the soul. Upon this misconception our rule was established. Since order depends upon principle, Locke came forward with the "natural rights of man." As Mr. Owsley says, the "most ominous result of discarding the doctrine of natural rights is that it removes the divine sanction to man's freedom and well being. It also destroys the theory of limited sovereignty and is paving the way for a totalitarian theory —first, total and unrestrained power in the sacred name of democracy...and then total power by entrenched government...." I don't see how any person, looking about him today, can disagree with this. At this remove from the past, however, I would like to take one exception: natural rights did not work because it is an unsound theory. In a Christian world there are natural attributes but no rights, just as there are no divine rights of kings. The deists who made the Constitution believed, so they thought, in a Creator; but he was an abstract one and very far away, no longer informing the temporal order, and far enough away not to interfere with what they did. The founding fathers, pious but profane men, forgot the sovereignty of God and, since they had to put it somewhere, put it in the people: that is, they made a contradiction of it, for he who is ruled does not rule. If they had been very clear about its being in the people of the state, the state might have been concrete enough and full enough of institutions to mitigate the chaos which resulted in this contradiction in terms. There is no such thing as divided sovereignty: its agencies can hold a divided authority, if the source, absolute and impeccable, is understood to be behind it. Perhaps, if he were alive, Mr. Owsley might consider further the reason behind the failure of what has caused the failure of constitutional government.

Certainly anybody apprehensive about our present state of being should read these essays. To know them is to inform ourselves upon the history of our common predicament. To act is another matter. It requires the appeal to a higher authority.

Andrew Lytle

February 1969
Monteagle, Tennessee

Introduction

The essays of Frank Lawrence Owsley collected in this volume have been selected as representative of the major fields of his research and writing. These papers fall into two classes. The first group are the strictly scholarly, heavily-documented pieces, based on thorough research. The second group of essays, while no less authoritative in their execution and research, embody philosophical insight and syntheses not always found in modern historical writings. With the exception of the last section of the volume, largely essay book reviews, they have been arranged according to an historical chronology rather than a chronology of time periods in which the articles were written. Several of the sections contain articles of both classifications and all of them deal with the South, which is as it should be, since the author was identified with that region throughout his career.

Frank Owsley spent most of his early life on farms near Montgomery, Alabama. He was born January 20, 1890, on a farm which had been his mother's share of her grandfather Abner McGehee's plantation. This great grandfather was one of the pioneer settlers of Alabama. During Frank's youth in the early 1900s, he knew many Confederate soldiers and he heard these veterans tell of their lives and the conditions in the country before the Civil War. Always interested in history, he remembered much that they told him. Many of these veterans had not been slaveholders but had owned good farms.

As an undergraduate and as a graduate student at Alabama Polytechnic Institute, Frank came under the influence of the great teacher, George Petrie, and in Professor Petrie's historical laboratory he learned the techniques of research. After receiving a master's degree at Auburn, he attended the University of Chicago where he studied with William E. Dodd, another outstanding teacher. Quite naturally, Frank's major interest was Southern history, intensified by his study with these two great Southern teachers.

The author of this volume of essays began his historical writings and publications after coming to Vanderbilt University as an assistant professor of history in 1920. His doctoral dissertation, *State Rights in the Confederacy,* was published in 1925 and several articles based on the research for this book were published in historical quarterlies at the same time. The Civil War, its causes, and the reasons for the South's defeat were all-engrossing subjects of study for him, culminating in the late twenties with the research for and writing of *King Cotton Diplomacy,* published for the first time in 1931.

On the basis of these works, Frank became known as a scholar who was not satisfied to follow the beaten paths of historical interpretation. Both of these books, *State Rights in the Confederacy* and *King Cotton Diplomacy,* were considered revolutionary at the time of their first appearance. In a review of the latter (*New Republic,* September 1931), Henry Steele Commager wrote, "Professor Owsley has here reevaluated the diplomatic history of the Confederacy, and his conclusions are decidedly at variance with those of his predecessors, who have been accustomed to emphasize moral rather than economic factors.... In the course of this argument many sacrosanct historical truisms are rudely discarded, and conclusions little short of revolutionary are advanced with a quiet audacity that is one of the rewards of scholarship.... Professor Owsley's massive volume not only challenges old beliefs and excites new controversies, but it supersedes all other studies of Confederate diplomacy by its thoroughness and its scholarship."

During this period of study, teaching, and research Frank Owsley became increasingly aware that the currently-accepted interpretations of the South and its history had no basis of fact. The histories of the region had been written almost altogether by Northerners who had never been in the South and they were based on assumptions which had not been thoroughly tested. With this discovery his sense of scholarly integrity and historical justice was aroused, and from that time until his death, he considered it his mission in life to correct these misconceptions. Because he felt this obligation so strongly, he undertook the writing of an American history textbook in order to convey the truth to future generations. No effort was too great, no research too tiring or time-consuming, if it helped him to accomplish this aim.

The 1930s began a new era for Frank. Having spent approximately fifteen years studying source materials, he was ready to state his opinions based on his research and historical judgments. At Vanderbilt he had become associated with a group, most of whom were connected with the English department, either as professors or outstanding former students. This group became known as the Southern

Delaware County Campus Library
The Pennsylvania State University
25 Yearsley Mill Road
Media, Pennsylvania 19063

Telephone
565-3300 x24 (day)
565-3303 (after 5)

Winter, 1974
January 1 –
March 31

Hours

Monday through Thursday	8:00 a.m. – 9:30 p.m.*
Friday	8:00 a.m. – 5:30 p.m.
Saturday (February 2, 9, 16, 23 only)	10:00 a.m. – 4:00 p.m.
*(Exception: January 28 to 31 – Monday-Friday	8:00 a.m. – 5:30 p.m.)

Item	Circulation	Renewal	Late Fines
Books	2 weeks	By telephone or in person. Present call number. Renewable for 2 weeks if not needed by another reader.	10¢ per day
Periodicals	overnight	non-renewable	25¢ per day
Reserve Items	2 hr. room use or overnight	non-renewable	50¢ per hour or part/hour
Records	1 week	non-renewable	25¢ per day
Pamphlets	1 week	non-renewable	10¢ per day

(For exceptions please see librarian)

Agrarians and set forth their belief in traditional values for society in the manifesto, *I'll Take My Stand,* published in 1930.

With a better perspective of this movement after twenty-six years, Frank stated at the Fugitive Reunion in 1956 that he thought the Agrarians were not only revolting against something but for something. "Many of us," he said, "had been working in different fields of human activity.... I was working in history...in Southern and sectional history, and more and more aware...that the people of America were losing the basic values of civilization, that we were going as a nation into materialism, that money value had become the real basic value, that the sense of community was disappearing, that the common courtesies of life were disappearing...that the whole civilization in this country was becoming cruder and cruder, that the things...we thought a civilized country stood for were disappearing.... I was very much aware of a crusade being levelled against the South, based on poor information, or bad reporting.... I think we all had the same feeling, that not only were we trying to reassert values that we thought were basic, but values that also had a considerable bit of sectional nature. That is, the attack was sectional.... We became, I think, in our writings very deliberately provocative. I certainly did, and I have been confronted with it from that time until now by the purists in my profession. In fact, there was a book written last year...in which I was spoken of as a 'modern fire-eater.'... We advocated...an agrarian way of life as...being the only examples in history where civilization had developed. And also a belief that the high-powered modern industrialization and materialism would not either develop or maintain a civilization very long."

Thinking historically along these lines Frank had written "The Irrepressible Conflict" in 1930 for *I'll Take My Stand.* Two other essays, "The Origins of the American Civil War" and "The Fundamental Cause of the Civil War: Egocentric Sectionalism," were later developments of his reflections on this subject. The latter essay is reprinted in this volume and is a final crystallization of this facet of his work.

Numerous essays, some in the form of essay-reviews, were written during the 1930s and were published in the *American Review, Southern Review, Virginia Quarterly,* and *Yale Review.* "The Pillars of Agrarianism," from the mid-thirties, contains the author's ideas for the solution of some of the South's problems.

By the end of the thirties Frank Owsley was again engaged in a major piece of research. This time the undertaking was so great that he enlisted not only the aid of his wife but also that of several of his graduate students. In the tax books and the unpublished census, used for the first time for historical research, he had found the South's nonslaveholding landowners, so long relegated to oblivion. Volumes and shelves of history had been written assuming that there were "only three important classes in the South—planters, Negro slaves, and poor whites." Only those who worked on this project can possibly know how many hours, days, and years went into the labor of copying and checking the census records, name by name, to discover the landowners and nonslaveholders. Adding machines, calculating machines, punch cards, and sorting machines were used to make the statistical tables necessary for this work. Once again no labor was too great, if it was necessary to set the record straight. Ten years was spent on this project by a half dozen or more persons. Several books on the subject—*Tennessee Yeomen, 1840–1860* by Blanche Henry Clark, *Mississippi Farmers, 1850–1860* by Herbert Weaver, and Frank Owsley's own *Plain Folk of the Old South*—were published in the 1940s. Other studies were made by Harry Coles on Louisiana and Davis Applewhite on South Carolina; and Chase Mooney published a book, *Slavery in Tennessee,* based on these sources. The conclusions of these studies have found their way into the thinking of most historians: and the fact that there was in the South a large class of nonslaveholding landowners can no longer be questioned.

After almost thirty years at Vanderbilt University, where among other duties he directed nearly forty doctoral dissertations and innumerable master's theses, Frank Owsley returned to his native state in 1949 to help inaugurate the graduate program in history at the University of Alabama. The first few vacation periods were spent in locating source materials on Alabama history. Several articles resulted from this research and subjects for theses and dissertations were investigated.

King Cotton Diplomacy went out of print in the late forties and it was decided to enlarge the book's scope before reissuing this volume and to include both Northern and Southern diplomacy. To accomplish this, it was necessary to study again in the English and French archives. For this purpose, Frank was given a Fulbright grant which required some lecturing at St. Johns College, Cambridge University, but which also allowed time for research. This work had barely begun when a fatal heart attack in Winchester, England, on October 21, 1956, brought it to a close. The Fulbright Commission continued to support the project and *King Cotton Diplomacy* was reissued in 1959 with some revisions based on the later research but the larger work had to be abandoned.

In all of Frank Owsley's major historical works he was blazing new trails. His research was thorough and of great magnitude and he boldly and courageously stated his conclusions. Half a century has passed since he began his career as an historian and author and almost thirteen years have elapsed since his death, but studies made by other scholars during these years have in no way undermined his research nor have they proved his judgments false.

Harriet Chappell Owsley

Nashville, Tennessee
March 1969

I

The Pattern of Migration and Settlement on the Southern Frontier

Plain Folk and Their Role in Southern History

The Pattern of Migration and Settlement on the Southern Frontier

The motives for migrating from the old, well-established communities of the United States into the fresh lands of the state and federal public domains varied with many individuals. A debtor might flee into the wilderness and divest himself of his debts as a cow rids herself of the swarms of tormenting insects by dashing through a thicket of bushes; the lawbreaker might thus get beyond the reach of the sheriff; the complexities of family and marital relations could be permanently simplified without wasting money on a lawyer and alimony by a move of a hundred miles in a well-chosen direction; old vices and old cronies could be left behind by the morally bankrupt who wished to begin life anew; tragedy might be put out of mind in a country so new and exciting. Thus sanctuary for all those desiring escape seemed to lie out beyond the fringe of settlement. Indeed, going from the old communities into the new country was, to many a migrant, like passing through a doorway, which closed behind him and through which he returned no more.

Others moved to the new country, not to seek escape but to be with their families and friends who were moving into the promised land. Love of adventure was often a powerful inducement to migrate. But the motive common to most immigrants was the desire to acquire the ownership or the free use of some portion of the public domain.

If one considers the landed resources that were available to the American people in the period between the Revolution and the Civil War, it would appear that the average American farmer, North and South, had ample opportunity of becoming a landowner; for a total of 1,309,591,680 acres had been federal lands during this time.[1] But there were also large bodies of state land on which immigrants might settle during the antebellum period. Much of the 22,400,000 acres that comprised the province of Maine was public land at the beginning of the period.[2] Perhaps 90 per cent of the 37,929,600 acres in Georgia was unsettled at the end of the Revolution.[3] Pennsylvania, New York, western Virginia, and western North and South Carolina contained large areas of lands yet to be disposed of by those states. Kentucky's 24,115,200 acres and Tennessee's 29,184,000 acres were just being pioneered at the close of the Revolution.[4] In

1845, Texas, having retained ownership of its public lands, possessed an imperial domain of 175,587,840 acres, about 100,000,000 acres of which were arable.[5]

The existence of these vast unsettled areas of public lands was an irresistible invitation to the land hungry to come and help themselves. And help themselves they did: speculators, land thieves, modest blackmailers who took only what the traffic would bear, squatters who wished to graze their hogs and cattle and to hunt, squatters who were carving out farmsteads and plantations, swarmed into what seemed a boundless empire.

During the interval between the Revolution and the Civil War the combined federal and state public domains in the South were greater than those in the North, while the population of the South was far less. In 1848, before the creation of Oregon as a territory, the area of the organized states and territories of the South was more than twice as great as that of the North, while the white population of the South was less than half of that of the North.[6] But the Southern agricultural immigrants had another great advantage over the Northern settlers, in that the grain and livestock farmers of the Upper South and the Southern highlands could move into the public domain of the Northwest, while the northern farmers could not profitably move farther south.

With such great landed resources so cheap and available and such a relatively small population, it was inevitable that the majority of the agricultural population, and even those dependent upon a grazing economy, should become freeholders in the newer portions of the Old South. But the continued emigration of vast numbers from the older Southern states caused a sharp decline in land values in those areas, so that those who were unable or unwilling to emigrate could purchase farms and plantations in their own community almost at frontier prices.[7]

In the settlement of the public domains of the South, there were usually two distinct waves of settlers rather than the three generally ascribed to the northern frontier. The first wave consisted of herdsmen, who subsisted primarily upon a grazing and hunting economy; and in the second wave were the agricultural immigrants, coming to possess the land. Though many families of the second wave moved regularly from one frontier to another in one generation, it seems to be true that the desire of most was to find a place for permanent settlement.

The herdsmen, who were the typical Southern pioneers, resembled in many respects the pioneer settlers of the Northwest, whom John M. Peck described in his *A New Guide for Emigrants to the West.* "First," observes Peck, "comes the pioneer, who depends for the subsistence of his family chiefly upon the natural growth of vegetation, called the 'range,' and the proceeds of hunting. His implements of agriculture are rude, chiefly of his own make, and his efforts directed mainly to a crop of corn and a 'truck patch.' The last is a rude garden for growing cabbage, beans, corn for roasting ears, cucumbers and potatoes. A log cabin, and, occasionally, a stable and corn crib, and a field of a dozen acres, the timber girdled or 'deadened' and fenced, are enough for his occupancy."[8] He occupies this place "till the range is somewhat subdued, and hunting a little precarious," and too many settlers come in; then he moves on to other frontiers.[9] But the pioneer whom Peck thus describes was usually a subsistence farmer and hunter, while the Southern pioneer as a rule was a livestock grazier and hunter who cultivated small truck gardens and corn patches for subsistence.

That the Southern pioneer should be a herdsman in a land which has not been noted for its livestock and the Northern pioneer should not be a grazier in a country of fine pasture lands, may seem odd. The explanation, however, is simple. The Southern pioneers were much nearer the markets than were the Northern settlers west of the mountains; but, of more importance, cattle and swine could be grazed in the South without having to be fed and sheltered during the winter, whereas in the Northwest the cold weather necessitated both feeding and housing of livestock. Livestock feeding, in contrast to grazing, of course, is the occupation of a well-settled farming community that has fair access to market. It must be observed, however, that the frontier ranges in the South were all that man and beast could desire as long as they were not overgrazed. The trees were loaded with nuts and mast for the swine, and the savannas and open forests, which had been kept clear of underbrush by the annual burnings by the Indians, billowed with wild oats and grasses, vetch, and peavines "tall enough to reach the shoulder of a man on horseback"; and the swamps and valleys were covered with dense canebrakes that furnished winter pasturage and protection from the cold.[10]

The best pasture lands were always those most suited for agriculture, and the herdsmen in quest of fine pastures naturally drove their herds into those parts of the public domain which the immigrant farmers would soon occupy. The result was that all the way from the Atlantic coast to the arid regions of the Southwest and from colonial times till after the Civil War, these pastoral folk were continuously crowded from the arable lands by the agricultural folk.

Livestock grazing was a major occupation in the South as long as there were large bodies of public lands. In colonial times many fortunes were made from herding livestock upon the wild lands of the proprietors or the king. Men owned herds ranging from a few dozen into the thousands of head.[11] Alexander Gregg says that in South Carolina "the number owned by a single individual were very large, almost incredibly so."[12] A British official in the late colonial period has left a vivid picture of cattle grazing in South Carolina and Georgia. He observed great droves of cattle "under the auspices of cowpen keepers, which move (like unto the ancient patriarch or the modern Bedowin in Arabia) from forest to forest in a measure as the grass wears out or the planters approach them."[13]

In the first thirty-odd years of the nineteenth century, as the herdsmen were forced by the agricultural settlers—who cleared and fenced the land and brought along their own smaller herds—to drive their livestock farther westward into the rich prairie and canebrake lands of Alabama, Mississippi, and Louisiana, both the size and the profits of the business increased. Contemporary travelers and writers were always impressed with the great herds of cattle and swine that they observed feeding upon the luxuriant pasture lands of the public domain. Estwick Evans in traveling through the South during the year 1818 saw thousands of cattle feeding along the banks of the Mississippi in the state of Mississippi;[14] Thomas Nuttall at about the same time noted huge droves of livestock on the prairies of southwestern Louisiana and in the Red River district of Arkansas.[15] William Darby, who dwelt in the Southwest for some time and traveled extensively throughout the region in the preparation of his *Emigrant's Guide to the Western and Southwestern States,* also took note of the large droves of cattle along the lower Mississippi and in the western portions of Louisiana.[16] Tilly Buttrick during the same period saw the cattlemen of Kentucky pasturing their herds north of the Ohio,[17] and Fortescue Cuming, on a journey into Arkansas, found the Kentuckians grazing the lush pastures of the public domain in that territory.[18] As late as 1837 John M. Peck remarked that "much of the forest lands, in the Western [Mississippi] Valley produces a fine range for domestic animals and swine. Thousands are raised, and the emigrant, grows wealthy, from the bounties of nature, with but little labor."[19] In northern Florida cattle grazing was the chief occupation until late in the antebellum period. One observer wrote in 1850: "So numerous were the herds of cattle in Alachua...that from 7000 to 10,000 could be seen grazing at once on Payne's Prairie; and there was a single grazier on the Wacasassa whose stock had increased in the course of a few years to the number of 3000 without any other expense than that of herding them."[20]

The grazing of livestock on the agricultural lands and the lives of the herdsmen followed a regular pattern from colonial days to the Civil War. When a cattleman became wealthy he settled down in some well-selected spot, usually as a planter, and placed his livestock in charge of cowboys, who pastured them out past the fringe of set-tlement, along with the herds of the smaller owners living upon the frontier. William Darby describes in his *Guide,* this planter-cattle-man combination in southern and western Louisiana, where the planters lived in the Teche country on their plantations, and em-ployed cowboys, for one-fifth of the increase of the herd, to graze their livestock on the prairies far to the West. Many such cowboys acquired wealth, after which they in turn settled as planters and hired other cowboys to tend their herds out on the frontier. Fre-quently, too, the smaller herdsmen settled as farmers on land which they had purchased, and allowed their livestock to graze, along with those of neighboring farmers, on the unfenced farm and government lands of the community.[21]

By 1840 the better agricultural lands in the older states and in many parts of the newer ones had been sufficiently settled by farmers to interfere with grazing upon the open range, and the herdsmen had largely disappeared from such lands. Those who had not desired to settle as planters and farmers,[22] but preferred their occupation and the frontier with its plentiful game, fresh cattle ranges, and scarcity of neighbors, took up their abode in the pine forests and in the mountains where occasional graziers had already settled. Here, protected by the sterile, sandy soils of the piney woods and the rugged surface of the highlands, the herdsmen and hunters found sanctuary from the pursuing agricultural settlers. Thus it was agri-culture rather than slavery that pressed these settlers into the less fertile and more rugged lands. This was an old phenomenon. From ancient times an agricultural economy has driven the livestock grazier into the deserts and the mountains, except in those states where the herdsmen control the government.[23]

The antebellum inhabitants of the pine belt and, to a lesser extent, of the mountains have been classified rather broadly as poor whites. While groups of the same type of people could be found scattered here and there in the rough, timbered areas that constituted numerous islands in the midst of the richer lands, the dwellers in the highlands and in the piney woods appeared to those who lived outside these regions to constitute the two chief bodies of poor whites. They lived in log cabins or hewn log houses. Their means of support visible to the usual traveler who made hasty detours through the edges of the great woods and mountains were meager indeed. There were usually a few acres of corn, patches of sweet potatoes, cabbage, collards, peas, beans, pumpkins, and turnips, and perhaps a few rows of cotton and tobacco in a "deadening" where blackened stumps of pitch pine or hardwood stood like a ghost forest. There would be a lean milk cow, two or three scrubby horses, a few razor-back hogs in a pole pen or roaming about the premises, and a pack of emaciated hounds. On the woodpile near-by would be a fine, bright bladed ax; and should the stranger peep into the cabin he would see homemade beds, tables, stools, and chairs, and the wall lined with pegs on which to hang things. Over the mantel and, if there was more than one male member of the family, on the wall in racks made of horns or pronged branches cut from trees would be the shiny, long-barreled "rifle guns." If the visitor were to go up in the "loft" he would probably find hanging from pegs numerous steel traps waiting to be set or repaired. The men seemed shiftless; for they would sit almost motionless for hours like a lizard on a sunny log, whittling transparent shavings from a piece of pine or spruce and occasionally squirting a liberal quantity of tobacco "juice" into the eye of a pig or chicken that came too close. While the men were thus taking their ease, the women hoed the corn, cooked the dinner, or plied the loom, or even came out and took up the ax and cut wood with which to cook the dinner.[24]

Of course the great error that contemporary travelers and later writers have committed concerning the mountain and piney wood folk of the antebellum South has been to consider them agriculturists. Had they lived upon the plains, their livestock economy would have been apparent; but because of the great forests their herds of cows and droves of hogs were seldom to be seen by anyone passing hurriedly through the country. Nor could the economic importance of their subsidiary occupation of hunting and trapping be realized except by one who tarried long and learned the way of these taciturn folk. Another error that has helped develop the idea that the backwoodsmen and mountaineers as a class were poor whites has been the failure to regard them, during the period under consideration, in their true character as frontiersmen. Much of the mountain and pine areas was, except for the absence of the Indians, frontier country as truly as was the outer or western frontier; indeed these regions might be called the inner frontier. Great portions of the mountain country and the pine belt from Georgia to Texas were public domain until after the Civil War, and were sparsely settled and bountifully stocked with game.

Local historians, biographers, genealogists, and writers of autobiography and reminiscences, particularly lawyers, preachers, small town newspaper editors, and doctors, who have lived in and near the pine belt and mountains, possessed fuller knowledge and understanding of the life and character of the folk in these regions than did the casual traveler from the outside. A brief examination of some of their accounts will be useful in giving a more authentic view of backwoods and mountain life.

In 1840 John F. H. Claiborne of Natchez traveled slowly and systematically through the piney woods east of the Pearl River in Mississippi as a newspaper reporter in the company of a group of politicians on a political speaking tour. Claiborne's reports go right to the heart of the frontier economy of these people. It was quite obvious to him on his leisurely journey that the real business of the piney wood folk was the grazing of cattle and hogs. The beauty and abundance of the range impressed him. Much of the country, he observed, "is covered exclusively with the long leaf pine; not broken, but rolling like the waves in the middle of the great ocean. The grass grows three feet high and hill and valley are studded all over with flowers of every hue.... Thousands of cattle are grazed here for market."[25] "The people are for the most part pastoral, their herds furnishing their chief revenue."[26] "These cattle are permitted to run in the range or forest, subsisting in summer on the luxuriant grass with which the teeming earth is clothed, and in winter on green rushes or reeds, a tender species of cane that grow in the brakes or thickets in every swamp, hollow and ravine."[27] The trade in cattle, observed Claiborne, "has enriched many people."[28] He was amazed at the ease with which fish, wild turkeys, and other edible game were procured, and the great variety of food supplied the table on the shortest notice.[29] Only one agricultural product seems to have connected these people in his mind with farming: the incredible quantities of sweet potatoes used at all meals and between meals. He recounted with gusto one occasion on which his kindly hostess surpassed the usual hospitality in dispensing sweet potatoes. He ate sweet potatoes with wild turkey and various other meats, had a potato pie for dessert and roasted potatoes offered to him as a side dish, drank sweet potato coffee and sweet potato home brew, had his horse fed on sweet potatoes and sweet potato vines, and when he retired he slept on a mattress stuffed with sweet potato vines and dreamed that he was a sweet potato that someone was digging up.[30]

William H. Sparks, the jurist, who dwelt in the Natchez district, appears to have ridden the judicial circuit as lawyer and judge in the region described by Claiborne, where he had an opportunity of becoming closely acquainted with the piney wood folk. Later, in writing his memoirs, he devoted considerable space to a description of these people. Those settlements east of the Pearl River, he said:

> . . .were constituted of a different people [from the agricultural population farther west]: most of them were from the poorer districts of Georgia and the Carolinas. True to the instincts of the people from whom they were descended, they sought as nearly as possible just such a country as that from which they came, and were really refugees from a growing civilization consequent upon a denser population and its necessities. They were not agriculturists in a proper sense of the term; true, they cultivated in some degree the soil, but it was not the prime pursuit of these people, nor was the location sought for this purpose. They desired an open, poor, pine country, which forbade a numerous population.
>
> Here they reared immense herds of cattle, which subsisted exclusively upon coarse grass and reeds which grew abundantly among the tall, long-leafed pine, and along the small creeks and branches numerous in this section. Through these almost interminable pine-forests the deer were abundant, and the canebrakes full of bears. They combined the pursuits of hunting and stock-minding, and derived support and revenue almost exclusively from these.[31]

Sparks knew some of these people quite well and he records a significant interview with a man whose grandfather and grandmother had settled in the Mississippi backwoods—then the Indian country—a few years after the Revolutionary War. The grandfather, he told Sparks, migrated from Emanuel County, Georgia.

He carried with him a small one-horse cart pulled by an old gray mare, one feather bed, an oven, a frying-pan, two pewter dishes, six pewter plates, as many spoons, a rifle gun, and three deer-hounds. He worried through the Creek Nation, extending then from the Oconee River [in Georgia] to the Tombigbee River [flowing through parts of eastern Mississippi and western Alabama].

After four months of arduous travel he found his way to Leaf River, and there built his cabin; and with my grandmother, and my father, who was born on the trip in the heart of the Creek Nation, commenced to make a fortune. He found on a small creek of beautiful water a little bay land, and made his little field for corn and pumpkins upon that spot, all around was poor, barren woods, but he said it was a good range for stock; but he had not an ox or cow on the face of the earth. The truth is it looked like Emanuel County. The turpentine smell, the moan of the wind through the pine-trees, and nobody within fifty miles of him, was too captivating a concatenation to be resisted, and he rested here.

About five years after he came, a man from Pearl River was driving some cattle by to Mobile, and gave my grandfather two cows to help drive his cattle. It was over one hundred miles, and you would have supposed it a dear bargain; but it turned out well, for the old man in about six weeks got back with six other head of cattle [he had obviously been engaged in a bit of cattle rustling]. From these he commenced to rear a stock which in time became large [which indeed, according to Sparks' account, developed into a sizeable fortune].[32]

The great pine belt of Alabama was primarily a cattle country. F. L. Cherry, writing in 1883, described one portion of the pine belt of that state, extending up into Russell County near which he had lived for fifty years:

There is a section of country about a hundred square miles or more, between the Chewakla and the Uchee Creeks, which fifty years ago [1833] would not number more than a dozen families and they were mostly cow "boys". This section was known as "Piney Woods" of Russell County, and as compared with the country on the creeks, was considered very poor, and profitably available only as a stock range.... As the land was nearly all public domain, and a market near at hand, the stock business was receiving considerable attention, and moderate fortunes soon accumulated.[33]

Cherry also said that piney woods people raised no corn the first few years, and "but little of anything else except stock which ran wild on the public domain."[34] In 1855 the pine lands of Alabama were still regarded as an unbroken forest affording "a fine stock range," practically undisturbed by the plowman;[35] indeed until after the Civil War little change had occurred and cattle grazing still prevailed.[36]

It is estimated that in the contiguous piney woods districts in northwestern Florida, southern Alabama, and southeastern Mississippi, there were 1,000,000 head of cattle in 1850.[37] This is probably too high, but there were certainly no less than 650,000 head of cattle in this area, and a proportionate number of sheep and swine.[38] The Alabama piney woods county of Covington may be taken as typical of this grazing region. With a population of 3,645 and with only 9,201 acres under cultivation in 1850, this county had 824 horses and mules, 10,617 head of cattle, 1,306 sheep, and 18,272 swine.[39]

In Georgia, and wherever there was a considerable area of sandy, pine-clad country, the story was the same. Simon Peter Richardson, a Methodist circuit rider and presiding elder on practically every circuit and district in northern Florida and southern Georgia during the late antebellum period, has left his impressions of the piney woods folk. In 1843 he was given the Irwin circuit, composed almost exclusively of the piney woods of southern Georgia. Richardson in his autobiography describes the country and the people of this circuit:

> [It]...reached from Mobly Bluff to the Okenefenokee swamp; a round of about two hundred and fifty miles, to be traveled in three weeks. The most of the people then lived by raising stock.... There were many good, kind families on the circuit. Everybody was hospitable in those days, whether he had much or little. I went round the circuit. The congregations were meager. All the church houses were small log cabins, and the seats were benches without backs. The people were nearly all dressed in homespun.... The whole country was a vast plain of long leaf pine forest. Sometimes the settlements were ten miles apart: but other parts were thickly settled.[40]

Richardson later occupied some of the richest charges in his conference, yet of the fifty charges he had held when he wrote his autobiography, he considered the Irwin circuit of the pine barrens one of the most satisfactory of them all.[41]

William P. Fleming, basing his account in part upon the testimony of surviving pioneers, gives a vivid picture of Crisp County, Georgia, and its grazing economy. The pine lands of Crisp, he said:

> were by that very classification, adjudged not the best for farm purposes, and, besides, these lands were fearfully "cumbered" with primitive forests of immense pines. Their adaptation to pasturage purposes, however, was apparent. Much of these lands, especially low lands hereabouts, grew wild oats in profusion, and the more elevated lands were heavily carpeted with wire grass, succulent and desirable to a prospective cattleman. A few

older people now living are familiar with the fact that droves of cattle and sheep, numbering thousands, might be hidden from sight in wild oats when only a short distance from some one searching for them.

Cattle, hog, and sheep raising, he continued, "was the principal business" until the sawmills cut the timber in the 1880's and 1890's.[42]

The importance of herding livestock in the Georgia pine belt and the almost exclusive devotion of its inhabitants to this business is shown in the census reports. In 1850, for example, the Georgia pine barrens, comprising about one-fourth of the area of the state and having about one-tenth of the population, produced over 400,000 head of cattle, 85,000 sheep, 356,000 swine, and 36,000 horses and mules.[43] This was nearly half the cattle, and about one-sixth of the sheep, swine, horses, and mules of the state. The huge county of Ware, with only 3,888 people and 11,316 acres under cultivation, had, according to the 1850 census, 781 horses and mules, 919 sheep, 20,993 head of cattle, and 26,054 swine.

The mountains were better ranges than the pine belt, for the soil was often fertile. In fact, more cattle, swine, and sheep per capita were raised in the Appalachians, the Cumberland Plateau, and the Ozarks than in the bluegrass basins of Kentucky and Tennessee.[44] But because of the difficulty of the terrain, cattle and herdsmen were unable to utilize as great a territory as could be grazed in the pine belt. Those who were fortunate enough, however, to gain control of the entrance of a high valley with ranges practically encircling it, had a natural pasture into which they might turn their cattle without danger of their straying. In May, cattle, horses, and sheep were turned into the mountains and allowed to remain there until October. The owners would visit their herds once a week and salt them to keep them gentle and prevent them from straying too far. In the fall they would drive them to market, usually on the coast. Through Buncombe County alone, high in the mountains of western North Carolina, 150,000 hogs and thousands of cattle passed annually on their way to market.[45] Unlike the pine belt, however, there were many rich valleys in which grain farmers raised huge quantities of corn to sell to the cattlemen to fatten the livestock for market or to feed them on their way to market. There were numerous "stock stands" along the French Broad River which fed 90,000 to 100,000 hogs a month while en route to market. Frequently, there would be 2,000 in one drove to be fed.[46] While cattle were grazed in large numbers just as in the piney woods, hogs were more important than cattle, for the hardwood growth produced immense crops of chestnuts, acorns, walnuts, and hickory nuts, and in the rich narrow valleys excellent corn could be grown. Not only did the mountains of North Carolina contribute to this stream of porkers and cattle; but many also came from those of Kentucky and Tennessee. In 1849–1850 at least 81,000 head of swine were driven to the east coast from the mountains in the two latter states.[47] The Cumberland Plateau was covered with grass "where an immense pasturage is afforded to the cattle," observed the British traveler, George W. Featherstonhaugh, in 1834.[48] Even the oak barrens on the highland rim in Tennessee to the west of the plateau were devoted primarily to grazing cattle and hogs.[49]

Frederick L. Olmsted has left what may be accepted as a very good generalized picture of mountain economy in the late antebellum period.

> The hills generally afford an excellent range, and the mast is usually good, much being provided by the chestnut, as well as the oak, and smaller nut-bearing trees. The soil of the hills is a rich dark vegetable deposit, and they cultivate upon very steep slopes. It is said to wash and gully but little, being very absorbtive. The valleys, and gaps across the mountain ranges, are closely settled, and all the feasible level ground that I saw in three weeks was fenced, and either under tillage or producing grass for hay.... Horses, mules, cattle and swine, are raised extensively, and sheep and goats in smaller numbers throughout the mountains, and afford almost the only articles of agricultural export.[50]

Ashe and Buncombe counties of North Carolina, located high up in the Smoky Mountains, may be considered typical of the mountains. In 1850 Ashe had a population of 8,777 and had only 64,805 acres under cultivation. There were in the county 2,713 horses and mules, 14,675 head of cattle, 18,250 sheep, and 25,267 swine. Buncombe's population at this time was 13,425, and there were 75,360 acres under cultivation. The county had 3,708 horses and mules, 16,349 head of cattle, 14,000 sheep, and 28,608 swine.[51]

There are no adequate statistics for the livestock business prior to the census of 1840; but grazing as distinct from livestock feeding was of greater relative importance in the antebellum South than in any other part of the United States. Indeed, the South produced a larger number of mules, swine, and beef cattle in proportion to population than any section until 1860, when the sparsely settled Pacific states led in cattle raising.[52] This leading position was due largely to the presence of vast bodies of unimproved land, not only in the mountains and pine barrens, but interspersed all through the less fertile and swampy areas of the arable lands. The table below[53] gives the total area of each Southern state with the improved acreage for 1850 and 1860, and it can be seen at a glance that the bulk of land in the South was unimproved.

States	Total Acreage	Improved Land	
		1850	1860
Arkansas	33,410,063	751,530	1,983,313
Florida	37,931,520	349,049	654,213
Texas	175,587,840	643,976	2,650,781
Kentucky	24,115,200	5,968,270	7,644,208
Tennessee	29,184,000	5,175,173	6,795,337
Missouri	41,836,931	2,938,425	6,246,871
Mississippi	30,179,840	3,444,358	5,065,755
Louisiana	26,461,440	1,590,025	2,707,108
Alabama	32,462,115	4,435,614	6,385,724
Georgia	37,120,000	6,378,479	8,062,758
South Carolina	21,760,000	4,072,051	4,572,060
North Carolina	32,450,560	5,453,975	6,517,284
Virginia	39,262,720	10,360,135	11,437,821
Maryland	7,119,360	2,797,905	3,002,257

The states of Arkansas, Texas, and Florida had scarcely been touched by the ax and the plow before the Civil War, and only a fraction of the land, ranging from about one-ninth of the total in Louisiana to nearly half in Maryland, had been put to agricultural uses in the other southern states.

A summary of livestock production in the Southern states and in the Old Northwest, the section in the North that ranked next to the South, is presented in the following table.[54] This will show the comparative value of livestock production in the South which was so largely based upon grazing the open range.

The relative importance of livestock production in the Northwest and the South can be more easily seen from a comparison of the average per capita ownership of livestock in each state. The following table, computed from the preceding table, gives the average ownership of each person in several states in terms of dollar evaluation.

The second wave of settlers to come into the public domain were, as previously observed, the farmers and planters who desired the ownership rather than the free use of some portion of the public domain. The migratory direction of an agricultural people is determined, where there is a choice, by several factors. The agricultural immigrant far more than the herdsman has a tendency to seek out a country as nearly as possible like the one in which he formerly lived, in the matter of soil, rainfall, temperature, and appearance—that is,

OLD NORTHWEST

State	Population	Horses Mules	Cattle	Sheep	Swine	Value of Livestock
Ohio	1,757,556	466,820	1,358,947	3,942,929	1,964,770	44,121,741
Indiana	931,392	321,898	714,666	1,122,493	2,263,776	22,478,555
Illinois	736,931	278,226	912,036	894,043	1,915,907	24,209,258
Michigan	341,591	58,576	274,449	746,435	205,847	8,008,734
Wisconsin ...	197,912	30,335	183,433	124,896	159,276	4,897,385

THE SOUTH

State	Population	Horses Mules	Cattle	Sheep	Swine	Value of Livestock
Virginia	1,421,666	293,886	1,076,269	1,310,004	1,829,843	33,658,659
N. Carolina ..	869,039	173,952	693,510	595,249	1,812,813	17,717,647
S. Carolina ..	668,507	134,654	777,686	285,551	1,065,503	15,060,015
Georgia	906,185	208,710	1,097,528	560,435	2,168,617	25,728,416
Alabama	771,622	187,896	728,015	371,880	1,904,540	21,690,122
Florida	87,444	15,850	261,085	23,315	209,453	2,880,058
Mississippi ..	606,526	170,007	733,970	304,929	1,582,734	19,887,580
Arkansas	209,897	71,756	292,710	91,256	836,727	6,647,969
Louisiana ...	517,762	134,363	575,342	116,110	597,301	11,152,275
Texas	212,592	89,223	330,114	100,530	692,022	10,412,927
Missouri	682,044	266,986	791,510	762,511	1,702,625	19,887,580
Kentucky	982,405	381,291	752,502	1,102,091	2,891,163	29,661,436
Tennessee ...	1,002,717	345,939	750,762	811,591	3,104,800	29,978,416
Maryland ...	583,034	81,328	219,586	177,902	352,911	7,997,634

having similar topography, streams, trees, and grasses. The similarity of appearance is of great importance for both psychological and practical reasons. The fact that the emigrant shakes from his feet the dust of his old community does not mean that he divests himself of the mental picture and love of the old countryside, of those rich limestone valleys, rolling hills, and sandy levels where the odor of the resinous pine scents the air and the tall trees moan in the wind, or of the rugged mountains with purple shadows and smoke hanging above the cove in the late afternoon, announcing the cheery news of supper a-cooking or the still making a run. A settler simply could never be entirely happy and at home unless he was surrounded by a landscape much like the one where he had spent his earlier years.

THE OLD NORTHWEST		THE SOUTH	
State	*Per capita value of livestock*	*State*	*Per capita value of livestock*
Wisconsin	$24.74	Arkansas	$31.67
Michigan	23.44	Florida	32.93
Ohio	25.67	Texas	48.98
Indiana	24.13	Kentucky	30.19
Illinois	32.85	Tennessee	29.89
		Missouri	29.15
		Mississippi	32.75
		Louisiana	21.53
		Alabama	28.10
		Georgia	28.39
		South Carolina	22.52
		North Carolina	20.38
		Virginia	23.67
		Maryland	13.72

Those accustomed to rugged country seldom debouched upon the plains, but migrated to a country where there were other hills and valleys—the Ozarks, for example, were largely settled by those from the Appalachians—while those who had inhabited level country usually avoided the hills unless they could settle in a wide valley with the hills in the distance. Those who had lived in a wooded country shunned the open prairies.

Aside from sentiment that grows into acute nostalgia in strange surroundings, the agricultural migrants—though to a much lesser degree the pastoral folk—have scientific and practical reasons for selecting a country similar to the one from which they emigrate. The basic and sound assumption of the farmer who seeks a country similar in appearance, climate, and soil to the old community in which he has lived is that he can continue in the new country to grow the field crops, fruits, and vegetables, the tillage, habits, and marketing of which are part of his mental furniture. "Men seldom change their climate," observed the superintendent of the Bureau of the Census in 1860, "because to do so they must change their habits."[55] William H. Sparks, who himself had migrated west, remarked that the emigrants were sure to select their new home, as nearly as possible, "in the same parallel, and with surroundings as nearly like those they had left as possible. With the North Carolinian, good springwater, and pine-knots for his fire, were the *sine qua non*."[56] Paul Vidal de La Blache, the geographer, applies this principle to the migratory movements of the Chinese into the unsettled areas within their own country. "How," he asks, "could such individuals contrive to get along there, if unable to live in customary ways, and with customary means?" They must "find an environment similar to the one which they have been obliged to leave."[57] Isaiah Bowman observes that the primary function of the individuals who went out upon the American frontier to locate a fit place for settlement for themselves and their neighbors usually "consisted merely in finding soils and slopes that resembled those back at home that were known to be good."[58] The letters and diaries of pioneers abound with reports to those in the East that the soil and climate of the new country were like those back at home. As a result of such reassuring knowledge, "one great bugbear of pulling up stakes and removing to a distant home was greatly neutralized by this comfortable feeling that, however great the distance and the consequent toil, men knew toward what kind of haven they were faring and that they would meet there conditions which they had mastered before."[59]

It was soon known by the average person in the eastern states that, outside the highlands, the temperature, rainfall, and soil of the country lying to the west, until the Great Plains were approached, were sufficiently like those in the East to permit the continuation of the same types of agriculture. This information was derived from land prospectors, and the emigrant guides prepared by such writers as William Darby, who made a careful study of these and related matters; but chiefly from the reports of the herdsmen, who had raised their little patches of corn, truck, tobacco, and cotton while hunting and grazing their livestock on the frontier. By 1860 the trend of migration had been scientifically examined by the Census Office on the basis of the nativity reports in the census tables of 1850 and 1860, and the superintendent of the census was able to state the fact that "the almost universal law of internal migration is, that it moves west on the same parallel of latitude."[60]

The necessity of continuing to grow the usual crops was not the sole practical motive that prompted the immigrant farmer to settle upon land like that which he had cultivated in the East. Of great importance was the need to continue to employ the methods and tools with which he was familiar. Those accustomed to the use of certain farm implements adapted to one kind of soil had great difficulty in changing to another type of soil, even though such a change did not entail any change in their farm economy. This was particularly true of those who, having cultivated sandy or loamy soils, moved into gummy clays and lime soils. Indeed there has been since ancient times a preference among agricultural folk for a soil with a sand or silt content because of the greater ease with which it can be cultivated.[61]

The implication of this prejudice in favor of a country similar in climate, surface appearance, streams and springs, soil, and the natural growth of grass, timber, and wild flowers, is this: the farmers making new homes in the West were, in the majority of cases, not in search of the richest lands of the public domain, but merely the richest of the particular type of land to which they were accustomed back in the East. Perhaps in most cases they were content with land almost identical with that left behind except that the new land was fresh.

Naturally, therefore, the rural folk of the upper South dwelling in the limestone valleys and highlands, whose pattern of farm husbandry had been the growing of grain and livestock, did not erupt into the lower South where climate and soil would force a radical change in farm economy and methods of cultivation. On the contrary, when they migrated it was usually into the highlands, limestone basins, and valleys of Tennessee, Kentucky, Missouri, and northern Arkansas and into the wooded lands across the Ohio River, where climate, soil, timber, and the grasses indicated that the new country would be hospitable to the familiar old crops. Both Darby and Peck, in their guides for emigrants, observed this westerly trend of the agricultural migrants,[62] and the federal censuses of 1850 and 1860 fully sustain their observations. In 1850 there were 142,102 free natives of Virginia living in the upper southern states of Missouri, Kentucky, and Tennessee, and 155,978 living in the Old Northwest; but in the lower southern states of Georgia, Florida, Alabama, Mississippi, Louisiana, Arkansas, and Texas there were only 38,311 such Virginians. The Virginians had settled chiefly in the tobacco, grain, and livestock regions. Maryland exemplifies better than Virginia the zonal trend of the migration of agricultural folk. In 1850 over 30,000 free natives of that state were living in Virginia and Pennsylvania— obviously the western portions—, 54,310 in the Old Northwest,

12,277 in Tennessee, Kentucky, and Missouri, and only 4,722 in the seven states of the lower South mentioned above. Thus Maryland contributed little either to the upper or lower southern states west of the mountains. North Carolina which, outside of the highlands, is essentially a state of the lower South, had 103,315 free natives living in Tennessee, Kentucky, and Missouri, 52,467 in the Old Northwest, and 107,912 in the newer states of the lower South.[63]

The Carolinas settled Georgia, and, with considerable aid from Virginia, settled Tennessee. The remainder of the states of the lower South were the children and grandchildren of the Carolinas, Georgia, and Tennessee. In 1850 there were 140,261 free native South Carolinians, 140,041 Georgians, 99,140 North Carolinians, and 79,640 Tennesseans living in the newer states of the lower South compared with about 43,000 from Virginia and Maryland. Though Tennessee and North Carolina had contributed heavily to the upper slave states and to the Old Northwest, South Carolina and Georgia had only 12,000 free natives in that region in 1850.

The census of 1860 continues to show the westward trend of population in the South, the newer states such as Alabama, Mississippi, Tennessee, and Kentucky contributing heavily to the states in the same zones to the west.[64]

The first agricultural settlers in the new farm lands in the Southwest as a rule came from the piedmont or "up-country" of the Carolinas and Georgia where they had already been engaged in the cultivation of cotton, and where the soil was similar in its clay and sand contents to much of the soil of the new country. Local pioneer writers agree that the early settlers of the Southwest—especially Alabama and Mississippi—were up-country Carolinians or Tennesseans, many of whom had originally come from up-country South Carolina. For example, most of the South Carolinians, who moved into Blount, Jefferson, and Pickens counties, Alabama, were from the York, Abbeville, and Fairfield districts,[65] very similar both in soil and in topography to the country in which they settled. More recent studies show that in all parts of Alabama as late as 1828, most of those immigrants whose origin could be ascertained came not from the tidewater regions of the South Atlantic states, but from the piedmont, where they had been cultivating the short staple cotton. Few of the tidewater planters migrated into the Southwest during this period, probably because their heavy investments in land, the stability of their principal money crops—rice, tobacco, and long staple cotton—and their established social position tended to hold them where they were.[66] But it may well be that the climate of the South-west, which was not hospitable to the culture of rice, tobacco, and long staple cotton, was a decisive factor in retarding the migration from the low country.

These up-country cotton farmers and planters who settled in the newer lands, as has been suggested, selected the lighter sandy loam and sand and clay soils in preference to the stiff clays and rich black prairie lands. A. J. Brown, in his history of Newton County, Missis-sippi, observed that the early settlers in that region preferred the poorer sandy lands to the richer prairies and clay soils. "The prairies of the county were very open; thousands of acres of this kind of land were entirely unobstructed by timber or undergrowth, and were very easily brought into a state of cultivation. The level, sandy and up-lands were much more in demand, as the people much preferred the level uplands to the ridges or prairies."[67] Nettie Powell noted the same thing in Marion County, Georgia. "The section south of where Buena Vista now is and leading towards Draneville was known as 'turkey ridge,' and was not attractive to early settlers on account of the hard red clay soil [indicating rich soil] which was not easy to cultivate with the wooden plows that were then in use. The most of this region was left vacant until the middle thirties."[68]

The method of migration and settlement in the South was fairly uniform during the pioneer period. Friends and relatives living in the same or neighboring communities formed one or more parties and moved out together, and when they had reached the promised land they constituted a new community, which was called a "settle-ment"—and still is so called. Settlements were frequently miles apart, and the inhabitants of a single settlement would be more scat-tered than they had been in the old community in the East; and other settlers would come in after the first trek in smaller groups or in single families and fill in the interstices. These later comers would often be relatives or friends of those who had come first, or friends of their friends. Frequently church congregations would move in a body into the Southwest or an entire hamlet or community would simply evacuate and march together into the "land of milk and honey." In describing the settlement of Wilkinson County, Georgia, Victor Davidson observes that "frequently large tracts were purchased and whole communities [from the older parts of the state and the Upper South] would move and settle on them. There were instances where congregations would follow their pastors here."[69] One entire community from Virginia "came in a body from that State and purchased lands near each other."[70]

The migration of a family group from Abbeville, South Carolina, to Cherokee County in the Coosa River Valley of Alabama in 1835, has been described by one of the members of the group. "In November 1835," he says, "we bade adieu to friends and left the old homestead never to look upon it again.... Late in the afternoon of our first day's travel we were joined, as we rolled on, by my maternal grandparents and several other members of the family, the party thus numbering forty or fifty souls."[71] Similarly, the migration from Alabama into Louisiana and Texas about 1840 was made in groups. On one occasion, for example, "some thirty families, forming a single party, are said to have met near Clarksville, and started together in their wagons for Louisiana and Texas."[72] One of the most interesting group migrations into the wilderness was that of the Presbyterian congregation of Bethel Church which came in a body from Williamsburg district of Columbia, South Carolina, and settled in Maury County, Tennessee, in 1808, where they established their church, "Zion," and their Zion community—which has remained virtually intact until this day.[73] The settlements at Watauga and in neighboring valleys, the Cumberland settlements, and those of the Kentucky bluegrass basin, such as Harrodsburg and Boonesboro, are all too well known as group undertakings to need more than mention. Such examples might be endlessly repeated. Thus the early communities of the newer states and territories were essentially transplanted organisms rather than synthetic bodies.

These groups did not move into the public domain in ignorance of their exact location; but rather, like the children of Israel, they sent their Calebs and Joshuas ahead to spy out the land and prepare the way. An early description of Blount County, Alabama, relates how the plain folk chose their location and how they made ready for the families to settle in a new community. As they prepared to move into the wilderness, the prospective immigrants usually sent

> ...a few strong men, generally their sons, without families, deep into the then wilderness in the fall, to make corn and prepare for them. The father generally went with them and chose the place, and then went back to prepare for moving when the corn was made. A bushel of meal will suffice a man one month, and if he has no other than wild meat, he will require even less bread. In the fall season, place three or four men, one hundred miles in a wilderness, with proper tools and two horses, they

will pack their bread stuff for the hundred miles—procure their meat—clear land—and produce corn sufficient to bread one hundred persons one year.[74]

Blount County, which comprised much of northern and western Alabama at the time of the first settlement in 1816 and 1817, was settled in this fashion.

The same preparations made in the migration of families of wealth are easily traced in the case of the family of Judge Charles Tait. The Taits lived in Elbert County, Georgia, from which many of the early settlers of Alabama migrated. In January, 1817, Charles Tait commissioned his son, Captain James A. Tait, to go into the public domain of Alabama territory to select a future home for the family. The father gave careful specifications as to the type of place to select. There were certain characteristics that the place must possess, he said:

> ...such as a stream near at hand for a mill and machinery—a never failing spring at the foot of a hillock, on the summit of which a mansion house can be built in due time; that it have an extensive back range where our cattle and hogs can graze and fatten without the aid of corn houses, that on the right and left there is an extensive body of good land where will settle a number of good neighbors and from whom the pleasure and benefits of society will soon be realized.[75]

In December of the same year Captain Tait wrote his father that he would go the next year to the Alabama territory, taking two or three Negroes with him, and would buy a few Negroes in Alabama, where they would make a corn crop. Later, when it was safe, the family was to be brought to the new home.[76] With several Negroes—and presumably several of his neighbors—he proceeded to the present Wilcox County and became a squatter on the public domain, where he raised a crop of corn just as had the small farmers who came to Blount County in northern Alabama in the same year. After a year on the public domain he purchased some land at two dollars an acre; but the government held most of the land off the market and he complained to his father that "we shall have to make another crop on the public land. The failure of the sale of all the townships advertised is a grievous and most mortifying disappointment to those generally settled on the land and to us in particular."[77]

In the meantime, the neighbors were moving into the Alabama territory, some of them to become neighbors of the Taits at their new home at Fort Claiborne—where a place on the bluffs of a river was selected with the requirements that met the elder Tait's specifications. The son's letters show that the trek from Elbert County had begun even before he himself set out to select a plantation. "Mr. Goode and family started yesterday for the Alabama territory," he reported in November, 1817. "Gov. Bibb will start on Thursday I believe, Esquire Barnet was to have broke ground on Thursday last, his son-in-law Taliafero, follows in about three weeks, and I suppose his son Thomas in the course of the winter. Thus you see the present inhabitants are moving off."[78]

In the main outline, then, migration and settlement on the southern frontier followed a pattern. The herdsmen who combined livestock grazing with hunting pioneered the arable lands, and they were closely followed, if not pursued, by the agricultural settlers. When the best lands had been taken up by the farmers, the smaller herdsmen who had not become farmers and planters retreated with their droves of cattle and swine into the pine barrens and highlands, where they would be protected from the encroachment of agriculture by poor or rugged land.

The agricultural folk in migrating into the public domain sought a country as similar as possible to the country in which they had lived. The reasons for this were the natural love of familiar environment and the necessity of continuing the accustomed farm husbandry, which only a country similar to the old one in climate, soil, and natural growth could meet. The migrants thus found themselves moving in a westerly direction along those isothermal lines or temperature zones in which they had lived in the East. Grain and cattle farmers of the upper South remained such and settled in the upper South to the west of the mountains and in the lower portion of the Old Northwest. Tobacco and cotton farmers did likewise and moved into the middle and lower southern territories and states. Before migrating, one or more representatives of a group spied out the land, whereupon the group—which was frequently a congregation or neighborhood—moved out together and became neighbors in the new country.

This pattern of migration and settlement had a significant bearing upon the social and economic structure of the Old South and the New. The herdsmen, who withdrew to the rugged and sterile lands in order that they might continue the occupation that they preferred, placed drastic limitations upon their own future economic well-being. As long as the pine belt and highlands were not overcrowded by man and beast, the range remained good and these semi-pastoral folk lived well and possessed a strong sense of security. They were certainly not poor whites as a class; but neither were many of them wealthy. Eventually, when these regions began to be crowded—and this was happening in a few places prior to the Civil War—the people would be compelled to graze fewer cattle and cultivate more and more land until they would find themselves farmers cultivating poor soil without much knowledge of agriculture.

Those agricultural immigrants who had deliberately shunned the fertile but tough clay and lime soils and had settled upon inferior sandy-loam lands placed limitations—though not as severe—upon their future economic prosperity in a way similar to the piney wood and mountain folk. While many became well-to-do, few became rich, for the economic level of an agricultural people can rise but little above the level of the fertility of the soil. On such lands were many large farmers and small planters with ten or fifteen slaves, but there were few if any large planters. Those agricultural migrants who moved into the rich lands were most fortunate; for, while most who settled in the Black Belt were possessed of only moderate means·at the time of settlement, nearly all rose greatly in the economic scale and many who were poor in the beginning became immensely wealthy before 1860. There were thus several regions differing greatly in fertility of soil, and consequently in wealth. As between these regions there was segregation; but within each region there was very little. In the Black Belt, for example, the property of the non-slaveholders and the great planters lay intermingled, and the census and tax lists show that the values of their lands and their agricultural productions per acre were about the same.

---

[1]Benjamin H. Hibbard, *A History of the Public Land Policies* (New York, 1924), p. 78, and Thomas C. Donaldson, *The Public Domain; Its History, with Statistics* (Washington, 1884), table on p. 13.

[2]Roy M. Robbins, *Our Landed Heritage; The Public Domain, 1776–1936* (Princeton, 1942), p. 9.

[3]Samuel G. McLendon, *History of the Public Domain of Georgia* (Atlanta, 1924), *passim*.

[4]Robbins, *Our Landed Heritage*, pp. 9, 26–27; Donaldson, *Public Domain*, p. 202; Hibbard, *Public Land Policies*, p. 78.

[5]*De Bow's Review* (New Orleans, 1846–1880), XIII (1852), 53. See Aldon S. Lang, *Financial History of the Public Lands in Texas* (Waco, 1932), and Reuben McKitrick, *The Public Land System of Texas, 1823–1910* (Madison, 1918), for detailed treatment of the landed resources of Texas.

[6]See Donaldson, *Public Domain*, pp. 28–29, for areas of states and territories.

[7]Avery O. Craven, *Soil Exhaustion as a Factor in the Agricultural History of Virginia and Maryland, 1606–1860* (Urbana, 1926), pp. 118, 120, 122–125; Avery O. Craven, *Edmund Ruffin, Southerner; A Study in Secession* (New York, 1932), pp. 52, 53, 63; Luther P. Jackson, *Free Negro Labor and Property Holding in Virginia, 1830–1860* (New York, 1942), pp. 35, 36.

[8]John M. Peck, *A New Guide for Emigrants to the West* (Boston, 1837), pp. 119–120.

[9]*Ibid.*, p. 120.

[10]Sallie W. Stockard, *The History of Guilford County, North Carolina* (Knoxville, 1902), pp. 55–56; Hope S. Chamberlain, *History of Wake County, North Carolina* (Raleigh, 1922), p. 69; Victor Davidson, *History of Wilkinson County* [Georgia] (Macon, 1930), pp. 107–108; William P. Fleming, *Crisp County, Georgia, Historical Sketches* (Cordele, Ga., 1932), pp. 24–25; Jethro Rumple, *A History of Rowan County, North Carolina* (Salisbury, 1881), pp. 28–29, 54; A. J. Brown, *History of Newton County, Mississippi, from 1834 to 1894* (Jackson, 1894), pp. 40–44; George G. Smith, *The Life and Letters of James Osgood Andrew, Bishop of the Methodist Episcopal Church South* (Nashville, 1883), p. 23; George E. Brewer, History of Coosa County, Alabama (ms. in Alabama Department of Archives and History, Montgomery), pp. 48, 49.

[11]Joseph Schafer, *The Social History of American Agriculture* (New York, 1936), pp. 93, 94, 95, 96; Lewis C. Gray, *History of Agriculture in the Southern United States to 1860*, 2 vols. (Washington, 1933), I, 148–151, 200–212; Bartholomew R. Carroll (ed.), *Historical Collections of South Carolina*, 2 vols. (New York, 1836), II, 129; Alexander Gregg, *History of the Old Cheraws* (Columbia, 1905), pp. 109, 110; William A. Schaper, *Sectionalism and Representation in South Carolina*, in American Historical Association, *Annual Report*, 1900, I (Washington, 1901), 295, 318–319.

[12]Gregg, *History of the Old Cheraws*, p. 109.

[13]Quoted in Schaper, *Sectionalism in South Carolina*, p. 295, and Gray, *History of Agriculture in the Southern United States*, I, 148.

[14]Estwick Evans, *A Pedestrious Tour*, in Reuben G. Thwaites (ed.), *Early Western Travels, 1748–1846*, 32 vols. (Cleveland, 1904–1907), VIII, 303.

[15]Thomas Nuttall, *Journal of Travels into the Arkansas Territory*, in *Early Western Travels*, XIII, 311.

[16]William Darby, *The Emigrant's Guide to the Western and Southwestern States; and Territories* (New York, 1818), pp. 76–77.

[17]Tilly Buttrick, *Voyages, Travels, and Discoveries, 1812–1819*, in *Early Western Travels*, VIII, 78.

[18]Fortescue Cuming, *Sketches of a Tour to the Western Country (1807–1809)*, *Early Western Travels*, IV, 298.

[19]Peck, *New Guide for Emigrants*, p. 41.

[20]Quoted in Gray, *History of Agriculture in the Southern United States*, II, 834. Chapter XXXV of this work gives a sketch of the cattle business in the South for the post-revolutionary and antebellum period. See also, Brown, *History of Newton County*, pp. 54, 55, 56; Simon P. Richardson, *The Lights and Shadows of Itinerant Life: An Autobiography* (Nashville, 1901), p. 86; Timothy H. Ball, *A Glance into the Great South-East; or Clarke County, Alabama, and Its Surroundings from 1540 to 1877* (Grove Hill, Ala., 1882), *passim;* Timothy Flint, *Recollections of the Last Ten Years* (Boston, 1826), p. 265.

[21]Pages 76–77. Cf. Schafer, *Social History of American Agriculture*, pp. 93–97.

[22]But it was no simple matter to change from a grazing economy to agriculture. Paul M. J. Vidal de La Blache, *Principles of Human Geography*, ed. Em-

manuel de Martonne, trans. Millicent T. Bingham (New York, 1926), p. 124, n. 15, quotes a letter from M. Woeikof in support of the difficulty of changing from a grazing to an agricultural economy: "As far as I know the change from nomad [livestock grazing] to farmer does not occur except under the influence and in imitation of agricultural neighbors." See also Norman S. B. Gras, *A History of Agriculture in Europe and America* (New York, 1925), pp. 9–10.

²³*Principles of Human Geography*, p. 54, n. 9, and pp. 130–131. Invaders like the nomadic Mongols and Huns into weak agricultural states have imposed their economic system upon the country. In a mountainous country like Greece and much of the Balkans, livestock grazing has been more important than agriculture and has been able to push the farmer out of many a small valley.

²⁴Frederick L. Olmsted, *A Journey in the Seaboard Slave States, with Remarks on Their Economy* (New York, 1856), pp. 348–351, gives a traditional picture of piney woods people. See also, *De Bow's Review*, XVIII (1855), 188–189.

²⁵"A Trip through the Piney Woods," *Mississippi Historical Society Publications* (Oxford-Jackson, 1898–1925), IX (1906), 514.

²⁶*Ibid.*, p. 515. Cf. *ibid.*, pp. 523, 533.

²⁷*Ibid.*, p. 521. Cf. *ibid.*, p. 530.

²⁸*Ibid.*, p. 522. Cf. *ibid.*, p. 521.

²⁹*Ibid.*, pp. 516, 522.

³⁰*Ibid.*, pp. 532–533.

³¹William H. Sparks, *The Memories of Fifty Years* (Philadelphia, 1870), p. 331.

³²*Ibid.*, pp. 332–333.

³³The History of Opelika and Her Agricultural Tributary Territory (ms. in Alabama Department of Archives and History), p. 160.

³⁴*Ibid.*, p. 163.

³⁵"On the Forests and Timber of South Alabama," in *De Bow's Review*, XIX (1855), 611–613. Cf. Lewis Troost, "Mobile and Ohio Railroad," *ibid.*, III (1847), 322.

³⁶Joseph Hodgson (ed.), *Alabama Manual and Statistical Register for 1869* (Montgomery, 1869), pp. 18–19. Cf. *ibid.*, for 1868, pp. 148–149.

³⁷Gray, *History of Agriculture in the Southern United States*, II, 834.

³⁸See *Seventh Census of the United States: 1850* (Washington, 1853), Table XI, pp. 407–409, 429–433, and 456–460, for livestock production by counties in Florida, Alabama, and Mississippi.

³⁹*Ibid.*, Table XI, pp. 429–433.

⁴⁰Richardson, *Lights and Shadows of Itinerant Life*, pp. 26 27. See also Smith, *Life and Letters of James O. Andrew*, p. 23.

⁴¹Richardson, *Lights and Shadows of Itinerant Life*, p. 43.

⁴²*Crisp County Historical Sketches*, pp. 24–25. See also Davidson, *History of Wilkinson County*, pp. 107–108, for a similar description of the range in the piney woods of Georgia at an earlier time.

⁴³*Seventh Census*, Table XI, pp. 377–384, for livestock, and Table I, pp. 364–365, for population.

⁴⁴Gray, *History of Agriculture in the Southern United States*, II, 876, 884.

⁴⁵John P. Arthur, *Western North Carolina; A History* (Raleigh, 1914), p. 285.

⁴⁶*Ibid.*, pp. 285–287.

⁴⁷"The Hog Business in the West," in *De Bow's Review*, XVI (1854), 539–540.

⁴⁸*Excursion through the Slave States*, 2 vols. (London, 1844), I, 185.

⁴⁹William Hale, *History of De Kalb County, Tennessee* (Nashville, 1915), p. 49.

⁵⁰*A Journey in the Back Country* (New York, 1860), pp. 222–223.

⁵¹*Seventh Census*, Table XI, pp. 318–324, for agricultural production, and Table I, pp. 307–308 for population.

[52]*Eighth Census of the United States, 1860: Agriculture* (Washington, 1864), pp. cxii–cxiii, cxxv–cxxvii, and cxviii.

[53]Donaldson, *Public Domain*, pp. 28–29, gives areas of states; *Seventh Census,* Table LV, pp. lxxxii–lxxxiii, and *Eighth Census, Agriculture,* Table I, p. vii, give amount of improved land of states in 1850 and 1860, respectively.

[54]*Seventh Census,* Table LV, pp. lxxxii–lxxxiii.

[55]*Eighth Census, Population,* xxxv.

[56]Sparks, *Memories of Fifty Years,* p. 20.

[57]*Principles of Human Geography,* p. 68. Cf. Timothy Flint, *The History and Geography of the Mississippi Valley* (Cincinnati, 1832), p. 217.

[58]*The Pioneer Fringe* (New York, 1931), p. 6.

[59]Archer B. Hulbert, *Soil: Its Influence on the History of the United States* (New Haven, 1930), p. 78. See also *ibid.,* pp. 21–23; Albert B. Faust, "German Americans," in Francis J. Brown and Joseph S. Roucek (eds.), *Our Racial and National Minorities; Their History, Contributions, and Present Problems* (New York, 1937), p. 171; and Laurence M. Larson, *The Changing West and Other Essays* (Northfield, Minn., 1937), pp. 11–12, 69–70, 71, for settlement of the Northwest by Europeans from similar regions.

[60]*Eighth Census, Population,* p. xxxv.

[61]Vidal de La Blache (*Principles of Human Geography,* p. 62) observes that the early agricultural communities of Europe were located on "the most easily cultivated" and "not always the most fertile" soils. "Mellow friable lands forming a sort of band from southern Russia to northern France" were the early abode of agricultural settlers. "Men began to seek out certain localities because they were easy to cultivate" (p. 65).

[62]Darby, *Emigrant's Guide,* pp. 121, 231; Peck, *New Guide for Emigrants,* pp. 62, 63, 108.

[63]*Seventh Census,* Table XV, pp. xxxiv–xxxviii.

[64]*Eighth Census, Population,* xxxiv, and 616–623. See also William O. Lynch, "The Westward Flow of Southern Colonists before 1861," *Journal of Southern History,* IX (1943), 303–327.

[65]George Powell, "A Description of Blount County," in *Transactions of the Alabama Historical Society, July 9th and 10th, 1855* (Tuscaloosa, 1855), pp. 37–41; Nelson F. Smith, *History of Pickens County, Alabama* (Carrollton, Ala., 1856), pp. 37–49. See also A. B. McEachin, History of Tuscaloosa (ms. copy in Alabama Department of Archives and History; also published in Tuscaloosa *Times,* 1880); and Ezekiel Abner Powell, Fifty Years in West Alabama (ms. copy in Alabama Department of Archives and History; also published in Tuscaloosa *Gazette,* August 12, 1886–September 5, 1889).

[66]See, especially, Thomas P. Abernethy, *The Formative Period in Alabama, 1815–1828* (Montgomery, 1922), pp. 25–26.

[67]*History of Newton County,* p. 54.

[68]*History of Marion County, Georgia* (Columbus, 1931), p. 21.

[69]*History of Wilkinson County,* p. 147.

[70]*Ibid.,* p. 162.

[71]J. D. Anthony, *Life and Times of Rev. J. D. Anthony: An Autobiography with a Few Original Sermons* (Atlanta, 1896), p. 14.

[72]Ball, *Glance into the Great South-East,* p. 207. See also, Louise F. Hays, *History of Macon County, Georgia* (Atlanta, 1933), pp. 112–113, 118–121, for an account of the settlement of that county, and particularly the town of Marshallville, by family and community groups from Orangeburg and Newberry, South Carolina.

[73]Records of the Zion Church, Maury County, Tennessee (microfilm copies in Joint University Libraries, Nashville, Tennessee).

[74]George Powell, "Description of Blount County," p. 42. See also Brewer, History of Coosa County, p. 48, for the example of Joel Speigner "spying out the lands for a group back in South Carolina."

[75]Charles Tait to James A. Tait, January 20, 1817, in Charles Tait Papers (Alabama Department of Archives and History). At the time this letter was written Charles Tait was a United States senator from Georgia. See sketch in *Dictionary of American Biography*, XVIII, 274–275.

[76]James A. Tait to Charles Tait, December 15, 1817, Tait Papers.

[77]January 17, 1819, *ibid*.

[78]November 10, 1817, *ibid*.

Plain Folk and Their Role in Southern History

*M*ost travelers and critics who wrote about the South during the late antebellum period were of the opinion that the white inhabitants of the South generally fell into two categories, namely, the slaveholders and the "poor whites." Moreover, whether or not they intended to do so, they created the impression in the popular mind that the slaveholder was a great planter living in a white-columned mansion, served by a squad of Negro slaves who obsequiously attended his every want and whim. According to the opinion of such writers, these "cavaliers" were the great monopolists of their day; they crowded everyone not possessed of considerable wealth off the good lands and even the lands from which modest profits might be realized; they dominated politics, religion, and all phases of public life. The six or seven million nonslaveholders who comprised the remainder of the white population and were, with minor exceptions, considered "poor whites" or "poor white trash" were visualized as a sorry lot indeed. They had been pushed off by the planters into the pine barrens and sterile sand hills and mountains. Here as squatters upon abandoned lands and government tracts they dwelt in squalid log huts and kept alive by hunting and fishing, and by growing patches of corn, sweet potatoes, collards, and pumpkins in the small "deadenings" or clearings they had made in the all-engulfing wilderness. They were illiterate, shiftless, irresponsible, frequently vicious, and nearly always addicted to the use of "rot gut" whiskey and to dirt eating. Many, perhaps nearly all, according to later writers, had malaria, hookworm, and pellagra. Between the Great Unwashed and the slaveholders there was a chasm that could not be bridged. The nonslaveholders were six or seven million supernumeraries in a slaveholding society.[1]

Frederick Law Olmsted, perhaps, contributed more than any other writer to the version of Southern society sketched above; for he was possessed of unusual skill in the art of reporting detail and of completely wiping out the validity of such detail by subjective comments and generalizations. For example, despite the fact that he saw little destitution and almost constant evidence of well-being among the poorer folk, he was still able to conclude "that the majority of the Negroes at the North live more comfortably than the majority of whites at the South"; that, indeed, the majority of the people of the South were poor whites. It was not, in his opinion, sterile soil and unhealthful climate that created the great mass of poor whites, but slavery. "For manual agricultural labor...," Olmsted wrote, "the free man looking on, has a contempt, and for its necessity in himself, if such necessity exists, a pity quite beyond that of the man under whose observations it has been free from such an association of ideas." Olmsted could make this generalization despite the fact that throughout his extensive travels in the South he had constantly observed Negro slaves and whites working in the fields together. Indeed, the degradation of free labor by slavery was Olmsted's major premise from which all conclusions flowed regardless of the factual observations that he conscientiously incorporated in his books.[2]

Other writers, who had little or no firsthand knowledge of the South, quite naturally relied on the writings of travelers, and particularly Olmsted, who was regarded as dispassionate and authoritative. Their tendency was to seize upon the generalizations rather than the detailed reporting of the travel literature, with the result that they further simplified the picture of Southern society. George M. Weston's *Poor Whites of the South* and his *Progress of Slavery in the United States* are excellent examples of this process of simplification. "The whites of the South not connected with the ownership or management of slaves," he wrote, "constituting not far from three fourths of the whole number of whites, confined at least to the low wages of agricultural labor, and partly cut off even from this by the degradation of a companionship with black slaves, retire to the outskirts of civilization, where they lead a semisavage life, sinking deeper and more hopelessly into barbarism with each succeeding generation. The slave owner takes at first all the best lands, and finally all the lands susceptible of regular cultivation; and the poor whites, thrown back upon the hills and upon the sterile soils—[are] mere squatters without energy enough to acquire the title even to the cheap lands they occupy, without roads, and at length, without even a desire for education...."[3]

J. E. Cairnes, the British economist, presented the final stereotype of Southern society in his book, *The Slave Power*. Cairnes appears to have rested his generalizations about the social structure of the South largely upon those of Olmsted, Weston, and Hinton R. Helper. It was a pyramid upon a pyramid. But it was a picture of Southern society that made a deep and lasting impression.[4] "The

constitution of a slave society...resolves itself into three classes,"
writes Cairnes, "broadly distinguished from each other and connected by no common interest—the slaves on whom devolves all the
regular industry, the slaveholders who reap all its fruits, and an idle
and lawless rabble who live dispersed over vast plains in a condition
little removed from absolute barbarism."[5] "These mean whites...are
the natural growth of the slave system"; "regular industry is only
known to them as the vocation of slaves, and it is the one fate which
above all others they desire to avoid."[6] "In the Southern States no
less than five million human beings [who have been expelled from
the good lands by the slaveholders] are now said to exist...in a
condition little removed from savage life, eking out a wretched subsistence by hunting, fishing, by hiring themselves out for occasional
jobs, and by plunder."[7]

The generalization that these writers made about the Old South
—which may well be considered the first version of *Tobacco Road*—
should be kept in mind, for they have been subjected to frequent
examination in preparing this study and will be points of reference
in it.

A few Southern historians have accepted in whole or in part the
picture of the society of the Old South, as portrayed by such writers
as those quoted previously; but most of them, without doubt, have
regarded it as fantastic. Sometimes with an expression of indignation
on their faces they will say, "folks are just not like that in the South.
Society is not and never has been divided into rich and poor." Those
who were born before 1890 had a firsthand acquaintance with one
and often two generations who had lived before 1860 and who were
not—nor had they ever been—either poor whites or planters. For
example, outstanding Southern historians such as J. G. de Roulhac
Hamilton, Charles W. Ramsdell, George Petrie, and Walter Lynwood Fleming grew up in communities where heads of many families, including their own, had been reared before 1860. It will,
perhaps, drive home the idea as to how well antebellum Southern
society was known by those born prior to the close of the last century
if it is remarked that Confederate soldiers in 1900 were about the
average age of veterans of World War I in 1949.

Possessed of this firsthand acquaintance with numerous representatives of the Old South, Southern historians have, with few exceptions up until this time, strongly maintained that the white people
of the antebellum rural South were not divided into the simple cate-

gories of rich planter and poor white. As time has passed, and with it the older generations, even stronger assertions are being made concerning the plain folk of the Old South and, indeed, concerning the whole society in that region. The tone of some of these claims is somewhat indignant just as the tone of anyone tends to grow indignant when he knows from his own observations and experiences whereof he speaks, but discovers that his star witnesses have disappeared from the court. The truth of the matter is that for good reasons, such as a lack of trained historians in the South until well after the opening of the present century, the testimony of these star witnesses, the survivors of the old regime, was not taken while they were numerous enough and young enough for their evidence to be both full and valid. It has been assumed, too, quite naturally, that since the farmers and small planters, unlike the large planters and businessmen, seldom preserved their private papers and business accounts, no record of their manner of life and their place in the Southern society remained after they passed on.

But these millions of people did leave records of their lives: the church records, wills, administration of estates, county-court minutes, marriage licenses, inventory of estates, trial records, mortgage books, deed books, county tax books, and the manuscript returns of the federal censuses. Other important sources from which much can be learned not only about the plain folk, but about society as a whole in the South, are the older county and town histories, biographies, autobiographies, and recollections of men and women of only local importance—preachers, lawyers, doctors, county newspaper editors, and the like, who knew every family in the county and frequently in a much wider area. Last but not least must be mentioned the writings of those sojourners in the South, who remained in one place long enough to become acquainted with the country and the people. Out of such documents a picture of the whole people can be constructed, not just that of the great planter and merchant, but, in the words of an old jingle: "Rich man, poor man, beggar man, thief, doctor, lawyer, merchant, chief...."

Of all these sources, the county records and the unpublished census reports, which are made by the county for each individual, are the most valuable documents from which to study the life of the people as a whole. It is only by employing them in great volume, however, and receiving a cumulative effect that they can at all be usefully employed.

Upon reading page after page of tax lists and census returns, both of which give the landholdings and much of the personal property of all individuals, the picture of the economic structure of the Old South gradually takes form. These sources reveal the existence of a society of great complexity. Instead of the simple, two-fold division of the agricultural population into slaveholders and nonslaveholding poor whites, many economic groups appear. Among the slaveholders there were great planters possessed of thousands of acres of land and hundreds of slaves, planters owning a thousand or fewer acres and two score slaves, small planters with five hundred acres and ten or fifteen slaves, large farmers with three or four hundred acres and five to ten slaves, small farmers with two hundred or fewer acres and one or two slaves. Among the nonslaveholders were large farmers employing hired labor who owned from two hundred to a thousand acres; a middle group which owned from one hundred to two hundred acres; "one horse farmers" with less than one hundred acres; and landless renters, squatters, farm laborers, and a "leisure class" whose means of support does not appear on the record. But the core of the social structure was a massive body of plain folk who were neither rich nor very poor. These were employed in numerous occupations; but the great majority secured their food, clothing, and shelter from some rural pursuit, chiefly farming and livestock grazing. It is the plain country folk with whom this study is most concerned—that great mass of several millions who were not part of the plantation economy. The group included the small slaveholding farmers; the nonslaveholders who owned the land which they cultivated; the numerous herdsmen on the frontier, pine barrens, and mountains; and those tenant farmers whose agricultural production, as recorded in the census, indicated thrift, energy, and self-respect.

It is impossible to convey the picture thus formed by comprehensive examination of tax lists and census reports to those who have not scrutinized these documents to some extent; but, as is so often true under such circumstances, it becomes necessary to resort to abstractions. In this case that means, of course, a statistical analysis, which is the basis for this study.[8] Only general conclusions will be presented here.

The slaveholding families composed nearly one third of the white population of the South, and most of them were small slaveowners and small landowners. As estimated, 60 per cent owned from one to five slaves, and another large group held from five to ten. Most slaveholders whose chief occupation was agriculture owned their farms, and the small slaveholders, as would be expected, were small landowners. At least 60 per cent of the small slaveholders had farms ranging in size from fifty to three hundred acres. Over 60 per cent of the nonslaveholders outside the upper seaboard states—who, it will be recalled, were classed as poor white trash—were also landowners. In the lower South and in portions of the upper south central states an estimated 70 per cent owned farms. The sizes of their holdings differed very little from those of the small slaveholders. About 75 per cent ranged from a few to two hundred acres and the other 25 per cent were above two hundred acres in size.

If one considers the landed resources that were available to the Southern people between the Revolution and the Civil War, it will become apparent why the bulk of the Southern rural population, nonslaveholder and slaveholder alike, acquired the ownership of farmsteads and plantations, and how it was that the herdsmen had such ample pasturage for their livestock. A goodly portion of the federal public domain, which totaled 1,309,591,680 acres,[9] and over 200,000,000 acres of state lands in Virginia, the Carolinas, Georgia, and Texas had been open to Southerners during this period.[10] The opportunity of acquiring land was greater in the South than in the North. For example, in 1848, before the creation of Oregon Territory the area of the states and organized territories of the South was more than twice as great as that of the North, whereas the population of the South was scarcely half that of the North.[11] At all times during the interval between the Revolution and the Civil War the combined federal and state public domains in the South were greater than those open to settlement in the North, and the population was increasingly less. But the Southern farmers had another great advantage over the Northerners in that the grain, livestock, and tobacco farmers of the upper South and the Southern highlands could and did move into the lower parts of the Northwest, whereas the Northern farmers could not profitably move South.

The tax lists and census reports enable us to determine with reasonable accuracy the social structure of the rural South, and they are in some degree a measure of the economic struggle of the people. They give us, however, only an impersonal, external view; they furnish, let us say, a picture of the economic man, not the social gregarious human. It is such documents as grand-jury reports, trial records, court minutes, and wills that furnish the vital spark and recreate the individual, the family, and the community. The wills especially, often so personal and intimate, go far toward supplying a substitute for the private letters and diaries which the common folk, unlike the planters, failed to preserve. The wills also reveal many family customs.

The role of the Southern folk was scarcely that of a supernumerary in any phase of Southern life. To deal with them—as has been the tendency in studying the plantation economy—either as a formless mass or filler that settles into the cracks and crevices left by the planters is to take a narrow and incomplete view of Southern society. On the other hand to deal with the plain folk as a class-conscious group, bitter and resentful toward the aristocracy because of exploitation and neglect of the latter, is even farther from reality.

The Southern folk were, as has been repeatedly said, a closely knit people; but they were not class-conscious in the Marxian sense, for with rare exceptions they did not regard the planters and men of wealth as their oppressors. On the contrary, they admired them as a rule and looked with approval on their success; and they assumed, on the basis of much tangible evidence, that the door of economic opportunity swung open easily to the thrust of their own ambitious and energetic sons and daughters. Indeed, it was considered a common occurrence outside the older states of Virginia and the Carolinas, for the rank and file to move upward in the economic scale, and for individuals in every community to become well-to-do planters, political leaders, and members of a learned profession. Relatively few of the plain folk, however, seem to have had a desire to become wealthy. Their ambition was to acquire land and other property sufficient to give them and their children a sense of security and well-being, to be "good livers" and "have something saved for a rainy day" as they would have put it. Nevertheless, the knowledge that the economic door was not bolted against themselves and their children tended to stifle the development of a jealous and bitter class-consciousness.

The abundance of cheap land, the generally high prices received for farm products and livestock, and the rapidly developing political democracy were the principal means of keeping the economic door unlocked, and preventing the development of a sense of frustration and resentment against the more wealthy. There were, also, other important forces that diminished the feeling of class stratification and helped in the creation of a sense of unity between the plain folk and the aristocracy. Such were the association of rich and poor in all religious activities and in the schools, the frequent ties of blood kinship between them, and the generally folkish and democratic bearing of the aristocracy. This sense of unity between all social and economic groups can not be stressed too much, in view of the strongly and widely-held opinion to the contrary. Indeed, when the entire social and economic structure of the Old South is placed in perspective, rather than viewing each segment as a separate thing, all parts will be seen as bearing a relation to the whole. It is then that the plain folk appear not as supernumeraries but as a vital element of the social and economic structure of the Old South. A grazing and farm economy rather than a plantation economy was practiced by nearly all the nonslaveholders and by 60 to 80 per cent of the slaveholders. Farm economy meant a diversified, self-sufficient type of agriculture, where the money crops were subordinated to food crops, and where the labor was performed by the family aided by a few slaves. Plantation economy depended upon slave labor, and usually specialized in the production of one or more of the staple crops, such as cotton, sugar cane, rice, and tobacco. Food crops and livestock were not neglected, as a rule, by the planters; in fact, they frequently produced enough corn for their own use, but such crops were generally subordinated to the money crops. As a result of the self-sufficiency of farm economy, the farmers were seldom involved in indebtedness, once they had paid for their lands.

Farm economy, together with livestock grazing, not only furnished support for the farmers and herdsmen who composed the bulk of the Southern population but supplied a large portion of the hogs, cattle, breadstuffs purchased for the plantations. Indeed, the farmers and graziers could have easily supplied the entire needs of the South for beef and pork, had not the greater portion of the cattle and hogs been driven to the seaports such as Philadelphia, Baltimore, Charleston, Savannah, Mobile, and New Orleans, where they were usually slaughtered and shipped to the Eastern markets or to the West Indies. Why these cattle and hogs were thus disposed of instead of being sold directly to the planters is a question that can be answered perhaps by a careful study of the weather map. The warm and damp winters of the lower South caused meat to spoil quickly and rendered large-scale slaughter and preservation of meat on the plantations a hazardous business, with the result that the larger drovers could not depend on the plantation markets. The planters often complained in their diaries and letters of their meat supply being spoiled by warm weather. For example Mrs. C. C. Clay of Huntsville, Alabama, wrote her husband on December 5, 1828, that "Augustine has gone to Tennessee in quest of pork. The weather bids fair for the same difficulty to exist in keeping pork that there was last year." On January 7, 1845, over sixteen years later, Mrs. Clay's son, Hugh Lawson Clay, writes his mother that "the weather is bad, very bad, warm and rainy—fair for spoiling pork and for nothing else. Many persons I hear have already lost most of their meat and are unable to buy more."[12] Because of this condition the seaport towns frequently had equipment for the slaughter of animals and the preservation of meat. Such places furnished a more reliable market, where the drovers could dispose of all their cattle and hogs at once instead of peddling them to the planters who might decide not to buy at all. In case such seaport towns were not satisfactorily equipped for slaughtering animals the livestock could be sent to Philadelphia, Baltimore, and Charleston, where they would be slaughtered and packed. It is not at all improbable that much of the meat of Southern livestock was sold back to the Southern planters; indeed, there is a tradition that such was the case. Other raw products such as cotton were treated in this fashion.

The Southern folk, with a more balanced economy than that of the planter groups, were obviously a source of strength when the Civil War came. Frequently all their men—including the heads of families—from 17 to 50 were in military service; but the younger children—boys and girls—the women, and the older men took the place of the absent men in the work and management of the farm. The plantations, however, were not as dependable as the farms in wartime because the slaves—except the house servants—usually fled to the Union lines as soon as the invading army came within reach, and thus completely paralyzed further agricultural production. The farms, on the other hand, continued to operate provided the farmers had been able to conceal their work stock from the Union troops, which was probably not difficult in a country so heavily wooded as the South.

It was, however, during the Reconstruction period that the plain folk revealed their real vitality and power of survival. Accustomed to every phase of work in any way related to farming and rural life, and often frontier life, they had no such readjustment to make as the planter who had usually little manual skill or experience in manual labor. With an ax, saw, auger, frow, drawing knife, and hammer, which might be assembled by a neighborhood pool, the farmers held their house-raisings and rebuilt with logs their houses and barns that had been burned during the war. With a sledge hammer and anvil they fashioned crude plows and hoes from the worn-out parts of old implements or from scrap iron and steel gathered here and there. They built crude wagons and carts, made horse collars by platting shucks, fashioned harness from hickory saplings with ax and drawing knife, and made traces and other parts of the harness from old pieces of chain or home-tanned leather. Often there would be a shortage of work stock, in which case what few old animals that were left would be passed around from place to place until they were unable to go. In some cases on record, men hitched themselves to the plow. In this way the plain folk by ingenuity, heartbreaking toil, patient endurance, self-denial, and physical toughness were able to survive the Civil War and Reconstruction, and restore their farm economy—a vital portion of Southern economy. This was accomplished when the plantation system was in shambles or severely crippled from the devastation of war and the destruction of the slave-labor system. It is not too much to say that the plain folk thus rescued the South from complete and, perhaps, final ruin with little or no aid or sympathy from any sources whatsoever outside the borders of their own section.

It has often been claimed that the planter class dominated politics and determined the policies of the government. If so, how did they control the mass of voters? Was it done by intimidation through threat of physical violence to the voter or his family?—a method quite common in Europe, today, and in many organizations in the United States. Such intimidation as a means of vote getting can of course be dismissed. It would have been physical and political suicide in a country where family ties and kinships were so numerous and close, and where such a threat would have been enthusiastically met—more than halfway—by men and boys handy with firearms. Did the aristocracy control the people by means of economic coercion? This also is a method too well known in the United States even to be discussed. This type of coercion was not possible in the antebellum South, however, since the Southern farmer usually owned his farm and was dependent on no one. All forms of coercion were in fact out of keeping with the character of either the common folk or the planters. What of the use of money to purchase votes necessary to win the election? Although there must have been in every community individuals whose vote could be purchased, there is no evidence of a widespread use of bribery to sway the vote of the people. Besides this, too, was not in keeping with the character of either group. Reuben Davis says in his *Recollections of Mississippi* that "there was little trickery and no corruption in the politics of those days, and a man who had dared tamper with a ballot box, or who had been detected in any fraud by the people, would have been torn in pieces without a moment's hesitation. The populace might be ignorant of many things, careless and indifferent about many more; but where honor and honesty were concerned the great heart of the masses beat true and fearless. Any man who aspired to lead them must be above reproach according to their standards.

"These standards were high enough and clean enough to force aspirants for leadership to at least outward conformity with the popular ideal, and the very existence of such an ideal kept the political atmosphere in a measure pure."[13] The truth of the matter is that whatever influence the planters exercised over the political action of the common people was of a personal and local nature. It was based upon the respect the plain folk of a community had for the character and judgment of individual planters in that community and such qualities of character and judgment in the planter were revealed only by his genuine participation in community affairs.

It must be remembered, however, that there were few genuine planters outside the Black Belt, and that such personal influence and leadership was relatively narrow. If the farmers who lived outside the Black Belt were to be brought to support the interest of the planters, a less personal means of gaining their votes would have to be used; and this method had to be that of persuasion. Such persuasion was then as now the chief business of the politicians; and unless the politicians were planters—and most, except on the national scale, were not—it would immediately become very much of a question as to whose interest was being served, whether that of the planters, or of the plain folk, or of the politicians and their political organizations.

The persuasive efforts made by both Whig and Democratic political leaders to win the political support of the rank and file was extraordinary. The two parties regarded few towns as too small for the establishment of rival newspapers. It was not uncommon for towns of less than one thousand people to have two ably-edited newspapers, whose emphasis would be political.[14]

Joint debates were a very popular mode of conducting a campaign. In these debates apt rejoinder, witty repartee, and side comments were often more effective than oratory. The common folk loved good oratory, but they revelled in the witty thrust and parry and in the practical joke. William H. Milburn tells of a political speaker, who, as he puts it, "was quite overthrown at the summit of a gorgeous flight of eloquence, and left to slink dumfounded from the stage" when an unscrupulous adversary bawled out at his back "guess he wouldn't talk quite so hifalutenin if he knowed his breeches was torn out behind."[15] These joint debates and political speeches, the one purpose of which was to gain popular support for political candidates, were usually successful in bringing together a great concourse of people. To make sure of a large attendance, scores of hogs, beeves, and young goats were barbecued, and barrels of lemonade were served. Seldom has the suffrage of the common folk been so courted as in the late antebellum South, and, as a result of this, seldom have the people been so well posted on the political issues of the day. "One of the most remarkable characteristics of the Southern people before the war," observes Reuben Davis, the Mississippi politician, "was their universal enjoyment of public speaking. . . . In consequence of this, the art of fluent speaking was largely cultivated, and a man could hope for little success in public life unless he possessed this faculty in some degree. Another consequence was that there was never a people better educated on political questions than the Southerners of that day."[16]

The significance of the role of the plain folk in politics may be partly evaluated from some of the provisions of the new state constitutions adopted under popular pressure between 1830 and 1860. Universal white manhood suffrage, the popular election of virtually all county and state officers, and the abolition of property qualifications for office holding in most cases were good examples. If the Democratic party, as it has been constantly asserted, was primarily the agency of the common people and the Whig party that of the planters and business interests, then more often than not in the lower South, at least, the party of wealth took a beating. Nor were the Democrats at all tenderhearted in the methods. In Alabama, for example, a Democratic legislature abolished the use of the three-fifths ratio in the election of Congressmen and placed representation thus on the white basis. This greatly reduced the power of the Black Belt, which was the Whig stronghold, and gave the white counties control. This law was followed by the reapportionment act of 1843 which gerrymandered the Congressional districts so as to ensure the continued control of the white counties. Then in the session of 1855–1856 the Democratic legislature in a redistricting act gerrymandered the Whig districts still further; and although the Whigs had an estimated 45 per cent of the population of the state they were able to elect only two congressmen out of the seven under this act.[17] Finally it was the Democratic party which took the lead in the secession of the Southern states. The Whig planters and businessmen generally were opposed to secession until the last and went out of the Union reluctantly.

Reference has been frequently made to the fact that outside the older states, individuals were constantly rising from the farmer to the planter class. There are indications, in fact, that in some areas a majority had thus risen from relative poverty as had the older planter class in the seaboard states. Much depended on where the immigrant settled, as was pointed out in discussing migration. Settlers on rich soils usually rose more rapidly and further than those on poorer soils. Indeed, it appears that in many parts of the Black Belt most of the settlers were either nonslaveholders or small slaveholders, and that frequently both nonslaveholders and small slaveholders became large slaveholders.

But the plain folk made a much larger contribution to the leadership in other classes than they did to that of the planter class. It appears to be true in the lower South and in Tennessee and Kentucky that the bulk of lawyers, physicians, preachers, editors, teachers, businessmen, and political leaders below the national level were members of families who were poor or only comfortably well off. A young man of ability, energy, and determination—barring unusually bad luck—could scarcely fail of considerable success in any of the professions. He might never set the world on fire—in fact, he probably would have no such desire as a rule—but he could nearly always rise to local leadership. After examining the life histories of a large number of individuals who have risen from obscurity and comparative poverty, one cannot fail to see that they all follow a similar pattern. First, the parents, though often very poor, usually possessed education beyond the limits of mere literacy and had great respect for education as a means of attaining success. Then, too, they had a

certain refinement, which their robust neighbors did not usually
have. Not that they were aloof or prideful in their bearing; only
they nursed a spark in their bosoms which they were able to pass on
to some of their children. Next the son, or sons, who felt this spark
of pride and ambition, utilized all possible opportunities at home
and at school to acquire education. After he had acquired sufficient
education and age he would teach school, clerk in a store, or find
other employment which would enable him to save enough money to
attend the academy or even college. Apparently most young men of
this type taught school. The third step was the preparation for his
profession, usually the law, medicine, or the ministry.

If he were to be a lawyer, oft-times he read law under the direction of an attorney while teaching school, though occasionally he
would attend a law school. When he had been admitted to the bar
he would usually enter a law office in a minor capacity—frequently
as a sort of secretary and copyist for the firm. If he were shrewd and
energetic—and young men of this type usually were—he would soon
rise into a prominent position in the firm or as an independent
attorney. The essentials to success were a practical knowledge of the
law, an understanding of country jurors, some oratorical talent, and,
always, cleverness in debate and repartee. There was much legal
business in the rural South and a lawyer of only modest talent could
earn a good income. Such well-known Georgians as Charles Tait,
United States senator and federal judge; William H. Crawford,
United States senator and secretary of the treasury; Richard Henry
Wilde, state attorney general and congressman; William Towne,
congressman and governor; Joseph E. Brown, governor, judge, and
United States senator; Alexander H. Stephens, Vice-President of the
Confederacy, congressman, and governor, followed the pattern
sketched above. Indeed, says William H. Sparks, from the ranks of
the poor but ambitious youth "arose most of those men so distinguished in...Georgia's earlier history."[18]

If the young man planned to become a physician, his preparation
could be as little or as much as he desired and was able to pay for.
The commonest procedure even for the most ambitious was to obtain employment with a practicing physician—such as keeping his
books, driving his buggy, and running errands. In his spare time, if
any, the apprentice read the medical books in the doctor's office and
perhaps dissected a cadaver—at least for a while, until it spoiled
completely. The doctor, no doubt, on his long drives would teach his

assistant, as best he could, the knotty problems in his books and in his practice. After two or three years of this apprenticeship, the student doctor could with no real difficulty obtain license to practice; in fact, he could without much risk set up most anywhere and practice without license. Perhaps the majority of apprentice physicians did not end their studies at this point but went off for a course of lectures and study in a medical college, which would extend over a period varying from a few months to several years.

Often, however, a poor young man planning to be a physician taught school or clerked in a store, just as had the prospective lawyer, for the purpose of saving enough money to complete his academic education and pay his expenses in a medical school.

An examination of the life histories of large numbers of the clergy seems to indicate that an overwhelming majority were recruits from the ranks of the people, and that they acquired their education in a fashion similar to that of the young men preparing for the other professions. Many began their careers as schoolmasters and, indeed, many continued throughout life to teach school.

The life histories of those who entered business, such as banking, merchandising, and real estate (better known as "land speculation") are not as well known as are those of men who entered one of the learned professions. The cases which have been examined, however, indicate that, although the field was more limited in the South than those of planting and the professions, the percentage of those from the ranks of the common folk was high.

Since education was for the poor but ambitious youth the gateway to success in business and the professions, what were the opportunities for acquiring the necessary education? Much has been said and even more has been assumed, and therefore implied, to the effect that the educational institutions of the South were practically closed to all but the well-to-do because of the great expense of attending them. It is certainly not the purpose of this study to go into the history and theory of education in the Old South, but a few facts will be pointed out which may indicate that the obstacles to acquiring an education were not very great if an education was desired.

The first thing is to observe that the common folk of the South obviously received relatively more schooling than has generally been supposed. By comparing the illiteracy of the Southern people with that of the people of New England, where for well-known reasons a common school system had long existed, the South has been made to appear as a land where mass ignorance prevailed. In 1850, for example, the census showed that only 1.89 per cent of the white population of New England above twenty years of age could not read; but in the South 8.27 per cent of this age group were illiterate. The fact was not advertised, however, that in the Northwest, where population was sparse and scattered somewhat as in the rural South 5.03 per cent of those above twenty were illiterate.

Just how illiterate, however, were the 8.27 per cent of the South and the 5.03 per cent of the Northwest? The answer is that in comparison with the situation in most countries of the world at that time the Southern folk were one of the most literate major groups of the entire world. In 1846, for example, of all the couples throughout England and Wales who got married, 32.6 per cent of the men and 48.1 per cent of the women affixed their marks instead of their signatures to applications for licenses. In the French army in 1851, of 311,218 conscripts 34 per cent could neither read nor write. The marriage and conscription records are very good cross sections of the young adult population; but in both France and England the young people were more literate than the older groups because of the improvement of the common school systems. In Spain, Portugal, Italy, the Balkans, Poland, and Russia illiteracy was between 90 and 95 per cent. Only in the Scandinavian countries, Belgium, and Holland, Prussia, and Saxony was the literacy of the people comparable with or greater than that of the South.[19] Most of the children in the rural communities of the South, including those of the well-to-do, learned to read and write and cypher in the old field schools. These were elementary schools, in which reading and writing and arithmetic and sometimes higher subjects were taught. They were financed primarily by subscription, each child being charged about two and one half dollars for a five or six months' term and one dollar for a six-week summer session. Toward the end of the period, many of these schools were receiving aid from both the state and county. Most of the academies, which will be discussed presently, had primary departments that taught the same things as the old field schools. The academies were usually located in a town or village.

Literacy is not education; however, if college attendance is any test of an educated people, the South had more educated men and women in proportion to population than the North, or any other part of the world. According to the 1860 census, out of a white population of 7,400,000 there were 25,882 students enrolled in

Southern colleges, whereas in the North, with a white population of over 19,000,000, there were only 27,408 students in college; and quite a large number of these were from the South. That is, there was one college student for each 247 white persons in the South and one in 703 in the North.

It was, however, the academy more than the colleges that gave the poor but ambitious youth their education. There were at the end of the antebellum period about 2,500 academies in the South. Most had primary departments to take care of the youngsters of the town and vicinity; they all had what would have been called high-school subjects, many of which are now taught in college; and all the larger, better equipped offered college work.

The tuition in these academies, most of which had ten-month sessions was low—about what the library, contingent, and athletic fee is in most of the schools today. The tuition per annum in the fifty-seven academies of Georgia in 1860 averaged $15.50 for the elementary branches and in the higher branches $26.00.[20] A study of over a score of academies in Alabama shows that the tuition for a student ranged from $15 to $25 in the primary departments and $25 to $35 in the high schools. Those academies that gave college work usually charged $40 to $50 a year. Board, room, and laundry ranged from eight to ten dollars per month. In short, for less that $150 a young man or young lady could attend an academy for ten months.[21]

Of course the quality of work offered by the academies varied with the quality of teachers and equipment. Edgar Knight in his *Public Education in the South* says that "the academy was a very highly respected means of education in the South, where it extended in greater numbers than in any other section of the country."[22]

The following subjects were usually taught in the academies: Elementary—spelling, reading, writing, arithmetic, English grammar, and geography. High school—chemistry, logic, ethics or moral philosophy, psychology (called intellectual science), physics, astronomy, political economy, composition and rhetoric, Greek, Latin, French, algebra, geometry, trigonometry, mechanical drawing, analytical geometry and calculus (by request). In the female academies, drawing, painting, fine needlework, and music were always offered, the tuition being extra. All of these, of course, were not required; in fact, a student could take one or all of them as it suited him or his purse. The struggling country youth eager to acquire an education would take every course possible.

It thus appears that the opportunity of acquiring an education — the gateway to the professions and to success — was quite favorable for the ambitious youth, however poor he might be. Indeed, it can be rather positively asserted that most young men, at least, who *desired* an education, could obtain one. The catchword, let it be observed, is *desired*.

[1]See A. J. N. Den Hollander, "The Tradition of the Poor White" in W. T. Couch (ed.), *Culture in the South* (Chapel Hill, 1934), pp. 403, 415, for a criticism of the traditional view of society in the antebellum South.

[2]*A Journey in the Back Country* (New York, 1863), pp. 237, 297, 298, 299, *passim*. See also *A Journey in the Seaboard Slave States, with Remarks on Their Economy* (New York, 1856), and *A Journey Through Texas* (New York, 1857), *passim*.

[3]George M. Weston, *The Poor Whites of the South* (Washington, D.C., 1856), p. 5. His *Progress of Slavery* was published in 1857.

[4]Allen Nevins drew upon Cairnes's *Slave Power* in his *Ordeal of the Union*, published in 1947; Thomas D. Clark has made large use of Olmsted in his book, *The Emerging South*, published in 1961; and Arthur M. Schlesinger, Jr., in his numerous publications has made constant use of these stereotypes of Southern society.

[5]J. E. Cairnes, *The Slave Power: Its Character, Career and Probable Designs* (New York, 1862), p. 60.

[6]*Ibid.*, pp. 78, 79.

[7]*Ibid.*, p. 54.

[8]The statistical data used in this article are taken from Frank L. Owsley, *Plain Folk of the Old South* (Baton Rouge, 1949), pp. 150–229.

[9]Benjamin H. Hibbard, *A History of the Public Land Policies* (New York, 1924), p. 78; and Thomas C. Donaldson, *The Public Domain; Its History with Statistics* (Washington, 1884), table on p. 13.

[10]Samuel G. McLendon, *History of the Public Domain of Georgia* (Atlanta, 1924), *passim*; Roy M. Robbins, *Our Landed Heritage; The Public Domain* (Princeton, 1942), p. 9; Reuben McKitrick, *The Public Land System of Texas, 1823–1910* (Madison, 1918); and Aldon S. Lang, *Financial History of the Public Lands in Texas* (Waco, 1932), *passim*.

[11]See Donaldson, *Public Domain*, pp. 28–29, for areas of states and territories.

[12]Clay Papers (Duke University Library). Similar references are found in many of the Clay Papers.

[13]New York, 1889, p. 112.

[14]Lewy Dorman, *Party Politics in Alabama From 1850 Through 1860* (Wetumpka, Alabama, 1935), pp. 19–20.

[15]*The Pioneers, Preachers and People of the Mississippi Valley* (New York, 1860), p. 467.

[16]*Recollections of Mississippi and Mississippians*, p. 69.

[17]Dorman, *Party Politics in Alabama,* pp. 25–26, 96–99. The development of political democracy is ably treated in Charles S. Sydnor, *The Development of Southern Sectionalism, 1819–1848* (Baton Rouge, 1948), Chaps. II and XII, and in Fletcher M. Green, "Democracy in the Old South," *Journal of Southern History,* XII (1946), 1–23.

[18]*The Memories of Fifty Years* (Macon, 1870), pp. 117–118. The best sources for the study of leadership in the learned professions in the antebellum South are county and local histories, memoirs, and autobiographies of lawyers, physicians, and preachers, and the state histories of religious demonstrations and of the bench and bar. Many such sources have been examined in this study, and only general reference is made here to this type of material.

[19]J. D. B. DeBow, *Statistical View of the United States, Embracing its Territory Population...Being a Compendium of the Seventh Census* (Washington, 1954), pp. 148–149.

[20]*A Gazetteer of Georgia, Containing a Particular Description of the State,* 4th ed. (Macon, 1860), pp. 143–148.

[21]The contemporary local newspapers contain much information about the academies, both in their advertisements and in their news and editorial columns. The county and town histories usually carry considerable information about the academies. The following works are useful in this connection: Edgar Knight, *Public Education in the South* (New York, 1922); M. C. S. Noble, *History of the Public Schools of North Carolina* (Chapel Hill, 1930); Charles W. Dabney, *Universal Education in the South,* 2 vols. (Chapel Hill, 1936); Robert H. White, *Development of the Tennessee State Educational Organization, 1796–1929* (Kingsport, 1929); Isabella M. E. Blandin, *History of Higher Education of Women in the South Prior to 1860* (New York, 1909).

[22]Page 73.

II

The Fundamental Cause of the Civil War:
Egocentric Sectionalism

Local Defense and the Downfall of the
Confederacy: A Study in State Rights

Defeatism in the Confederacy

Why Europe Did Not Intervene

The Fundamental Cause of the Civil War: Egocentric Sectionalism*

Before attempting to say what were the causes of the American Civil War, first, let me say what were not the causes of this war. Perhaps the most beautiful, the most poetic, the most eloquent statement of what the Civil War was not fought for is Lincoln's Gettysburg Address. That address will live as long as Americans retain their love of free government and personal liberty; and yet in reassessing the causes of the Civil War, the address whose essence was that the war was being fought so "that government of the people, by the people and for the people shall not perish from the earth" is irrelevant. Indeed, this masterpiece of eloquence has little if any value as a statement of the basic principles underlying the war.

The Civil War was not a struggle on the part of the South to destroy free government and personal liberty nor on the part of the North to preserve them. Looked at from the present perspective of the world-wide attempt of the totalitarians to erase free governments and nations living under such governments from the face of the earth, the time-worn stereotype that the South was attempting the destruction of free government and the North was fighting to preserve it seems very unrealistic and downright silly. In the light of the present-day death struggle against the most brutal form of despotism ever known, the Civil War, as far as the issue of free government was involved, was a sham battle. Indeed, both Northern and Southern people in 1861 were alike profoundly attached to the principles of free government. A systematic study of both Northern and Southern opinion as expressed in their newspapers, speeches, diaries, and private letters, gives irrefutable evidence in support of this assertion. Their ideology was democratic and identical. However, theoretical adherence to the democratic principles is not sufficient evidence that democratic government exists. I believe that I shall not be challenged in the assertion that the economic structure of a section or a nation is the foundation upon which its political structure must rest. For this reason, therefore, it will be necessary to know what the economic foundations of these sections were. Was the economic struc-

*This essay was originally Mr. Owsley's presidential address to the Southern Historical Association in November 1940.

ture of the North such as to support a political democracy in fact as well as in form? And was the economic structure of the South such as to permit the existence of free government? By utilizing the county tax books and the unpublished census reports a reasonably accurate and specific picture of wealth structure of the antebellum South, and to some extent that of the other sections has been obtained. As has been generally known, the Northwest was agricultural and its population was predominantly composed of small farmers, though a considerable minority were large farmers comparable with the larger Southern planters. It seems that in 1860 about 80 per cent of the farmers in the Old Northwest were landowners. A fairly large fraction of the remaining farm population in that area were either squatters upon public lands or were the members of land-owning families. Only a small per cent were renters. In those regions farther west the ownership of land was not as widespread because farmers had not yet completed their titles to the lands that they had engrossed. Taken as a whole the people of the Northwest were economically self-sufficient. They could not be subjected to economic coercion and, hence, they were politically free. Their support of free government—as they understood it—was effective.

The Northeastern section of the United States had already assumed its modern outlines of a capitalistic-industrial society where the means of production were either owned or controlled by a relatively few. That is to say, New England and the middle states were fast becoming in essence a plutocracy whose political ideology was still strongly democratic; but the application of this democratic ideology was being seriously hampered by the economic dependence of the middle and lower classes upon those who owned the tools of production. The employee unprotected by government or by strong labor organizations was subject in exercising his political rights to the undue influence of the employer.

To sum up: the economic structure of the Northwest was an adequate foundation for free government; but that of the East, though still supporting democratic ideals, was often too weak to sustain these ideals in actual government.

Turning to the South, which was primarily agricultural, one finds the situation completely contradictory to what has usually been assumed. While the plutocracy of the East owned or controlled the means of production in industry and commerce, the so-called slave oligarchy of the South owned scarcely any of the land outside the

Black Belt and only about 25 per cent of the land in the Black Belt. Actually, the basic means of production in the Black Belt and in the South as a whole was well distributed among all classes of the population. The overwhelming majority of Southern families in 1860 owned their farms and livestock. About 90 per cent of the slaveholders and 70 per cent of the nonslaveholders owned the land which they farmed. The bulk of slaveholders were small farmers, not oligarchs. While taken together they owned more slaves and more land than the large planters, taken individually the majority of slaveholders owned from one to four slaves and less than three hundred acres of land. The nonslaveholders—70 per cent of whom, as just noted, were landowners—were not far removed economically from the small slaveholders. While the majority of slaveholders possessed from one to three-hundred acres of land, 80 per cent of the landed nonslaveholders owned from one to two hundred acres of land and 20 per cent owned from two hundred to a thousand. To repeat: the basic fact disclosed in an analysis of the economic structure of the South, based upon the unpublished census reports and tax books, is that the overwhelming majority of white families in the South, slaveholders and nonslaveholders (unlike the industrial population of the East) owned the means of production. In other words, the average Southerner like the average Westerner possessed economic independence; and the only kind of influence that could be exercised over his political franchise by the slave oligarchy was a strictly persuasive kind. The South, then, like the Northwest, not only held strongly to the democratic ideology; it also had a sound economic foundation for a free government.

If the destruction of democratic government by the South and its preservation by the North were not the causes of the Civil War, what then were the causes? The immediate answer to this question is that in 1861 the Southern people desired and attempted to establish their independence and that the North took up arms to prevent the South from establishing this independence. This is only another way of saying that by 1861 the South had developed a Southern nationalism. The war for Southern independence was and remains unique: it is the only war ever fought upon the principle of the right of a people to choose their own government, for the purpose of separating from a government founded upon this principle. Looking immediately behind this desire of the South to establish a separate government, and of the North to prevent it, we discover a state of mind

in both sections which explains their conduct. This state of mind
may be summed up thus: by the spring of 1861 the Southern people
felt it undesirable and dangerous to continue to live under the same
government with the people of the North. So profound was this feeling among the bulk of the Southern population that they were prepared to fight a long and devastating war to accomplish a separation.
On the other hand, the North was willing to fight a war to retain
their reluctant fellow citizens under the same government with
themselves.

That state of mind, which manifested itself in a desire of the
South to separate from the North, and a desire on the part of the
North to conquer and break the South, we may well call a war
psychology. Its origin was in the sectional character of the United
States. In other words, Southern nationalism and the resultant Civil
War had one basic cause: sectionalism. But to conclude that sectionalism was the cause of the Civil War, and at the same time insist—as
has usually been done—that the Civil War was the climax of an
irrepressible conflict is to seem to accept a pessimistic view of the
future of the United States. For if the antebellum conflict was irrepressible and the Civil War unavoidable, we are faced with future
irrepressible conflicts, future civil wars, and ultimate disintegration
of the nation into its component sections. I say this because I do not
see any way by which sectionalism can be erased from the political,
economic, racial, and cultural maps of the United States. Our national state was built, not upon the foundations of a homogeneous
land and people, but upon geographical sections inhabited severally
by provincial, self-conscious, self-righteous, aggressive, and ambitious
populations of varying origins and diverse social and economic systems; and the passage of time and the cumulative effects of history
have accentuated these sectional patterns. That is to say, the United
States has always been and probably will always be more of an empire than a national state.

Before accepting the possibility of future wars and national disintegration as inevitable because of the irrepressible conflict between
permanent sections, let me hasten to say that there are two types of
sectionalism: there is that egocentric, destructive sectionalism where
conflict is always irrepressible; and there is that constructive sectionalism where good will prevails—two types as opposite from one another as good is opposite from evil, as the benign is from the malignant. It was the egocentric, the destructive, malignant type of sec-

tionalism that destroyed the Union in 1861, and that would do so again if it existed over a long period of time.

Before discussing that destructive sectionalism which caused the Civil War, some observations should be made of the constructive type, since, as I have suggested, the very nature of the American state makes one or the other type of sectionalism inevitable. The idea of either good or bad sectionalism as an enduring factor in American national life has received scant consideration by historians as a rule, either because they have desired to justify the conduct of their section on occasion as being the manifestation of nationalism when in truth it was sectionalism writ large; or because they have apparently been unable to reconcile sectionalism with nationalism.

Since sectionalism from the very nature of our country must remain a permanent and basic factor in our national life, we should look it in the face and discriminate between the good and the bad features. Above all else, we should recognize the fact that sectionalism when properly dealt with, far from being irreconcilable with nationalism, is its strongest support. It is only the malignant, destructive type that conflicts with nationalism or loyalty to the national state or empire. Great Britain once failed to make this distinction and to grasp the fact that the American colonials could be good Americans and good Britishers at the same time, and the result was the loss of the American colonies. After the lesson learned from the American Revolution, the British mind has grasped the fact that good Canadians or good Australians are all the better Britishers because of their provincial or—may I say?—sectional loyalty. Provincialism, dominionism, and, in the case of the United States, sectionalism, far from excluding nationalism, when properly recognized and not constantly frowned upon, and the interests of sections ignored and their ambitions frustrated, are powerful supports of nationalism. Such provincialism or sectionalism becomes a national asset. It is a brake upon political centralization and possible despotism. It has proven and will prove to be, if properly directed, a powerful force in preserving free institutions. It gives color, variety, and vitality to all segments of the national state. Because of this vitality in all its parts, the United States, unlike France, whose lifeblood seems to flow entirely through Paris, would prove a difficult country to subjugate by a foreign enemy, and its government and society more difficult, if not impossible, to overthrow by violent revolution. It is because Great Britain has, as the result of her lesson learned from the American

Revolution, fostered a good sectionalism within her empire, that she stood alone in 1940–1941 and baffled the orderly mind of the Germans and defied conquest. By loosening the ties that bind the component parts of this straggling union of colonies and dominions, Great Britain has made these bonds all the stronger. She and her commonwealth of nations—her sections—thus live in all their parts. Tragically, the American people failed to learn adequately the very lesson that they so thoroughly taught Great Britain: that local differences and attachments were natural, desirable, and formed the very rootbed of patriotism; indeed, that such differences, when given decent recognition, greatly strengthened nationalism and the national state. It was this failure to recognize or respect local differences and interests—in other words, the failure to recognize sectionalism as a fundamental fact of American life—that contributed most to the development of that kind of sectionalism which destroyed national unity and divided the nation.

There were three basic manifestations of that egocentric sectionalism which disrupted the Union in 1861. First was the habit of the dominant section—that is, the section which had the larger share in the control of the federal government—of considering itself the nation, its people the American people, its interests the national interests (in other words, the habit of considering itself the sole possessor of nationalism, when, indeed, it was thinking strictly in terms of one section) and conversely the habit of the dominant section of regarding the minority group as factional, its interests and institutions and way of life as un-American, unworthy of friendly consideration, and even the object of attack.

The second manifestation of this egocentric sectionalism that led to the Civil War was the perennial attempt of a section to gain or maintain its political ascendency over the federal government by destroying the sectional balance of power which, both New England and the South maintained, had been established by the three-fifths ratio clause in the federal Constitution.

The third and most dangerous phase of this sectionalism, perhaps the *sine qua non* of the Civil War, was the failure to observe what in international law is termed the comity of nations, and what we may by analogy designate as the comity of sections. That is, the people in one section failed in their language and conduct to respect the dignity and self-respect of the people in the other section. These three manifestations of sectionalism were so closely related that at times they can be segregated only in theory and for the sake of logical discussion. Indeed, as I have suggested, all were manifestations of that egocentric sectionalism that caused a section to regard itself as the nation.

Let me review some familiar facts of American history that illustrate each of these phases of sectionalism. During the first twelve years of the government under the federal Constitution, the old commercial-financial aristocracy of New England, with the aid of the same classes of people scattered throughout the urban centers of the seaboard, controlled the national government through the instrumentality of the Federalist party. An analysis of the chief measure of the Federalist regime and of the mental processes behind their enactments—as disclosed in speeches and letters and newspaper editorials—reveals the dominant section, New England, with its compact, homogeneous population, its provincial outlook, thinking, talking, and acting as if it were the United States; its way of life, its economic system, and its people the only real Americans; while the remainder of the country, the people, and their interests and ways of life were alien and un-American. Most of the laws enacted during the control of the New England Federalists were considered by the South and much of the middle states as being for the sole benefit of the commercial and banking interests of the East, and as injurious, even ruinous, to the agricultural sections. In order to give constitutional sanction to these centralizing sectional laws, the Federalist party under the brilliant leadership of Alexander Hamilton evolved the doctrine of implied powers, which seemed to the agricultural sections, by this time under the leadership of Thomas Jefferson, to be pulling the foundations from under constitutional government. This sectional and centralizing policy of the New England-dominated Federalist party culminated in the Alien and Sedition Laws, which were met by the Virginia and Kentucky Resolutions. These resolutions may be regarded as a campaign document to be used in ousting the Federalists and New England from power. They were also a threat of the minority section to withdraw from the Union should Federalist New England continue in power, and continue its policy of ignoring the agricultural sections of the country or of running roughshod over their interests.

The overthrow of New England's control of the national government by the Jeffersonian party in 1800 resulted in a twenty-four-year regime of the Virginia dynasty, during fifteen years of which—that

is, until after the War of 1812—the government was distinctly dominated by the South and Southwest. If Hamilton had been positive
that the welfare of the nation depended upon reinforcing and maintaining by special government favor the capitalistic system of the
East, Jefferson was more positive that democratic and constitutional
government and the welfare of the American people depended upon
maintaining the supremacy in government and society of a land-
owning farmer-people whose center of gravity was in the South and
middle states. To Jefferson commerce, finance, and industry were
only necessary evils to be maintained purely as conveniences and
handmaidens of agriculture. Such a doctrinaire conception of government and society boded ill for New England; and the period
from 1801 until the end of the War of 1812 was filled with laws,
decrees, and executive acts that seemed to threaten the economic and
social existence of that section. One measure in particular seemed to
be destined to end forever in favor of the South the sectional balance of power, namely, the purchase of Louisiana. During all this
time New England's standing committee on secession, the Essex
Junto, was maneuvering to bring about the withdrawal of New England from the federal Union; nor is there any sufficient reason to
suppose that it would not have eventually succeeded in the disruption of the Union had not the ending of the war with Great Britain
brought a termination of the policies that seemed so detrimental to
the social and economic interests of the East; and had not the out-
burst of genuine nationalism at the victorious ending of the war
actually resulted in the adoption of measures distinctly favorable to
New England. The point I wish to emphasize is that the rise to
power of the South and middle states was marked by the same
egocentric sectionalism which characterized the dominance of Federalist New England: the agricultural sections thought of themselves as
the United States, thought of the American farmers as the only
simon-pure Americans, and looked upon the interests of the agricultural population as the national interests.

It is not the ambition of this essay to attempt a summary of the
antebellum history of the United States; but simply to use the twelve-
year sectional regime of the Federalists and about the same length of
rule by the Jeffersonian party to illustrate that tendency of the
dominant section to consider itself the United States and its people
the American people, and by the same token to ignore or treat with
contempt the peculiar needs of the minority sections.

The second manifestation of that egocentric sectionalism which led to the American Civil War was the attempt of one section to gain a permanent ascendency by destroying the sectional balance of power or by permanently undermining the prestige of the other section. Let me pause for a moment, in discussing the overthrow of the balance of power, and review very briefly just how and why there had been an approximate balance of power established between the slaveholding and nonslaveholding states during the constitutional convention. The delegates to the convention, from both the Northern and Southern sections of the country, were unanimously in favor of a constitution that would establish a much stronger and more effective government than that which had so signally broken down under the Articles of Confederation. There was a fundamental difference, however, as to what specific powers should be granted to this new government. New England and the capitalistic segments of the middle states were above all else determined that the new government should be able to control foreign and interstate commerce and to make commercial treaties that could be enforced. The agricultural sections of the country looked with considerable disfavor upon such a grant of powers. The South was so much opposed that it quietly passed out the word that it would never enter a Union where commerce was so thoroughly controlled by the national government unless it were assured a position of approximate political equality in that government. Otherwise, the power over commerce would be used by the North, dominated by the East, for its sole benefit and to the detriment of agriculture and the South.

Finally, the balance of power was worked out by the technique of counting three-fifths of the slaves in apportioning representation in Congress and in the electoral college. This was called the three-fifths compromise between the North, which wanted to count all the slaves in apportioning direct taxes and none in apportioning representatives, and the South, which wanted to count all the slaves in making up representation and none in making up taxation. But an examination of the speeches and correspondence of the delegates indicates that it was also, and more important, a means of giving the South approximate equality in the federal government in return for granting New England's profound desire to have the federal government control interstate and international commerce.

That the sectional balance of power should be obtained by the process of counting three-fifths of the slaves in determining representation was a natural but unfortunate arrangement. It was natural inasmuch as the Southerner regarded his slave as a human being and as part of the population; it was unfortunate in that it quickly identified the political influence of the South with the institution of slavery, and in doing so it went far toward engendering or increasing hostility in New England and finally in the whole North toward both slavery and the South.

As long as New England was able to dominate the federal government there was no important opposition to the theoretical balance of power obtained by the three-fifths ratio; but when New England lost her status with the collapse of the Federalist party, her leaders immediately seized upon the three-fifths ratio as the explanation. During the period that ended with the Hartford Convention and the treaty of peace the New England leaders were unceasing in their attack upon "slave representation," as they called it. At the Hartford Convention it formed the leading grievance. The convention demanded an unconditional repeal.

During this same time Jefferson purchased the Louisiana territory, not for the purpose of destroying the sectional balance of power, but complacent in the belief that it would do so. We thus behold, during the earlier Jeffersonian period, the spectacle of the agricultural South and the commercial East tampering with the sectional balance of power. Of course, permanent balance of power was impossible in a rapidly expanding country, and both sections must have realized that eventually the forces of nature would tip the balance in favor of one section or the other or in favor of a section not yet born. Such eventualities were regarded as remote and were not permitted to disturb the peace of mind. It was the overthrow of the sectional balance by artificial, political methods which caused uneasiness and wrath, for it indicated intersectional ill will or gross selfishness.

The Missouri controversy (1819–1820) marked the decline of the agitation by the Northeast to repeal the three-fifths ratio clause as a means of weakening the political power of the South and inaugurated the second and final phase of the struggle of the North to destroy by artificial methods the sectional balance of power. This second phase was to prevent the formation and admission into the Union of any more slave states, which meant, from the political and social point of view, the exclusion of Southern states. While the demand for exclusion was based partly upon what we may call moral reasons, Rufus King and the other Northern leaders in this debate were quite frank in asserting that the Missouri debate was a struggle between the slave and free states for political power.

The first two phases of that sectionalism which led to the Civil War, while causing a slow accumulation of sectional grievances, were not marked during the thirty years prior to the Missouri debates by excessive ill will or serious disregard for the comity of sections. Indeed, up until the time of the Missouri debates, despite the rivalry of sections which almost disrupted the Union, there was maintained a certain urbanity and self-restraint on the part of the leaders of the rival sections; for as long as the founding fathers lived and exercised influence over public affairs, there seems to have been a common realization—indeed, a common recollection—that the nation had been founded upon the principle of mutual tolerance of sectional differences and mutual concessions; that the nation had been constructed upon the respect of each section for the institutions, opinions, and ways of life of the other sections. But the years laid the founding fathers low, and their places were taken by a new and impatient generation who had no such understanding of the essence of national unity. The result was that urbanity, self-restraint, and courtesy—the ordinary amenities of civilized intercourse—were cast aside; and in their gracious place were substituted the crude, discourteous, and insulting language and conduct in intersectional relations so familiar in the recent relations between the totalitarian nations and the so-called democracies. It was the Missouri debates in which intersectional comity was first violated; and it was the political leaders of the East, particularly the New Englanders and those of New England origin, who did it when they denounced in unmeasured terms slavery, the slaveholder, and Southern society in general. It is noteworthy that the Southern leaders, with the exception of one or two, including John Randolph, ignored this first violent, denunciatory, insulting language of the Northerners during and immediately after the Missouri controversy; ignored them at least in that no reply in kind was made with the possible exception of two or three, including John Randolph, who demanded that the South withdraw from the Union before it was too late. The private correspondence of the Southerners, however, reveals them as resentful and apprehensive of future bad relations with the North.

Ten years after the Missouri Compromise debates the moral and intellectual leaders of the North, and notably those of New England origin, took up the language of abuse and vilification which the political leaders of that section had first employed in the Missouri debates. Quickly the political leaders resumed the tone of the Missouri controversy: and thus was launched the so-called antislavery crusade, but what in fact was a crusade against the Southern people. For over three decades this attack upon slavery and the entire structure of Southern society grew in volume and in violence. (A discussion of the motives behind this crusade would lead us far afield and into bitterly controversial questions. It does seem clear, however, that political and economic considerations were thoroughly mingled with the moral and religious objection to slavery.) One has to seek in the unrestrained and furious invective of the totalitarians to find a near parallel to the language that the Abolitionists and their political fellow travelers used in denouncing the South and its way of life. Indeed, as far as I have been able to ascertain, neither Dr. Goebbels nor Virginio Gayda nor other Axis propaganda agents ever plumbed the depths of vulgarity and obscenity reached and maintained by George Bourne, Stephen Foster, Wendell Phillips, Charles Sumner, and other Abolitionists of note. Let me cite a few of these—most of them are too indecent to quote. Phillips characterized the South as "one great brothel, where half a million women are flogged to prostitution." Bourne raised Phillips' estimate and insisted that there were a million slave women in the South who constituted "one vast harem where men-stealers may prowl, corrupt and destroy." However, Bourne was not satisfied with implicating the entire white male population of the South in the charge of miscegenation; he gave what he claimed were authentic examples of the same practice among the young white women of the South and insinuated that such practices were common. Foster and Bourne both attacked the morality of the Southern ministry. Bourne said that the pulpits of the South were often filled with "man stealing, girl selling, pimping and slave manufacturing preachers," and that the churches were "synagogues of Satan." It would be far better, he insisted, "to transfer the inmate from the state prison, and the pander from the brothel to the pulpit" than permit a Southern minister "to teach us righteousness and purity" in a Northern church. Foster, in a book significantly entitled the *Brotherhood of Thieves,* charged that the Methodist Church was "more corrupt than any house of ill fame in New York," arguing that the fifty thousand adult female slaves who were members of that church "were inevitably doomed to lives of prostitution" under the penalty of being scourged to death. Foster, Bourne, Phillips, William Lloyd Garrison, Theodore Parker—indeed, most of the Abolitionists—put forward such attacks upon

Southern morality. No one was spared in this charge. All crimes were laid at the door of these people: they were kidnappers, manstealers, pimps, robbers, assassins, free-booters, much more "despicable than the common horse thief." Good taste permits no real analysis of this torrent of coarse abuse; but let it be said again that nothing equal to it has been encountered in the language of insult used between the nations today—even those at war with one another.

This crusade against the South has often been brushed aside as the work of a few unbalanced fanatics. Such is not the case at all. The genuine Abolitionists were few in number in the beginning; but just as radicalism today has touched so many intellectuals of the East, so did abolitionism touch the intellectuals of the East and of the North generally. So did it touch the moral and political leaders. The effects upon the minds of those millions who did not consider themselves Abolitionists were profound. In time the average Northerner accepted in whole or in part the abolitionist picture of Southern people: they became monsters. Such a state of mind is fertile soil for war. The effect upon the minds of the Southern people was far more profound, since they were recipients of this Niagara of insults and threats. To them the Northern people were a combination of mad fanatics and cold-blooded political adventurers. As years passed, slow and consuming fury took hold of the Southern people; and this fury was combined with a deadly fear which John Brown's raid confirmed: a fear that most of the Northern people not only hated the Southern people but would willingly see them exterminated. This fear was further confirmed when such a kindly philosopher as Ralph Waldo Emerson approved of the incendiary John Brown, by likening him to Jesus.

The political, intellectual, and moral leaders of the South did not remain silent under the abuse of the crusaders and the fellow travelers and well-wishers, but replied in a manner that added fuel to the roaring flames which were fast consuming the last vestiges of national unity. The language of insult which the so-called fire-eaters employed, however, was not usually coarse or obscene in comparison with that of the Abolitionists; it was urbane and restrained to a degree—but insulting. Thus in language of abuse and insult was jettisoned the comity of sections. And let me repeat that peace between sections as between nations is placed in jeopardy when one section fails to respect the self-respect of the people of another section.

Local Defense and the Downfall of the Confederacy: A Study in State Rights

In recent years it is becoming more apparent to students of Confederate history that the Confederacy collapsed more from internal than from external causes and the most disastrous of these internal ailments was the attempt of the Southern people to practice their theory of state rights during the war. This destroyed the possibility of coöperation, embittered and demoralized the people, and pitted the state governments against the Confederate government like hostile powers. This struggle between the states and the Confederate government extended into many fields, mostly related to the conduct of the war. One of the most important of these fields was the matter of local defense. It is the object of this article to present a careful study of the policy of local defense in the Confederacy, and show how it contributed to the downfall of that government.

The military frontiers of the Confederacy stretched over many thousands of miles. Every state save Tennessee and Arkansas had long reaches of undefended sea coast, Florida alone having practically as much as the Union. Then there was the upper tier of Confederate states whose borders lay alongside the hostile frontiers of the Union, penetrated by navigable rivers radiating into the heart of the country. As if this were not enough exposure for the new-born republic, Texas and Arkansas were frontier states: to the north of them in the territories of New Mexico, Arizona, and Indian Territory lived many wild tribes of aborigines, while to the west of Texas lived the half-breed Mexicans, whose depredations under the leadership of the chieftain, Cortinas,[1] were keeping the Rio Grande country in constant turmoil. Last, but, to the Southern people apprehensive of servile insurrection, not least in importance, was the "home front," liable at any moment to become the most horrible and bloody battle-ground of the war. If one can visualize this situation and keep in mind the fact that the people were thoroughly steeped in the doctrines of state rights and local patriotism, he will be prepared for the inevitable military policy that undertook the defense of all these far-flung lines. The "sovereign states" built up small armies of their own, inefficient and undisciplined, withdrawing at times a hundred thousand or more men, together with arms and equipment to fit them out, all of which was sorely needed on the battle front.

However, the Confederate government did not accept this individualistic policy with meekness. Its leaders, being in a position to see the whole situation, made a stupendous effort to gather in their hands the reins of power necessary for success and to obtain possession of the men and material retained in the state forces. The constant pull of the states to retain as large forces as possible and the counter pull of the Confederate government, with the general staff point of view, to force the states to disgorge, resulted in a veritable tug of war between the central and the local governments.[2]

The study of the problem of local defense falls naturally into two periods: (I) from secession to the passage of the first conscript law in 1862; and (II) from the adoption of the conscript law until the war ended.

I. January 1861 to April 1862

The period that ends with the first conscript law may be characterized by two distinct phases: (1) the withholding by the states from Confederate service of arms and munitions of war; and (2) the withholding of men.

1. Arms

There were on hand two available supplies of arms and munitions of war in the South when the Confederacy was organized, and both of these were held by the states. There were the arms taken with the United States forts and arsenals, which were distributed among the states about as follows: 47,327 in Louisiana, 19,455 in Alabama, 22,469 in South Carolina, 22,714 in Georgia, 10,000 in Arkansas, 37,000 in North Carolina,[3] and 35,000 in Texas.[4] There were also a few thousand in Virginia and scattered around in other states, making a total of about 190,000 small arms, many of which were old-fashioned and of little use until repaired.[5] In addition to the arms thus captured, each state had on hand a supply, part of which had been purchased immediately after John Brown's raid and the election of Lincoln. Alabama had, during the winter of 1860–1861, purchased 9,000 stand of arms, 10 brass cannon, 2 columbiads, and a large quantity of ammunition,[6] which, added to the arms already on hand, made no bad show. Mississippi, already equipped with 2,127 rifles and other small arms, purchased about this time 5,000 stand of muskets.[7] Texas had several thousand in addition to a large supply of private arms.[8] Georgia[9] and North Carolina[10] each, apparently, had several thousand, and South Carolina had 11,000, just purchased,[11] and had an old stock that was in the hands of the militia.[12] Virginia had on hand 100,000 stand of small arms in the fall of 1860 and evidently made extensive purchases afterwards.[13] In addition to these available supplies there were a large number of private arms in the South, due to the rural and frontier character of the section. But at best the supply of munitions of war was definitely limited. Yet if the individual states had immediately placed the arms in their possession in the hands of the Confederate armies, if the state authorities had made the proper effort to obtain the private arms of the citizen instead of discouraging him from selling them to Confederate agents, the Confederate government would have been able to put a much larger army in the field in 1861.

Theoretically, the states did transfer the arms and munitions captured with the United States arsenals, but in actual practice the several governors each disposed of a large part of these arms according to the interests of their respective states or according to their individual judgment.[14]

As to the arms actually owned by the states, the governors either refused to allow them to be carried out of the state or gave them up reluctantly and sparingly. In March 1861 Governor A. B. Moore of Alabama wrote Secretary Walker, who had applied to the governor for arms, that he was not prepared to say what the state convention then in session would do about the matter, but that he was "inclined to the opinion that they should be retained by the state to enable her to meet any emergency and protect and defend her citizens."[15] Again on July 4, 1861, the governor found it out of the question to arm 3,000 men called out by the Confederate government for general service, because, as he said, "it leaves the state almost defenseless;"[16] but at the same time he was able to arm six regiments and 2500 other special emergency troops for a defense of the coast which was in no immediate danger.[17]

Governor Thomas Moore of Louisiana informed Secretary Walker on May 20, 1861, after the latter had besought the Governor to arm a few thousand Confederate troops being raised in that state, that he was doubtful whether he would arm any more troops for general service as he was "emphatically unwilling to leave the state without sufficient arms for home protection." At this moment the governor had, apparently, a supply of arms lying idle in the state arsenal.[18] Again in July he refused to arm five or six regiments for the Confederacy because, he said, it would take all the guns in the arsenal, "and surely we ought not to be without arms when we may expect an invasion ourselves in the fall."[19]

Nor was Mississippi any more generous than the other states in giving up her arms and munitions of war to the central government. On July 17 Governor Pettus wired Secretary Walker, who as usual was out in his futile quest for state help, that he had no power under the state law to arm the regiments just raised at Iuka.[20] The persistent refusal of his own state to supply Confederate troops with arms, or, in rare cases where it did supply them, its continuous discrimination in favor of short-term organizations, at length evoked a rebuke from President Davis.[21] Governor Pettus's reply was that he had only been carrying out the state law and orders of the military board, which laid the injunction upon the governor that "no arms should be given to any companies until all the companies mustered into the service of the state were armed." Only in very rare cases, he added, had the military board allowed a departure from these standing orders.[22]

North Carolina, like the other seaboard states, lived in constant dread of a mammoth expedition against her coast, and she soon began to discourage the removal of her arms into the other states. In the spring of 1862 the governor became so much concerned over the matter that he issued a belligerent proclamation against the purchase of arms or the impressment of any kind of military equipment by Confederate agents. He promised to use force, if it became necessary, to protect the citizens against the Confederate government.[23] Not only was he unwilling for them to leave the state, but in January 1862 he was compelled, he said, "in view of the immediate and pressing necessity for arms for our defense" to ask the return of a quantity of arms that had been taken out of the state into Virginia.[24]

Governor Pickens of South Carolina wrote to Secretary of War Benjamin in September 1861 that he felt that the state was not able to arm any more Confederate troops because it had to arm the 15,000 state troops.[25] Not satisfied with keeping 15,000 stand of arms out of general service, he requested the return of some that had been taken out of the state.[26]

Tennessee, in the first few months, not only contributed no arms to the Confederate government, but actually received 6,000 stand with which to equip her state organizations, which steadily refused to be mustered into Confederate service.[27] Texas refused to comply with the requisitions from the Confederate authorities;[28] and in Arkansas the same situation existed. General Hindman notified President Davis that "the state authorities refuse arms of any kind, retaining them for the militia."[29]

Virginia, with her 100,000 stand of small arms and the Harper's Ferry machinery, together with other quantities of war material, showed the same reluctance in pooling her military equipment. The state authorities refused for a while to issue any of the tools and lead stored in the armory at Richmond, and Major Gorgas, Confederate munitions chief, complained that the refusal had done "great injury to the common defense;"[30] and when he suggested that the stock of small arms belonging to Virginia, stored in the Richmond armory, be transferred to the Confederate authorities for general issue, Secretary of State Munford quickly rejected the proposal. Virginia, he protested, "wishes to reserve the arms now left in the armory for a case of emergency, when it may be necessary to give them to her unarmed militia."[31] Finally, because of haggling on the part of the Virginia authorities the most priceless months of Confederate history were allowed to slip by before the Harper's Ferry and Richmond armory machinery was transferred to the central government.[32]

Georgia not only proposed to keep what she needed of the supply of arms within the state but also to get as much more as possible out of the Confederate government. Furthermore, Governor Brown in carrying out this selfish policy did not refrain from engaging in frequent unnecessary and far-fetched quarrels with the sorely-beset Richmond government. With no uncertain motives he promptly negatived the attempt of volunteers who had not been organized through his office to carry state arms out of Georgia. In May 1861 he issued a proclamation that any officer who permitted or encouraged his men to carry state arms out of Georgia would be punished to the limit of the law.[33] The governor also put in a claim for 29,000 pounds of powder stored in the Confederate arsenal at Augusta,[34] for he was determined that the state should have what belonged to it even if it broke up the whole system of defense worked out in Richmond. However, the Confederate authorities refused to deliver the powder before making an inquiry as to the facts in the case,[35] since powder was a very important commodity at the time. Whereupon Brown, angered by the delay, ordered the state arsenal at Savannah closed to all Confederate officials. His injunction to the arsenal keeper was "not to issue anything to the order of a Confederate officer for the present."[36] Secretary Walker protested against this abrupt procedure. Brown's reply indicated that the arsenal at Savannah had been closed in retaliation for the delay of the secretary in releasing the powder claimed by the state at Augusta. Besides, without reference to other issues, Brown reminded Walker that "the arsenal and its contents are the property of the state" and that no Confederate officer had any rights there except at the sufferance of state authorities. In plain English, the arsenal belonged to Georgia and it was nobody's business outside of Georgia as to what it pleased her to do with it.[37]

In April 1862 Brown wrote Secretary of War Randolph asking the return of all the rifles in the hands of the twelve-months troops whose term was soon to expire. He was not willing, he said, that the superior model rifles belonging to Georgia should be thrown into the Confederate arsenals for general issue. Then, he added, figuratively lowering his voice to a knowing whisper, "If I have not mistaken your character you belong to that class of statesmen known as states rights men. I cannot, therefore, doubt what will be your decision of this question."[38] Outside of the fact that the twelve-months troops would soon be returning to Georgia, there was another reason why Brown raised the issue at this particular time: the Confederate Congress had passed a law requiring that all arms of the twelve-months or other troops whose term expired before the termination of the war should be kept within control of the president.[39] This law, Brown evidently expected to question when he wrote Randolph, and undoubtedly he looked to the new secretary of war for substantial aid in defeating its terms. But Randolph proved an apostate, at least in the opinion of Joe Brown, for he assured the governor that "the exigencies of the times require many things which would under other circumstances be wholly unjustifiable....," and that the act retaining the state arms within control of the president was one of the things necessary. He also dropped a hint to the factious Brown that a little patience and forbearance would mend matters very greatly.[40]

Not content with retaining her own arms and a good part of

those captured with the United States arsenals, Georgia attempted to obtain possession of cargoes of Confederate rifles that landed in her ports. The hysteria caused by rumors of a gigantic expedition against Brunswick gripped the people in the summer and fall of 1861. Apparently, Governor Brown was largely responsible for this, because he was continually advertising the exposed condition of Georgia's coast. He called wildly for help, dancing a frantic jig up and down Georgia and accusing the Confederate government of gross neglect. If he could not get the Confederate government to return the Georgia boys in Virginia to protect their sacred homes and "rally around the green graves of their sires," he demanded that it give him plenty of rifles to arm those still at home. On September 18, 1861, he wired Benjamin to supply him with arms sufficient to equip four regiments for local defense. He suggested that he be allowed to help himself from the Confederate cargo just landed at Savannah.[41] Benjamin promptly wired him that this cargo was wanted for the poorly-armed troops in Virginia, where real fighting was being done.[42] But Joe Brown, who was successfully attempting to bring under his control the entire management of the coast defense of Georgia,[43] could not let such a rare opportunity escape to get something at the expense of the central government: he apparently induced the Confederate General Lawton, by the application of high pressure,[44] to seize the cargo and place the rifles in the hands of the local-defense troops.[45] Lawton immediately notified Adjutant General Cooper that the pressing necessity in Georgia had forced him to seize these arms. He pictured the people to be in a state of the "greatest alarm at the intelligence, which seems reliable, that the mammoth expedition now being fitted out in New York is intended for Brunswick on the lower part of the coast of Georgia." The cargo was needed to arm the thousands of able-bodied men being called out by Brown.[46] Secretary of War Benjamin, though the hands were those of Esau, recognized the voice of Jacob. He peremptorily ordered Lawton to recover at once all but a thousand rifles, with the caustic remark, evidently intended for the officious Brown, who had been tampering with the Confederate general, "that it is scarcely necessary to observe that if the government cannot have its property intended for public defense landed or deposited at any point of the Confederacy without being exposed to having it seized and appropriated to meet supposed local exigencies it would be better to abandon at once all attempts to conduct the defense of the country on an organized system and deliver over the control of the military to the local militia and popular meetings."[47] But Governor Brown, who only thrived upon such words as these, did all in his power to grab the next cargo that landed in Georgia.[48]

The results of such a policy were disastrous. With the enthusiasm of the year 1861 (almost without a parallel in history) the Confederate government could have placed an army of perhaps 600,000 men in the field within a few months if it had had the arms. The several reports of the secretary of war bear out this rather bold assertion. Secretary Walker, in his report of July 24, 1861 said: "It is with mingled feeling of pleasure and regret that this Department mentions the fact that many more have come forward to volunteer for the war than it was possible for the government to arm. From the applications on file in this office there can be no doubt that if arms were only furnished no less than 200,000 additional volunteers for the war would be found in our ranks in less than two months."[49] Secretary Benjamin, who succeeded Walker in the fall of 1861, stated in his report of December 14 that when he assumed control of the War Department it was not unusual "to refuse offers of 5000 men per day;"[50] and in March 1862 he expressed the opinion to President Davis that he could put 350,000 additional men in the field, if arms could be had.[51] But the arms were not to be had, mainly because the states refused to part with them, and only about half of 600,000 went into the Confederate armies before 1862. The result was that Albert Sidney Johnston[52] in the West had to lie idle at Bowling Green when with a few more thousand, as he lamented, he would have been able to take the offensive and "Tennessee, the valley of the Mississippi, and the Confederacy" would have been safe; and Joe Johnston and Beauregard in the East were unable to move for lack of men.[53] The initial advantages of superior trained soldiery and better generals[54] were lost and the popular enthusiasm for war was dissipated: State rights had reaped its first harvest.

2. Men

But no sooner had the Confederacy begun to obtain arms in sufficient quantities to meet the exigencies of the situation than another obstacle placed in its path by state rights loomed up: the War Department could not get men. The individual states had capitalized the enthusiasm and the fears of the people and had caught the overflow in their own local military organizations. These organizations had their inception at the very period of secession. They had been very small at first and had interfered little with the Confederate attempts to build up an army, except, of course, in the matter of arms, but gradually they grew in size and importance until they absorbed a great part of the man power that should have gone into the general service. An account of these organizations, state by state, will help us to an understanding of their importance as a factor in the overthrow of the Confederacy.

In January 1861 Governor A. B. Moore suggested to the legislature that Alabama should have a "regular army" for its protection in case of trouble with the United States growing out of secession.[55] A few days after this the state convention adopted this suggestion of the governor and authorized the organization of a state army.[56] As a result, Moore was able in the fall of that year to report that the local troops—not to be confused with the militia—consisted of six regiments, and 2,500 other special troops all well-armed and equipped, and several other units in the process of formation.[57] About the same time that the Alabama convention authorized the formation of a regular army Louisiana made a similar step,[58] with about the same results.[59] In Mississippi, by the first of March 1861 there were, according to Governor Pettus's count, between thirty and forty companies of state troops,[60] and by the passage of the first conscription law this force had been built up to almost 5,000 regularly enlisted state troops.[61] North Carolina kept up a large force, under constant fear of an attack from the sea. In the late spring of 1862 the state forces numbered 10,000 men[62] in actual service and 10,000 organized ready to be called out,[63] making a total of 20,000. During the first year of the war there were between 15,000 and 20,000 state troops in South Carolina,[64] in addition to the militia and Confederate troops in that state. Governor Harris of Tennessee reported on May 28, 1861, several thousand state troops, all of whom seemed unwilling to enter the general service;[65] and on July 31 the Tennessee adjutant general's report showed 19,400 infantry, 2,079 cavalry, and 558 artillery in the state forces.[66] Virginia had, according to the paymaster of state troops, 40,000 men thus organized about the first of July.[67] Arkansas had usually about 8,000 state troops during this period;[68] and it was due largely to the divided authority over state and Confederate forces that Missouri and most of Arkansas were lost to the South during the first year of the war.[69] Texas, as we might expect, from her exposed frontiers insisted upon keeping a well-organized state force.[70]

Georgia, in all probability, kept no more local troops than South Carolina or even North Carolina; but Governor Brown, whose patriotism reached very little farther than the borders of his own political opportunities, which coincided with the boundaries of the state of Georgia, assumed the attitude now, as always, of "every man for himself and the devil for us all." In the early part of 1861, the Georgia state convention under the guidance of the energetic governor provided for a force of two regiments of regulars and 10,000 volunteer troops to be held in readiness for any emergency that might threaten the safety and peace of the state.[71] Even at this early period, Brown showed himself alert for symptoms of encroachments upon Georgia's rights. The Confederate government had just taken over, by law, the defense of all the states, in short had assumed its legitimate control of war, and the governor was careful to point out to the state convention that there were very definite limits upon the powers of the Confederate government in the matter of controlling and directing the defense of the state of Georgia. On March 15 he reminded the convention that it was one of Georgia's reserved rights to have a well-organized force, and that in joining the Confederacy she had not surrendered the right to protect herself when she was threatened.[72] As the year wore on, the fear of invasion grew, especially, as we have already seen, under the inspiration of Brown, and he conceived the ambitious plan of directing the whole coastal defense himself. In carrying out this plan, he demanded that the Confederate government move no more native troops from the state;[73] he demanded that Stovall's battalion be returned from Lynchburg, Virginia;[74] and he demanded other impossible and foolish things. In the meanwhile, he recruited an entire division and organized the coast defense without reference to Confederate plans.[75] General Lawton of the Confederate service wrote Secretary Benjamin that Brown was planning to put General W. H. T. Walker, who had left the Confederate service embittered against the government, in charge of the state defense, and he was so dejected over the prospect that he predicted disaster and asked to be relieved of his place.[76] There is no way of knowing the exact size of Brown's state army during this period, for it was composed of all kinds of troops, militia, short-term volunteers, and regularly enlisted men. However, in the spring of 1862, when the conscript law was passed which robbed the governor of some of his troops, there were, according to Brown's report to Secretary Randolph, 8,000 regularly enlisted men in state service,[77] and many had already served out enlistments and gone home.

This policy of each state maintaining its own troops for local defense, and its effect upon the general Confederate service, was well summed up by Secretary of War Benjamin in one of his reports. Due to the great enthusiasm of the people, he said, the Confederate government was just on the eve of success in putting into the field a powerful army, when it "was embarrassed and impeded by a very unexpected cause. In several of the states the governors, apprehensive of attack at home and actuated by the natural desire of aiding in the defense of their own states, failed to perceive that the only effective means of attaining that end was by a concentration of the common strength under one head, and that an attempt by each state to make a separate defense against so powerful an enemy...could result in nothing but the defeat of each in detail. In disregard of so obvious a truth several of the states undertook to raise independent armies to repel invasion, retained at home arms and munitions, and called for volunteers for short terms...for service within the state. The fatal effect of so short-sighted a policy became instantly apparent. Companies already organized and ready to be mustered into Confederate service for the war, marched out of the camps of rendezvous to enlist in the state service for three, four, or six months."[78]

II. April 1862 to April 1865

No sooner had the conscript law of April 1862 broken up the state military organizations, than several of the states began to rebuild them. Presently, as a result of this movement, there were as many men held back for local defense as there had been the first year of the war. Yet this formidable aggregation of state troops was absolutely worthless from all points of view: they were of no value to the Confederacy and they were of none to their state. General Brandon described them as "being composed of men who have been skulking from the service" by hiding in the local organizations under state protection; and who had no discipline since they were amenable only "to their own courts-martial, composed of the same class of men" whose decisions were always "in accord with the general feeling of the men and officers." The men, he said, were always "going and coming when they please," and they were "but little better than an armed mob." Not being subject to Confederate courts-martial the generals could not enforce discipline and order, "and disaster and disgrace will result when they are brought into the field."[79]

Nine-tenths of the men in many of the organizations were subject to general service, which, added to the notorious inefficiency and cowardice of such organizations, made it absolutely necessary that the Confederate government should obtain control of them, both to obtain men fit for recruiting its armies and for the purpose of discipline and unity of purpose. So the Richmond government set out to accomplish this end, and the whole period from the beginning of conscription till the end of the war is marked by its desperate but futile efforts to extend its control over state troops. Secretary of War Seddon sounded the keynote of this policy in a circular letter to the state governors. He said: "The numerically superior armies of the enemy confronting us in the field at all the most important points render essential for success in our great struggle...greater concentration of our forces and their withdrawal in a measure from the purposes of local defense."[80] Let us follow out the successful efforts of each state after the first conscript act to rehabilitate its local troops and the unsuccessful efforts of the Confederacy to obtain control of these troops.

In the summer of 1862 Alabama, under the direction of Governor Shorter, began to salvage its old military organizations and to rebuild them, at first, out of material not taken into the Confederate service. On August 28 the governor called for 500 men to guard a certain vital point in the state where several public works were located.[81] In December he followed up this call with a stirring proclamation for men and boys to volunteer for the defense of their state.[82] There was no intention, at first, of absorbing conscript material into the local units, but the desire for men was so great that usually no embarrassing questions were asked when a man presented himself for local defense. One step led to another until presently Governor Shorter came out with the bold request that the War Department allow him to enlist for state defense all the conscripts in the counties of Barbour, Pike, Henry, Dale, Coffee, and Covington.[83] Finally Seddon yielded to the pressure which had been backed with a strong popular clamor, and wrote the governor that he might enlist the conscripts as he had requested.[84] Emboldened by this success, the governor immediately dispatched Colonel Clanton to Richmond with a personal letter to the War Department asking for all the rest of the conscripts in Alabama who showed any reluctance to going into Confederate service.[85] Judging from later conditions, Clanton evidently met with some success.

Soon after the second conscription act (October 1862) Governor Brown influenced the Georgia legislature to pass an act providing for a state force to be composed of any of the men not in actual Confederate service.[86] Spoiling, as usual, for a quarrel with President Davis, he wrote the latter that Georgia had a right to every able-bodied man not in actual Confederate service, but that the legislature had adopted the idea of concurrent jurisdiction and had confined its claims to those conscripts not enrolled. He enforced his arguments by a garbled quotation from Davis himself. President Davis had said with reference to the militia: "Congress may call forth the militia to execute Confederate laws. The state has not surrendered the power to call them forth to execute state laws. Congress may call them forth to repel invasion; so may the state, for it has expressly reserved this right...for the power is implied reserved of governing all militia except the part in actual service of the Confederacy." Certainly Davis had had no intention of surrendering conscripts to Brown when he wrote this, but this was Brown's favorite way of exasperating his antagonist—taking a quotation out of its proper surroundings and twisting it to suit his own interpretation. He concluded his letter with the admonition that the president must instruct his enrolling officers to act accordingly.[87] By 1863 he had two regiments of regularly enlisted state troops and was calling out for state defense all men between the ages of 18 and 45 not in the Confederate service.[88]

In Louisiana the legislature passed a law on January 3, 1863, drafting all able-bodied men not in the actual military service of the Confederacy.[89] Immediately the law was put into operation by General Order number 8 and the Confederate government was wheedled into allowing conscripts to enter the service of the state: always "until the emergency is over"[90]—which, of course, was never over until the war was ended. On July 27, 1863, General Ruggles reported that "the state organizations are composed to a great extent of men subject to conscription...that a mutual understanding had existed...between the state executive and the Confederate department commander, based upon orders of the War Department allowing states to retain conscripts in existing state organizations...which has allowed the state to absorb most if not all of the conscript material."[91]

By the fall of 1862 Mississippi had a considerable state guard in addition to her active militia,[92] most of whom had been recruited from conscript material either by the consent of the War Department or the district commander.[93] In December Governor Pettus added further to the state forces by having the legislature enact a law drafting for state service all men between the ages of 16 and 60 not in the actual service of the Confederacy.[94] In the summer of 1863 Governor Pettus, just as these old state organizations were approaching the termination of their enlistment, obtained further permission to recruit them again for local defense.[95] In November 1863 these troops were reported to the governor as numbering about 5,000,[96] five-sixths of whom were between the ages of 18 and 45 and would have been subject to conscription if the state organizations had not absorbed them, frequently with the consent—though ofttimes unwilling—of the War Department.[97]

In the fall of 1862 there was a pronounced feeling in North Carolina that the Confederacy had drafted the state's troops and left it in the lurch in the matter of coast defense. Governor Vance championed the popular discontent and fanned the flames higher. Under his guidance the people began to show distinct signs of unwillingness to leave the state to fight. On October 25 Vance wrote Davis "that many openly declare they want not another man to leave the state until provision is made for her own defense."[98] Not obtaining reinforcements in the necessary quantities, Vance turned to his legislature, which was very decidedly anti-Davis, and arraigned the central government on the charge of bad faith. He had supported conscription, he said, because he thought he would "actually be providing for state defense," but he had been tricked; the citizens of North Carolina had been taken from their state, leaving her stripped and defenseless; and despite the fact of her vast, unprotected sea coast, "she has fewer troops given her for its defense" than any other state. He recommended the "raising of at least ten regiments" for state defense.[99] These words fell upon sympathetic ears: the legislature immediately enacted his proposal into a law.[100] Vance then addressed himself boldly to President Davis, asking for rifles with which to arm his troops and requesting that he be allowed to enlist all the conscripts he might need, without interference.[101] Seddon was unable, of course, at this time to supply rifles for state troops and he told Vance that the president did not feel authorized to relinquish claims to those who were subject to conscription.[102] But Vance did not wait for this reply; he ordered the Military Board of North Carolina to call out the necessary men to fill up the ten regiments. The Board made a clean sweep of able-bodied men and a large organization was formed.[103] A few men in the legislature who were not hostile to the administration introduced a resolution in the Senate declaring that the military bill raising ten regiments for state defense out of any material at hand was not intended to create a conflict with the Confederate government; but the Senate immediately defeated the resolution by a vote of 27-5.[104]

By December 1862 Texas had a state force of at least 5,000 men.[105] South Carolina seems to have kept her local defense troops in spite of the conscription law—due to the fact that they had been regularly enlisted as "troops of war," which a state might unquestionably retain in time of war if it insisted on doing so. In May there were 17,000 local defense troops in the state, and even those who were being recruited for Confederate service were unwilling to leave the state. Among the latter was the Eighteenth South Carolina Regiment.[106] Virginia, also, was raising a force of about 10,000 in September 1862.[107]

Thus, state by state had the local defense organizations grown up and multiplied until, like the barnacles on the hulk of a foundering ship, they threatened to drag the Confederacy down to destruction. Hoping to remove the necessity for state organizations and to divert all able-bodied material absorbed by them into the general service as well as place local defense under Confederate control, Secretary Seddon on June 6, 1863, proposed to the several governors that they organize all the men and boys above and below military age, able to bear arms, into local-defense and limited-service companies under Confederate authority. This could be done under acts of Congress of August 21, 1861, and October 13, 1862. However, the secretary, uncertain whether the governors of the several states would make any effort to accomplish the proposed object, hit upon the alternative of making a requisition of from 5,000 to 10,000 men on each state. These men were to be mustered into the Confederate service for six months.[108] The secretary, as he explained then and several times afterwards, had no intention of having the governors raise these troops for six months, but he thought this requisition might be used as a club to induce the formation of the proposed Confederate local defense units.[109] However, Seddon failed to take the proper measure of state rights and state dignity: practically none of the governors made any move to organize the Confederate local defense troops, but they took advantage of the requisition made upon them to acquire the residue of the able-bodied men for the state forces. Nor did they transfer their troops to the Confederate service for six months.[110] They pursued their customary policy of "loaning" them to the district commander during an emergency.

Governor Vance was a shining example of the governors who neither raised local Confederate troops nor transferred the state troops to the Confederacy. In his proclamation calling for the organization of state volunteers to meet the secretary's requisition he was very careful to assure the touchy North Carolinians that "the control and management of these troops raised under this proclamation will be retained by the authorities of the state."[111] Not only did he keep the guiding reins over the state troops; he had the audacity to suggest to President Davis that he be given permission to include 1,200 deserters in his organization. They were, he said, willing to come out and "enlist for defense of their state alone." He admitted that "the effect on the army might be injurious," but this did not deter him from asking the privilege, since the Confederate authorities would never be able to get them anyway.[112]

When the requisition was made upon South Carolina she pursued the same policy. Already possessed of a large force, in which there were seven conscripts out of every eight men,[113] the state authorities obtained permission from the War Department to keep the conscripts "until the exigency was passed."[114] After obtaining this concession the state refused to transfer the troops because it was feared that the Confederate officers would remove those subject to conscription from the state to the Confederate armies, and thus deprive the state of South Carolina of her chief material for local defense. Thus Adjutant General Garlington, who spoke for the governor, wrote General Thomas Jordan, chief of the staff.[115]

Nor did Mississippi show a different spirit. Instead of turning the able-bodied men of military age over to the Confederacy and helping to recruit the local-defense companies as requested by the Secretary of War, that state only took a firmer grip on both local defense and her able-bodied population. The state, like North and South Carolina, got permission to retain the conscripts it already had and to use others in districts exposed to invasion in making up the troops asked for.[116] Like the two Carolinas, Mississippi also practically refused to muster her troops into Confederate service, after she had been allowed to preëmpt the conscripts. Governor Clark well expressed the position of his state in his message to the legislature in November 1863. "It is not to be expected," he said, "that the Confederate troops will be so disposed as to give protection to all portions of this state. They will occupy certain lines and move for defense of certain points as exigency may require" and, he thought, like his predecessor, Pettus, that "a large force [of state troops] was necessary to our defense." The result was that out of 7,000 troops called for only 26 companies of about 1,500[117] men were organized under the Confederate law for local defense and the remainder were either retained entirely by the state or were mustered temporarily into Confederate service.[118]

The reaction of Governor Brown of Georgia toward Seddon's proposition was characteristic. He refused to lift his hand until the Secretary promised not to take any part whatsoever in the direction of the matter. "If the President," he said, "will accept 8,000 men organized by the state...and tendered for six months...I think I can have them ready by August the first. If this is satisfactory, say so...and instruct Confederate officers not to attempt to get up conflicting organizations."[119] Seddon showed a reluctance in forbidding Confederate officers to organize local companies as it was strictly within their rights under the new law to do so, and Governor Brown instantly washed his hands of the whole affair with the remark that he could do nothing toward organizing troops under Confederate law other than to "invite" men to form themselves into such units.[120] Seeing the futility of attempting to coöperate with Brown, Seddon finally decided to let the governor handle the whole matter, as the latter much desired. He wrote Brown that if he would undertake the matter so as to obtain the whole number required, he would agree to leave the organization of the entire outfit in his hands.[121] The result was Brown made a wonderful showing on paper and advertised his ability to raise troops all over the South. To the Confederate government, however, his energies were of little benefit; the troops he turned over to the War Department were nothing but limited-service state troops: very few Confederate local-defense troops were formed.

As soon as Governor Brown had obtained all the concessions he wanted in raising these troops he found fresh ground on which he began a quarrel with the Confederate authorities. After the battle of Chickamauga he thought that the Secretary of War should allow the six-months troops to go home until another big battle was to be fought, in order that they might attend their crops and other duties. His opinion was that the Confederacy had promised to use them only in emergency and that it was in honor bound to release them when there was no emergency.[122] This was true of the Confederate local-defense troops, but as Brown's stubbornness had resulted in the formation of state troops who had been mustered for six months, this rule did not apply. As a result Secretary Seddon kept them in continuous service, and Governor Brown's wrath knew no bounds. After haranguing his legislature on the subject,[123] November 13, 1863, he wrote Davis that the Confederate government had broken faith with the Georgia troops, and that as a result of his keeping them in service their crops had been ruined. He demanded that they be allowed to go home at once "till another exigency calls for their service."[124]

In January 1864 he again resumed this quarrel and denounced the Confederate authorities for their failure to keep faith with "part of the state guard called out early in September last and kept constantly" in the service. He asserted there was no emergency that demanded their services, and that this act of injustice on the part of the Confederate government had "engendered a feeling which will render it very difficult to enlist another similar force in the state."[125] Seddon's reply was that the military situation had been one of constant emergency—so much so that a "judicial administration did not justify the disbanding of any troops under the control of the Department." Seddon also reminded the irate governor that the latter had furnished state troops when the call had really been made for special-service and local-defense Confederate organizations, and that as a result it had been impossible to dismiss and recall them: such organizations were too unwieldy for that. Finally, the fault really was Brown's.[126]

Governor Brown was not the man to let anyone else have the last word, and without any delay he shifted the quarrel over to the question as to the kind of troops Seddon had called for in his original proposal, attempting to prove by his usual clever method of making quotations apart from their connections that Seddon had simply told a lie when he stated that the original call was for local-defense Confederate troops.[127] But Brown had so many controversies on his hands at this time that it is a marvel to one who has gone over the voluminous correspondence involved how he managed to keep track of them all and remember who his enemies were and what their points of difference were. It profits us nothing to follow this particular controversy any further as we may safely assume that the governor never ceased night or day in his waking hours—and perhaps in his dreams —to throw obstacles in the path of the Confederacy.

After this vain effort to obtain control of the state troops and of local defense, the next step was to draft the state forces into the military service of the Confederacy and form them into "reserves" for state defense. The conscription act of February 17, 1864 had this for its main object. All men between the ages of 17 and 18, and 45 and 50 were drafted for state defense, and it began to look as if the War Department was about to consummate its oft-defeated ideal of a unified and concentrated military system. But once more, its bête noir, state rights, overthrew its calculations. This time two elements, heretofore of minor importance in all the states except Georgia and North Carolina, assumed a prominent rôle in causing the states to retain troops of their own. First was the necessity of retaining as many producers at home as possible in order to relieve the great suffering and want that was being felt all over the South by 1864. Men who belonged to state organizations could be sent home on indefinite furloughs until called out by the governor to meet an emergency, after which they might be furloughed again. This would enable the men to tend their farms and manage their business. On the other hand, if a man belonged to the Confederate reserves, he would in all probability be kept in constant service and his business would go to ruin, his farm grow up in weeds, and those dependent on his labors would suffer.

In the second place, there was a growing sensitiveness on the part of the states as to their constitutional right to maintain "troops of war." Many things had been happening during late years that raised the heretofore mild form of state sovereignty into an active, dangerous type. The Confederacy had long been impressing what it needed with a heavy hand; it was putting men into prison without warrant and executing them, so men said, without trial; provost marshals were requiring the civil population to carry passes miles away from the military lines; the Confederate government had destroyed the state troops in 1862 by conscription; it had attempted to get them in 1863 by a ruse; and now it had drafted them outright—it began to appear even to otherwise calm, well-balanced men that the Confederate government was building up a military despotism at the expense of the sovereignty of the state. The Stephens-Toombs-Brown-

Vance party won many new adherents at this point. They all belligerently asserted the constitutional right to maintain "troops of war" in order to preserve the sovereignty and the dignity of the state.

We might safely assert that the greater part of the hostility to conscription, except in Georgia and North Carolina, developed after the passage of the law of February 1864 and that it was largely due to the fact that the law proposed to divest the states of their right to maintain "troops of war"—the sine qua non of their sovereignty.

Governor Clark of Mississippi, whose state had always been able, without resorting to hostilities with the Confederate government, to retain a force of several thousand men was, after the passage of the conscript law of February, 1864, at last confronted with the alternative of an utter abandonment of the state's right to "troops of war" or defiance of the Confederate law. The governor made inquiries through his friend, Mr. Watson, whether the state would be permitted to retain its troops; and on February 26 Secretary Seddon wrote Governor Clark that the Confederate government laid claim to all men who were not regularly enlisted as "troops of war," and that he considered the Mississippi organizations as nothing but ordinary militia, which would be subject to conscription.[128] The governor now saw that it had been put squarely up to him whether he would insist on what he considered the rights of the state, or whether he would back down and allow the Confederate government to have his troops. He was not noisy, like Brown and Vance. But he quietly insisted on his right to "troops of war," as he called the state organizations, and to any citizen "not actually brought under the authority of the Confederate government;"[129] and kept one of the largest forces heretofore raised for local defense in the state during the spring and summer following the last conscription law.[130] As the year wore on and the Federal armies pressed more and more into the state, the governor included yet larger numbers in the state organizations. In September 1864 he issued a proclamation in which he asserted his right to all persons, without regard to age, if they would enlist in the state forces.[131]

The effect of the attitude taken by Governor Clark was the failure of the Confederate government to organize an effective reserve force in Mississippi. General Brandon wrote General Cooper in the fall of 1864 that "the enlistment of men in state organizations had virtually arrested...the...enrollment of the reserves.... All are rushing into the state organizations;"[132] and about a month later, in

November, he wrote President Davis to the same effect and added that the men liable to service were going into the state regiments "even after being enrolled."[133] The state forces thus built up at the expense of the Confederate armies, as early as August, 1864 numbered 5,000 enlisted men and 8,000 militia in active service,[134] and as General Brandon had pointed out, there were many enlistments in the state organizations during the months after August which must have added very materially to the 13,000 men already reported in active state service. These troops were kept by the state of Mississippi until the war was practically over, when the governor was finally induced to agree to part with those claimed by the Confederate government.[135]

Governor Watts of Alabama, who had a considerable organization of local-defense troops when the last conscript law was passed, refused to allow them to enter the Confederate Reserves. His first tilt over this matter happened when he learned that the Confederate government was about to conscript a special regiment of young men whose officers held their commissions through the influence of the governor, and who were from the best families of the state and probably very influential. He won a partial victory by forcing the Confederacy to accept them as organized, thus ensuring these young officers their commissions and at the same time saving his dignity.[136] But the other state organizations he absolutely refused to hand over to the reserve officers. These were composed mostly of men above forty-five who had farms and business interests as well as families, which explained the fact that he refused to let them go when he had allowed the Confederate authorities to take over the regiment of youngsters.

In pursuance of his policy of retaining his state forces, Watts became involved in a controversy with the Confederate authorities, who insisted upon their right to all men of military age not exempt by law. On May 31 he wrote Seddon that the enrolling officers were taking his men to camps of instruction for the reserves, and that this was doing great injury to the planting interests. This, he thought, was the "most egregious folly, to call it by no harsher name" he had ever heard of. Not only was it foolish to take "men over forty-five and boys under eighteen from their farms...placing them in camps to do nothing" while their crops were ruining, but it was also an injustice to the men and an encroachment upon the reserved right of the state to maintain "troops of war." He could see no object the

Confederate government could have in taking men out of one local-defense organization and putting them in another "unless it is to prevent any state organization" whatever; and, if this were the case, he said, while he had heretofore confined himself to remonstrance against taking his troops, he might feel himself "justified in going farther unless some stop is put to the matter." He was determined that under no conditions would he "permit the troops organized for state defense...to be taken out of the control of the state."[137]

What was left of Louisiana went busily ahead organizing or continued to keep the state troops already on hand. Attempts were made to prevent the recruiting of these state forces at the expense of the Confederate government, but they proved futile. Preston Pond, who helped the governor look after the interests of the state, wrote Governor Allen on May 8, 1864, that the Confederate officers of that district had issued an order to prevent the organization of state troops. However, he said, "Major Cockern is proceeding strictly according to law. He came to me for advice and my advice was to disregard all such orders, maintain his organization, and proceed to complete it according to law and the orders received from you; that whether the state had the right and power to form troops of her own out of any material she pleased," was not a question to be "settled by any Confederate officer."[138] Governor Allen then protested to the War Department that the action of the Confederate government was a personal offense and an insult to the state.[139]

Florida seems to have asserted the state's right to troops rather successfully during the last year of the war. Adjutant General Hugh Archer reported September 19, 1864, "that there have been organized and commissioned thirty-nine companies of state troops embracing an aggregate of 2,780 men."[140] In Texas during the latter part of 1863 and the first half of 1864 the situation was about as bad as one could imagine. The large state force, made up chiefly of conscript, had been mustered into Confederate service for six months about the middle of 1863,[141] and its term of service had expired by the end of the year. Immediately, General Smith called upon the governor to let him continue to use these troops, but the latter refused on the ground that the situation was not as bad as General Smith had described, and further, because all the Confederate troops had been sent out of Texas into Louisiana.[142] Governor Murrah was backed in his position on this question by the Texas legislature, which passed a law in February 1864 claiming every conscript in Texas not in actual

Confederate service.[143] The governor thus gained a firm hold upon his troops. He allowed them to reorganize under new officers who were "fixed" and to go on detail as wagon drivers. He flatly refused to listen to the importunities of the Confederate generals of that department to give them succor, although at the time he had 5,000 men who belonged to the state force, hauling cotton.[144] However, when half the year had passed Governor Murrah was finally brought to see the Confederate point of view after General Magruder had threatened to take the conscript material by force, or else to march out of Texas and leave the defense of that state to the governor's "wagon drivers."[145] But great hurt had been done the Confederate cause by the time the governor promised to surrender his organizations. In truth, General Magruder said, Murrah had done more harm to the cause in Texas than the Federals by "his factious opposition to the laws of Congress on such grounds as the 'dignity of the state'. . .and the extreme state rights construction of the laws of Congress."[146] Magruder pointed out very aptly the effect of such a controversy and a conflict of authority between the Confederate and state authorities. He had "complete and practical evidence that wherever the Confederate authorities and that of the state come into conflict, men unhesitatingly make use of that conflict to avoid military service and certainly that of the Confederate states." He said that when the governor of Texas had issued his proclamation claiming all the conscripts according to the state law of February 1864 "whole brigades disbanded and returned home," and immediately afterward "desertion from the Confederate troops became much more extensive."[147]

In Georgia, as might be expected, a very poor showing was made in the matter of organizing the state troops into reserves.[148] Governor Brown, in accordance with a resolution of the legislature, promised not to do anything that would interfere with the law providing for their organization, but he paid no attention to this promise. He had already had great success in urging the legislature to appropriate $8,000,000 as a fund to maintain the state troops and to pass new laws reorganizing the militia.[149] He started the year 1864 with 8,000,[150] and under local stress he added to them as the year wore on.[151]

The War Department utterly failed, as a matter of course, to get these troops through the law of February. It then attempted to induce Governor Brown to transfer them under a requisition, with the result that it became involved in the bitterest controversy of the whole war. In order to understand this ugly quarrel between the governor and the Confederate authorities it will be necessary to go back to another controversy—having to do with local defense—that led into this one. In June 1864 Sherman was striking at the city of Atlanta and Brown was in a state of frenzy. On June 28 he wired Davis to send Generals Forrest and Morgan to cut off Sherman's line of communication to force his withdrawal or capture. Brown had never shown any disposition to go to the aid of other states, but now that Georgia was threatened he demanded that all else must be stopped and reinforcements sent to his state. "This place," he urged Davis, "is to the Confederacy almost as important as the heart is to the human body." It must be held at all odds.[152] On the following day Davis wired Brown that Morgan and Forrest were engaged in a special work and that their services were indispensible in their "present field." Moreover, he assured Brown, "the disparity of forces between the opposing armies in north Georgia is less...than at any other point.[153] This reply to Brown's demands was perfectly courteous, yet, on receipt of the telegram, the governor flew into a rage both on account of Davis's refusal of reinforcements and what he was pleased to regard as an "exhibition of temper" on the part of the president. He dispatched a hot message to Davis attacking the Confederate military policy of dispersion, which, he himself above all others had foisted upon the Richmond government; and he assured the president that "if Atlanta is sacrificed and Georgia overrun while our cavalry is engaged in distant raids, you will have no difficulty in finding from correct sources of information what was expected of you."[154]

Receiving no aid from Richmond, the governor took matters into his own hands. The old quarrel arising over conscription, over his jealousy of the president's power of detail, over the right to "state troops of war," over his claim to detail whom it pleased him, he settled in his favor with a stroke of the pen. He literally made a clean sweep of the political board. By a proclamation declaring that Georgia was abandoned to her own defense, he drafted into the state forces all the Confederate details, agricultural, mechanical, and industrial, with the exception of those engaged in the Confederate arsenals—unless these details had been countersigned by the state of Georgia; he drafted all Confederate exempts, unless he had also exempted them, members of the Confederate local defense companies, and all persons subject to military service but not yet actually under Confederate control. On the other hand, he exempted all persons employed in the mills and factories—now working for the state—on the railroads, all policemen, mayors, firemen, guards of the penitentiary, employees of the state armory, and all state-house employees.[155] Thus he took the Confederate details and exempts and left his own unmolested. Those whom the Confederate government had desired to leave at home, he took; those the Confederate government had desired to see in military service Governor Brown left alone.

It was typical of the man. But he must needs add insult to injury. On July 19 a few days after this famous proclamation, he wired the President to instruct his officers to cease "throwing obstacles in the way of getting these men [Confederate details] into active service."[156] Of course Davis did all he could to check the governor's course in laying claim to Confederate details and conscripts. He instructed Seddon that the details must not be allowed to go into Georgia organizations, but that they were subject in emergency "to be ordered out with the reserves."[157] Similar instructions were sent to Howell Cobb, general of reserves in Georgia,[158] and on the same day Brown was notified that the detailed men were in Confederate service and could not be incorporated in the state forces.[159] But these instructions and warnings were all for nought: the governor continued the course of opposition he had marked out for himself. At length, when he had raised and equipped as many as he wanted, he "loaned" his troops to General Hood—subject always to the condition that he might withdraw them and send them home when he desired.[160] This was a poor makeshift in a crisis like that facing the Confederate armies, for Brown had no better military judgment than to withdraw his militia in the midst of a pitched battle. This was an intolerable situation—a state force filled with conscripts, exempts, and Confederate details, liable at any moment without notice to be withdrawn from service. If only they could be mustered into Confederate service, the tangled thread could be straightened: the details could be transferred to the reserves where they really belonged, the exempts could be sent home, the conscripts put into general service, and the details Brown had made put back in the militia; and the troops would be subject—not to the whims of a suspicious and vindictive governor—but to the orders of a Confederate general. Hence, on August 30 Seddon made a requisition upon the governor for his 10,000 militia, hoping thus to settle the matter.[161]

But the very thing that the Confederate authorities had planned to prevent now happened: as if to anticipate the requisition Brown sent his troops home on a thirty-day furlough, during the most critical moments of the campaign around Atlanta. This was simply a maneuver in local politics—the governor was taking care to mend his fences even while Atlanta was falling into the hands of the enemy. In his proclamation the governor praised the troops for their service and gallantry, and told them that it was their due, as the emergency was over, that opportunity be given them to put their houses in order and take a breathing spell.[162] Two days after sending the troops home to rest, Brown received the requisition from Seddon. Without a doubt the governor was the angriest and bitterest person on the continent at the moment. With his pen fairly reeking with gall he wrote the secretary a flat, unconditional refusal. The president, he said, had scattered his forces "from Texas to Pennsylvania while a severe blow was being struck at the heart of the Confederacy;" and that with 30,000 men lying idle in Texas, and the reserves guarding prisoners back of the lines, he had refused to send a man to reinforce the Confederate army defending Atlanta. If the president had had control of the militia, he said in all probability he would have sent it to some other state to fight, or he would have disbanded it and placed over it "his own partisans and favorites." But most important of all, Brown actually feared that the requisition for his militia was a move on the part of Davis, whom he already regarded as a regular Nero, to disarm Georgia so as to prevent resistance to further encroachments on her reserved rights. He would refuse to "gratify the President's ambition...and surrender the last vestige of the sovereignty of the state."[163]

On October 8 Seddon refuted Brown's unjust accusations concerning the motive of the president in making the requisition. There were, he said, two motives back of that measure. In the first place, it was desired to put the state troops under the control of the Confederate generals where they could be relied upon at all times. For "it is easy," he wrote, "to see how uncertainty as to their control or retention must impair reliance by the commander on these troops, and embarrass all calculations for their employment and efficiency in combined operations." The second reason had been that the troops requisitioned contained conscripts and Confederate details "which had engendered controversy and endangered collision between the local Confederate and state authorities" which it was thought might be terminated by gaining control over the troops. The secretary then accused Brown of playing into the hands of the enemy, who believed from his words and actions that he was prepared to "entertain over-tures of separate accommodation." He also arraigned the governor for refusing to obey the provision of the constitution that made the president commander-in-chief of all the military forces. This, he pointed out, was a repetition of what Massachusetts and Connecticut had done during the War of 1812, which had resulted in casting a shadow over the loyalty of those states.[164]

Brown's reply to this letter again accused the president of aiming at absolute power by grasping the entire control of the Confederate and state forces. As to the president's attempt to settle the quarrel over the details and conscripts in the state force by requisition, Brown sarcastically remarked that it was a "new discovery of the president of the mode of settling a controverted right," by which the stronger took from the weaker, "and the magnanimity and states-manship displayed by him in this affair cannot be too highly appre-ciated." He flatly denied that the president was commander-in-chief of the militia (except when it was actually in Confederate service) with the power to call it out at his discretion.[165] Seddon immediately cited the Confederate laws of February 28 and March 6, 1861, which conferred plenary power upon the president to employ all military forces of the Confederate states, including militia, the regular army, or any other forces organized in the Confederacy. "In my judgment," said he, "these acts...bind you both as a citizen and an officer and you owe prompt, cordial, and unhesitating obedience to them."[166] Brown's rejoinder was that the acts were not susceptible of any such construction, but that if, as Seddon contended, they were, then "Con-gress had no power or authority to pass them."[167]

The argument had lasted six months, but it had booted the Con-federate government nothing. Brown kept the state troops and all Confederate details; as late as March 13, 1865, when it was all about over, Governor Brown issued the following defiant order: "All per-sons belonging to Major Smith's division are in the actual military service of the state. No one of them, whether detailed agriculturists [Confederate] or not, will obey any order from a Confederate offi-cer.... The Confederate officers can take no control over them with-out the consent of the state till they are disbanded by the state. They are now on furlough."[168]

Having failed to gain control of the state forces by all the methods heretofore tried, President Davis turned in despair to the Confederate Congress and asked it to pass a law which would enable him to take them over in a body by some form of requisition.[169] But Congress by this time was dominated by the idea of state rights and state sovereignty. Brown, Stephens, Toombs, Vance, Rhett, Pollard, and their like, rather than Davis, were the leaders to whom Congress now looked for inspiration. His appeal fell upon deaf ears. The Committee on Military Affairs reported that in its opinion any law transferring the control of the state troops to the president would in reality be equivalent to another conscription act, which it was not willing to adopt.[170]

In retrospect, we see that the states were so strongly imbued with the idea of their own separate identity and rights that they attempted their own defense. This resulted in withdrawing arms from general service during the first year of the war when the Confederate government was unable to obtain an adequate supply elsewhere, and thereby prevented the recruiting of the Confederate armies; it resulted, especially after the first year when arms were more plentiful, in withdrawing large numbers of men from the general service. The attempts of the Confederate government to obtain control of the men and arms thus withheld aroused many bitter feuds between the state and Confederate authorities. Altogether, local defense contributed very materially to the defeat of the Confederacy.

[1]*Montgomery Weekly Advertiser*, March 30, 1861; *The War of the Rebellion: a Compilation of the Official Records of the Union and Confederate Armies* (Washington, 1880–1901), Ser. IV. Vol. I, 74. Cited henceforth as *Rebellion Records*.

[2]See Duncan Rose, "Why the Confederacy Failed," *Century*, LIII (November 1896), 33–38, and the replies by Gen. Stephen D. Lee, Brig. Gen. E. P. Alexander, Maj. Gen. O. O. Howard, and Gen. D. C. Buell in the February 1897 issue (pp. 626–633) as to the effects of "dispersion" caused by local defense.

[3]*Rebellion Records*, Ser. IV, Vol. I, 292. For North Carolina see Walter Clark (ed.), *Histories of the Several Regiments and Battalions from North Carolina in the Great War, 1861–'65* (Raleigh, 1901), pp. 40–43. Cited henceforth as *North Carolina Regiments*.

[4]*Montgomery Confederation*, June 21, 1861.

[5]For instance, there were 20,000 rifles at Harper's Ferry with the stocks destroyed. J. B. Jones in his *A Rebel War Clerk's Diary at the Confederate States Capitol* (Philadelphia, 1866), I, 78, gives the total number of arms as only 15,000, but this is plainly a rough guess.

[6]*Rebellion Records*, Ser. IV, Vol. I, 52.

[7]*Ibid.*, pp. 63, 67, 68.

[8]*Ibid.*, pp. 713–722.

[9]*Ibid.*, pp. 319, 332, 350, 355, 366, 367, 401, 402, 473, 491, 1046, 1047, 1063–1067.

[10]*North Carolina Regiments*, I, 40–43.

[11]*Rebellion Records*, Ser. IV, Vol. I, 479.

[12]*Ibid.*, pp. 634–636; *ibid.*, Ser. I, Vol. I, 265.

[13]*Ibid.*, Ser. IV, Vol. I, 379–393.

[14]*Montgomery Mail*, May 14, 1861; *Rebellion Records*, Ser. IV, Vol. I, 228, 292.

[15]*Ibid.*, p. 121.

[16]*Ibid.*, p. 420.

[17]*Ibid.*, pp. 702, 704–705.

[18]*Ibid.*, p. 337.

[19]*Ibid.*, p. 422.

[20]*Ibid.*, p. 484.

[21]*Ibid.*, p. 712.

[22]*Ibid.*, pp. 712–713.

[23]*Appleton's Annual Cyclopaedia, 1862*, p. 660.

[24]*Rebellion Records*, Ser. IV, Vol. I, 827–828.

[25]*Ibid.*, pp. 624, 634, 635; see also *ibid.*, p. 479.

[26]*Ibid.*, Ser. I, Vol. VI, 372.

[27]*Ibid.*, Ser. IV, Vol. I, 358, 479.

[28]*Ibid.*, Ser. I, Vol. III, 623.

[29]*ibid.*, p. 588.

[30]*Ibid.*, Ser. IV, Vol. I, 469–473.

[31]*Ibid.*, p. 511; see also *ibid.*, p. 722.

[32]*Ibid.*, pp. 358, 468–473, 476, 481, 482, 488, 489, 491, 492, 504–512, 530, 534.

[33]*Ibid.*, Ser. I, Vol. LII, Pt. II, 97; see *ibid.*, Ser. IV, Vol. I, 319, 332, 350, 355, 366, 367, 401, 402, 473, 491 for controversy with the Confederate authorities over this question. See also below.

[34]*Ibid.*, Ser. IV, Vol. I, 368.

[35]*Ibid.*, pp. 406, 407, 410, 411.

[36]*Ibid.*, p. 401.

[37]*Ibid.*, p. 416.

[38]*Ibid.*, pp. 1046–1047.

[39]*Ibid.*, p. 1059.

[40]*Ibid.*, pp. 1058–1059.

[41]*Ibid.*, p. 614.

[42]*Ibid.*, p. 615.

[43]*Ibid.*, Ser. I, Vol. VI, 307.

[44]*Ibid.*, Ser. IV, Vol. I, 668. Brown had shown Lawton a message from Richmond that convinced the latter of an imminent invasion. From the well-known tactics of Brown one can readily understand what that persistent individual was up to.

[45]*Ibid.*, pp. 617–618.

[46]*Ibid.*

[47]*Ibid.*, pp. 624–625.

[48]*Ibid.*, Ser. I, Vol. VI, 318–319.

[49]*Ibid.*, Ser. IV, Vol. I, 497; cf. *ibid.*, p. 349.

[50]*Ibid.*, p. 795.

[51]*Ibid.*, pp. 970, 1168; *ibid.*, Ser. I, Vol. VII, 907. A prominent author of the history of the North Carolina regiments says that at least 100,000 more men would have been in the ranks by 1862 if arms had been furnished (*North Carolina Regiments*, I, 40–43).

[52]*Ibid.*, Ser. I, Vol. VII, 794–795.

[53]*Montgomery Weekly Advertiser*, August 31, 1861.

[54]The statement that the South had the better generals and better-trained soldiery at the outbreak of the war will probably go unquestioned at the present day, for all recall the fact that the prominent Southern families took a special pride in sending their sons to West Point and to the several well-equipped military academies in the South, and that the mass of Southern people were accustomed to the use of the rifle and pistol and to horseback riding and other exercises closely related to military training and, moreover, the institution of slavery tended to develop the militant temperament. This condition would naturally lead one to expect the South to show the advantage at first, and the fact that Lincoln changed generals after almost every important battle, until those splendid leaders, Thomas, Sheridan, Sherman, and Grant were brought to the top showed that the Confederacy came up to expectations. The situation is well characterized by the following quotation from the New York *Tribune:* "Most of them [Southerners] have been trained from the cradle to consider personal bravery the very first essential of manly character and skill in the use of arms the first necessity of a gentleman. The revolver and rifle have been their playthings from boyhood.... They have many of the very best of our late army officers and their soldiers will at first be better led and better handled than ours." Quoted in the *Montgomery Weekly Advertiser,* May 14, 1861.

[55]*Rebellion Records,* Ser. IV, Vol. I, 50.

[56]*Ibid.,* Ser. I, Vol. LII, Pt. II, 15.

[57]*Ibid.,* Vol. I, 702, 704–705; cf. *Annual Cyclopaedia, 1862,* p. 9, and Miller, *History of Alabama,* pp. 156, 157, 179 for references to state troops.

[58]*Rebellion Records,* Ser. IV, Vol. I, 172–173, 177–178.

[59]*Ibid.,* pp. 753, 754, 755; *ibid.,* Ser. I, Vol. LIII, 612.

[60]*Ibid.,* Ser. IV, Vol. I, 174; cf. *ibid.,* p. 63.

[61]*Ibid.,* Ser. IV, Vol. II, 178–179.

[62]*Ibid.,* I, 1092; cf. *ibid.,* pp. 827–828.

[63]*North Carolina Regiments,* I, 8–12. 10,000 were turned over at the time of conscription, but six infantry, three artillery, and one cavalry regiment were left in the state. *Ibid.,* p. 12.

[64]*Rebellion Records,* Ser. I, Vol. I, 624, 634–635; *Annual Cyclopaedia, 1862,* p. 759.

[65]*Rebellion Records,* Ser. I, Vol. I, 358.

[66]*Ibid.,* Ser. I, Vol. LII, Pt. II, 123–124.

[67]*Ibid.,* Ser. IV, Vol. I, 860–863; cf. *ibid.,* pp. 963, 1114–1115, and *ibid.,* Ser. I, Vol. LI, Pt. II, 495. These troops were mustered into Confederate service, as sometimes happened in other states, but they retained their local character, being mustered only for limited periods and for state defense. The object of being carried on the Confederate rolls was to obtain Confederate pay.

[68]*Ibid.,* Ser. I, Vol. III, 595, 732; Vol. VIII, 748; Vol. XIII, 29–32.

[69]*Ibid.,* pp. 29–32.

[70]*Ibid.,* Ser. IV, Vol. I, 250–252, 717, 978–979.

[71]*Ibid.,* pp. 167–168.

[72]*Ibid.,* p. 168.

[73]*Ibid.,* Ser. I, Vol. LI, Pt. II, 359.

[74]*Ibid.,* Vol. VI, 284.

[75]*Ibid.,* p. 307; *The Confederate Records of the State of Georgia,* 6 vols. (Atlanta, 1909–1911), II, 93–95, 131–132, 138–144, 146, 154.

[76]*Rebellion Records,* Ser. I, Vol. VI, 284.

[77]*Ibid.,* Ser. IV, Vol. I, 1063, 1067.

[78]*Ibid.,* p. 795; cf. Brown's message to the Georgia Assembly, December 5, 1861, in *Confederate Records of Georgia,* II, 154. Louisiana, North Carolina, Virginia,

Tennessee, and probably other states, he said "have called into the field large numbers of state troops to repel invasion and protect their property." This policy of local defense was evidently generally known throughout the Confederacy.

[79]*Rebellion Records,* Ser. IV, Vol. III, 740.

[80]*Ibid.,* Ser. IV, Vol. II, 580.

[81]*Ibid.,* pp. 70–71.

[82]*Ibid.,* pp. 253–256.

[83]*Ibid.,* Ser. I, Vol. LII, Pt. II, 414–415.

[84]*Ibid.,* pp. 414–415; see also *Montgomery Mail,* January 25, 1863.

[85]*Rebellion Records,* Ser. IV, Vol. II, 419–420.

[86]*Ibid.,* p. 264; *Confederate Records of Georgia,* II, 257–258, 274.

[87]*Rebellion Records,* Ser. IV, Vol. II, 263–264.

[88]See *Confederate Records of Georgia,* II, 447–449, 507–508.

[89]*Rebellion Records,* Ser. IV, Vol. II, 398–399.

[90]*Ibid.*

[91]*Ibid.,* p. 677.

[92]*Ibid.,* pp. 178–179; cf. *ibid.,* pp. 16, 17.

[93]*Ibid.,* pp. 667, 754, 759–761.

[94]*Ibid.,* p. 249; *ibid.,* Ser. I, Vol. LII, Pt. II, 453.

[95]*Ibid.,* Ser. IV, Vol. II, 697, 701, 754, 760, 765.

[96]*Ibid.,* pp. 927–936: "3 regiments, 3 battalions, 10 unattached companies, etc."

[97]*Ibid.,* pp. 775–776.

[98]*Ibid.,* pp. 146–147. This feeling became worse as time passed. See Jones, I, 303, 325; II, 37.

[99]*Rebellion Records,* Ser. IV, Vol. II, 180–181.

[100]*Ibid.,* p. 210.

[101]*Ibid.;* also Jones, I, 198.

[102]*Rebellion Records,* Ser. IV, Vol. II, 225, 226.

[103]*Richmond Examiner* and *Raleigh Standard* quoted in *Montgomery Mail,* December 6, 1862; *North Carolina Regiments,* I, 13, 14, 51–52. North Carolina already had six local defense regiments in the Confederate service, besides the Sixty-Seventh and Sixty-Eighth North Carolina Regulars, and this new levy increased the number to about 17,000. These local defense troops were usually mustered in to the Confederate service for limited periods—for state defense—in order to draw Confederate pay, etc. See *Confederate Records of Georgia,* II, 160–165, 173.

[104]*Richmond Whig,* quoted in *Montgomery Mail,* January 28, 1863.

[105]*Rebellion Records,* Ser. IV, Vol. II, 548–549; *ibid.,* Ser. I, Vol. XXVI, Pt. II, 497–498; Vol. LIII, 840; *Montgomery Mail,* December 14, 1862.

[106]*Annual Cyclopaedia, 1862,* p. 759; cf. *Mobile Register,* quoted in *Montgomery Mail,* December 12, 1862, April 11, 1863; *Rebellion Records,* Ser. IV, Vol. II, 665, 702, 788, 803; *ibid.,* Ser. I, Vol. XIV, 784.

[107]*Ibid.,* Ser. I, Vol. LI, Pt. II, 620.

[108]*Ibid.,* Ser. IV, Vol. II, 580–582; cf. Jones, I, 347–348.

[109]*Rebellion Records,* Ser. IV, Vol. II, 580–582; cf. Jones, I, 347–348.

[110]Probably Texas and Georgia transferred them for six months—only to involve the Confederate Government in a quarrel for keeping the troops in the field too long.

[111]*Rebellion Records,* Ser. IV, Vol. II, 596.

[112]*Ibid.,* p. 674.

[113]Report of C. D. Melton, Commandant of Conscripts, South Carolina; *ibid.,* pp. 812–814.

[114]*Ibid.,* pp. 665, 702, 803, 813.

[115]*Ibid.,* p. 702.

[116]*Ibid.*, pp. 677, 697, 701, 754, 759–761.

[117]*Ibid.*, p. 936.

[118]*Ibid.*, pp. 926, 928, 976–978.

[119]*Ibid.*, p. 584.

[120]*Ibid.*, pp. 590–591.

[121]*Ibid.*, p. 595.

[122]*Ibid.*, p. 824.

[123]*Confederate Records of Georgia*, II, 523–526.

[124]*Rebellion Records*, Ser. IV, Vol. II, 952–953.

[125]*Ibid.*, Vol. III, 61–62; cf. Jones, II, 145–146.

[126]*Rebellion Records*, Ser. IV, Vol. III, 164–165.

[127]The original proposal of Secretary Seddon shows that he, and not Brown, was right. *Ibid.*, Vol. II, 580–582.

[128]*Ibid.*, Vol. III, 172–174, 821–822; Jones remarks at this point that it seemed "the states respectively mean to take control of all their men not now in the Confederate states armies," and that he feared there would be "confusion worse confounded" (II, 377; cf. *ibid.*, 199).

[129]*Ibid.*, Ser. IV, Vol. III, 903, 904.

[130]*Ibid.*, pp. 307–309; *ibid.*, Ser. I, Vol. XXXII, Pt. III, 650–651.

[131]*Ibid.*, Ser. IV, Vol. III, 710, 740.

[132]*Ibid.*, p. 740.

[133]*Ibid.*, pp. 823–824.

[134]*Ibid.*, p. 590; *ibid.*, Ser. I, Vol. LII, Pt. II, 726.

[135]For the controversy over the surrender of these troops see *ibid.*, Ser. IV, Vol. III, 902–903, 904, 1162–1167; *ibid.*, Ser. I, Vol. LII, Pt. II, 810–811.

[136]*Ibid.*, Ser. IV, Vol. III, 276, 472.

[137]*Ibid.*, pp. 463–464. The governor sent a few more threatening letters to Richmond, with the result, apparently, that he desired. Preston made the remark on receiving one of these letters that "the tendency of the action of the state authorities is to absorb the whole class of reserves" (*ibid.*, pp. 464, 466).

[138]*Ibid.*, p. 400.

[139]Jones, II, 324.

[140]*Rebellion Records*, Ser. IV, Vol. III, 669.

[141]*Ibid.*, Ser. I, Vol. XXVI, Pt. II, 497–498.

[142]*Ibid.*, Ser. I, Vol. XXXV, Pt. II, 1087–1095, 1103.

[143]*Ibid.*, Ser. I, Vol. XXXV, Pt. III, 786–789.

[144]*Ibid.*, p. 726.

[145]*Ibid.*, pp. 786–789.

[146]*Ibid.*, p. 727.

[147]*Ibid.*, pp. 786–789.

[148]The number of reserves raised in Georgia was so small that General Cobb was compelled to use them all in guarding the 30,000 Federal prisoners in that state (*ibid.*, Ser. I, Vol. LII, Pt. II, 736–740).

[149]*Annual Cyclopaedia, 1863*, p. 448; *Confederate Records of Georgia*, II, 601–610.

[150]*Rebellion Records*, Ser. IV, Vol. II, 977. Governor Clark referred to this number in his message to the Mississippi legislature as showing what other states were doing in the matter of local defense, and as proof of what Mississippi should do. Cf. *Confederate Records of Georgia*, II, 601–610.

[151]On August 30, 1864, for instance, when Secretary Seddon made his requisition upon Georgia, there were 10,000 organized and others reported as available (*Rebellion Records*, Ser. I, Vol. LII, Pt. II, 727; cf. *Confederate Records of Georgia*, II, 774–775).

[152]*Rebellion Records,* Ser. I, Vol. LII, Pt. II, 680–681.

[153]*Ibid.,* p. 681.

[154]*Ibid.,* p. 687.

[155]*Ibid.,* pp. 688–691. Confederate details were obnoxious in Brown's sight. By the law of February 1864 all men between the ages of 17 and 18, and 45 and 50 had been subject to service in reserve unless "detailed" by the president. Brown regarded this as one of the last moves of Davis to gather complete power over the entire population of Georgia (*Confederate Records of Georgia,* II, 601–610).

[156]*Rebellion Records,* Ser. I, Vol. LII, Pt. II, 709–710.

[157]*Ibid.,* p. 710.

[158]*Ibid.*

[159]*Ibid.,* p. 711.

[160]*Ibid.,* pp. 717, 724, 725.

[161]*Ibid.,* p. 727.

[162]*Ibid.,* pp. 735–736; cf. Jones, II, 311.

[163]*Rebellion Records,* Ser. I, Vol. LII, Pt. II, 736–740; cf. Jones, II, 292. Brown's opposition to the law of February 1864 conscripting all between the ages of 17 and 18, 45 and 50 for service in the Confederate reserve was largely an outgrowth of fear that Davis was attempting to deprive Georgia of her militia and thus deny her right to "troops of war" (*Confederate Records of Georgia,* II, 601–610).

[164]*Rebellion Records,* Ser. I, Vol. LII, Pt. II, 754–758.

[165]*Ibid.,* pp. 778–790.

[166]*Ibid.,* pp. 796–799.

[167]*Ibid.,* pp. 803–807.

[168]*Ibid.,* Ser. IV, Vol. III, 1138. In the controversy, which lasted from July 16, 1864, to January 1865, the Confederate authorities had finally, when they were seeking an honorable surrender to Brown, consented that conscripts and details might remain in Brown's militia until the militia was disbanded. The result of this promise was that Brown never disbanded his militia, but sent them home on indefinite furloughs, thereby preventing the Confederate Government from asserting its claims over them.

[169]*Ibid.,* p. 1133; *Journal of the Congress of the Confederate States of America, 1861–1865,* 7 vols. (Washington, 1904–1905), IV, 704–705.

[170]*Rebellion Records,* Ser. IV, Vol. III, 1145–1146.

Defeatism in the Confederacy*

There have been few wars in history in which a country has presented such a solid front or offered such a large percentage of its population to the god of war as the South did in 1861. Six hundred thousand out of a population of eight million whites offered their services to the Confederacy the first year of the war, and it was only the lack of arms that prevented the South's putting an army of that size in the field.[1] The French revolution with all its enthusiasm for war against the enemies of liberty, equality, and fraternity, with a population almost three times this, seldom had armies so large.

By 1863 this spontaneity and enthusiasm had disappeared from great sections of the population of the Confederacy and was rapidly dying among the soldiers at the front. Defeatism—though not known, perhaps, by the term—had sapped and mined the moral foundations of the South until the whole war structure was crumbling, and by 1865 a complete collapse was impending, even had the Confederate army remained undefeated.

Yet over much of this period Confederate arms were eminently successful in winning battles. Lee was, up to the end of 1864, still able to destroy one-third of Grant's army with an army only one-third as large in the short space of a summer. Why, then, this psychology of defeat in the midst of so much victory?

The answer is that the will to war had been broken by causes other than military defeat—and perhaps one might add that the hearts of many were also broken. One of the most fundamental causes for this condition was that a great part of the Southern people had nothing more than an academic interest in slavery and secession. True, the average backwoodsman and up-countryman hoped some day to own slaves, but, after all, the fact remained that he did not and, so, had nothing to lose by emancipation. The great mass of blacks were owned by a relatively small group who lived in the tidewater and river-bottom regions of the South, and in all probability, because of poor soil and poor farming methods in the hills, the slaves would have continued to be owned largely by the planters in

*The writer wishes to express his appreciation of the excellent study, "Peace Moves in the Confederacy," made by Miss Georgia Lee Tatum as an M.A. thesis at Vanderbilt, which he has found invaluable in preparing this article. [F.L.O.]

the Black Belt. On account of the lack of slaves in the back counties, and a different social and economic structure, sectionalism developed all the way from Maryland to Texas, and manifested itself in an unjust distribution of representation and bitter feelings. The small slave group kept the power in their own hands and often abused this power.[2]

Hope of an ultimate settlement, lack of economic interest in slavery and sectionalism had prompted the up-country elements in the various Southern States to oppose secession. In Alabama, William R. Smith, Robert Jamison, D. P. Lewis, Jeremiah Clemens, and Nicholas Davis led the Northern section in opposing secession, 31 delegates refusing to sign the ordinance of secession.[3] Stevens and H. V. Johnson, old whig leaders, championed the opposition in Georgia and about one-third of the convention opposed secession.[4] In Texas there was a strong up-country opposition led by Sam Houston.[5] In Mississippi about one-third of the delegates led by A. J. Brown, W. M. Yerger, Judge Sharkey, and Poindexter opposed secession.[6] Virginia,[7] North Carolina,[8] Arkansas,[9] and Tennessee[10] opposed and defeated secession until Lincoln began his policy of coercion, whereupon they seceded,[11] leaving the leaders and a small group of irreconcilables disgruntled and bitter.

With the exception, however, of this small knot of unionists and of east Tennessee and west Virginia the up-country people accepted the verdict and displayed much enthusiasm. They had not wanted to secede, and above all, even when they had contemplated ultimate secession of their states as a redress of admitted wrongs, they had desired to exhaust all resources before the final step was taken. On the other hand, they disliked "Yankees" and feared Negro equality in case of emancipation, and were stung to great anger when Lincoln pitched his armies into the South, invading their homes and threatening the dreaded liberation of the blacks.

This resentment at invasion and dread of Negro equality could not take the place of a similar state of mind on the part of the Black Belt, plus an economic interest rather than an academic interest in Negro slavery—not in the face of what turned out to be a long and grim struggle. The up-country people could easily fight a ninety-day war as some of their leaders had promised this one would be, but not a war that lasted over several years. Anger and enthusiasm are too transient to serve as a basis of war. So the opposition began to show its head under the up-country irreconcilables.

The suffering of the soldiers and their families was a great factor in producing defeatist psychology. Frequently, the entire able-bodied male population of an up-country district was in the army, leaving women, children, and old men to plow the fields and gather the crops. Frequently, there were no men at all left in a family and few in a neighborhood. The writer knows of a case in Coosa County, Alabama, where out of a family of nine sons and two daughters, all married, the nine sons and the two sons-in-law went into the army, leaving their eleven families under the care of one aged grandfather. This was by no means an unusual example. The result was extreme destitution when taken in connection with the fact that a soldier's pay in this period was hardly worth 50 cents a month in gold, and the prices of goods were higher than even depreciated currency should have made them because of heartless speculation.[12]

The raids of the enemy and the occupation of the country also added tremendously to the destitution of the people. Frequently this destitution was made more appalling by the terror-stricken women and children fleeing back into the Confederate territory where they were without homes, food, or any means of support save what the charity of others almost as poor might offer.[13]

Impressment of supplies by the Confederate armies, especially when made by able-bodied officers who should have been in the fighting line, added to the bitterness and want. While impressment was necessary, its manner was often harsh and at best it was always distressing to those whose goods were taken. In addition to the impressment of supplies the Confederacy finally resorted to the tax in kind by which one-tenth of what a man produced must be surrendered to the government agents.[14]

Suffering was not confined to the people at home. That of the soldier was proverbial and when he received letters from home, depicting such terrible conditions and at the same time telling of able-bodied speculators who should have been in the army, it was often more than he could bear. The morning sun often shone upon an empty tent, the former occupant of which was far on his way back home, presenting his cocked musket as a furlough, to any who questioned his going.[15]

We have noted that invasion produced great physical suffering which contributed much to defeat, but the greatest suffering was not material but mental. The fear that women had at home and the dread that soldiers at the front had for their wives, sweethearts, and mothers, and other loved ones was all-compelling at times. Rape, murder, and other nameless violations hovered always as a dark specter in the minds of the soldiers from the invaded districts. This fear, of course, affected both rich and poor alike, except, of course, the rich could move their women out if they felt the need. An example of this mental effect is seen in the case of Arkansas soldiers in the spring of 1862 when all the troops were withdrawn from the state and sent to Shiloh. A wail of despair from the invaded country, voiced by the governor, was heard by the soldiers upon the east bank of the Mississippi. Arkansas was deserted! Abandoned to shame and destruction by her own friends! If we are abandoned, he cried, "let Southern Missourians, Arkansans, and Texans know it and prepare for the future. Arkansas abandoned...is not Arkansas as she entered the Confederacy. Her children fleeing from the wrath to come will build them a new ark and launch it upon new waters."[16] Thousands of soldiers deserted back to the Arkansas shores.[17]

Frequently, people in the up-country were indifferent to the war. They asked only to be let alone, and if allowed would have remained neutral or under any government which did not molest them.[18] Any kind of molestation by either North or South would be resented and would throw these people over into the opposing camp. This was exactly what happened when the Confederacy adopted the policy of conscription. It was a potent factor in inclining them toward peace.[19]

Perhaps the most fundamental and far-reaching cause of defeatism was the ever-growing idea of the favoritism of the Confederate government. It was felt that all the favors were showered upon the planters and people of the Black Belt, while the burden of the war was being shifted upon the backs of the poor small farmer and backwoodsman. The old leaders of the poor districts and white counties began to speak openly and to proclaim that this was a rich man's war and a poor man's fight and the old sectional jealousy at once became alive and burning in the breasts of those who were suffering so terribly, with no prospect of material returns to pay for their sacrifices. The conscript law dragged the poor man from his cabin leaving his family to the chances of war, while the rich man of the Black Belt was permitted to go free because he was able to hire a substitute.[20] The fact that able-bodied men were thus permitted to stay at home and become speculators, often in the necessities of life, charging exorbitant prices for things the soldier's meager pay could not provide for his family, was maddening. The poor soldier and his family felt that not only was the war a rich man's war and a poor man's fight, but that everything else also belonged to the rich man, even to the pittance he and his own family obtained. He felt the truth of the scriptures that to him who hath it shall be given and from him who hath not it shall be taken.[21] Jones, in his diary, complains constantly that the people of wealth who had most at stake were more and more allowing the burden of the war to be carried by the very people who were least able to carry it and who would benefit least by success.

The substitute law was repealed in 1864,[22] but a loophole still remained in the form of the twenty Negro or later fifteen Negro law, through which a planter might escape service if he desired, for at first, any man who owned twenty slaves and later fifteen might be exempted to oversee his Negroes.[23] The planter class probably furnished throughout the whole war a larger percentage than any other class in any country has ever furnished for military service. They were able to do this because of the fact that the Negro slaves relieved them of the task of making a living for their families. However, there were numerous able-bodied men out of the service for whom there was no excuse, men who took advantage of the substitute and twenty-Negro law to stay out. Those men were very obvious and obnoxious because of their tendencies to grind the face of the poor, and the principle involved in the twenty-Negro clause and the substitute law was thoroughly vicious and bound to rouse the suspicion of the poor. Hence the belief that the Confederacy was practicing rank favoritism was perfectly logical and inevitable, especially since the up-country people had been accustomed from time immemorial to being dealt with unfairly by the Black Belt people who dominated the state governments.

Other examples of apparent injustice and favoritism were the numerous group of able-bodied officers who were able to escape service by being detailed as conscript commandants, provosts, or supply officers. Vance thoroughly advertised this type of officer whom he described as of petty mind "dressed up in a little brief authority."[24]

The flames of angry discontent were fanned by the numerous controversies between the state and Confederate governments over states' rights, and by the propaganda of the peace societies that began to show great strength by 1863.

These disloyal peace societies were the expression in an organized way of the desire for peace resulting from the causes discussed above. However, as suggested above, they were also a potent cause in producing further converts to the peace idea.

Symptoms of the peace organizations began to be apparent in north Alabama as early as April 1862 in connection with the passage of the conscript law. Meetings and conventions expressing a desire to remain neutral were held in Winston, Fayette, and Marion counties.[25] Leaders of the old Unionist element began to come out in the open. Clemens and Judge Lane had several Confederate sympathizers jailed by the Federal officers, and Clemens asked to be allowed to go to Washington to find out how peace might be obtained.[26] The draft boards in north Alabama began to show distinct signs of disloyalty as the greater part of the conscripts were discharged on the slightest excuse.[27] Trading with the enemy became common at this time.[28]

By 1863 signs of peace and disloyal sentiments could be seen in the hill and backwoods districts of central and southern Alabama.[29] In Randolph County the people stormed the jail and freed all the draft dodgers and deserters, and about the same time the Third Alabama Reserves deserted en masse. This trend of affairs was brought to a climax in the fall of 1863 when many of these up-country and backwoods counties elected a solid phalanx of peace men and open Union sympathizers to county and state offices, and made almost a clean sweep of Confederate officers by electing six avowed Unionists to Congress.[30] Similar conditions in the other states caused an investigation to be made.

This investigation of the Confederate authorities revealed a startling situation throughout the entire South. In Alabama, Arkansas, Georgia, Texas, and Mississippi there existed a disloyal chain of organizations known as the "Peace Society,"[31] and in Virginia, Tennessee, North Carolina, and perhaps South Carolina disloyal societies known as "Heroes of America."[32] The "Peace Societies," in different districts, had different signs and passwords. The "Heroes of America" seem to have had one set of passwords, signs, and grips.

The following is an illustration of the method of recognition used in central Alabama by the members of the "Peace Society": First the grip would be given by turning the side of the thumb instead of the ball to the back of the hand of the person who was being tested. The one thus approached, if a member, would ask:

"What is that?"

"A grip," would be the reply.

"A grip of what?"

"A constitutional peace grip."

"Has it a name?"

"It has."

"Will you give it to me?"

"I did not so receive it neither can I impart it."

"How will you impart it?"

"I will letter it to you."

"Begin you."

"No, you begin."

Then peace was spelled out by alternate letters. There were several signs of recognition. A stick was taken, held in both hands and then thrown to the right. The countersign was to put the right hand to a lock of hair or right side of the head as if brushing something to the right. In battle a soldier made his identity known by leaning his gun to the right. The sign of distress was made by holding the right arm out horizontally and bringing it down to the side by three distinct movements. In case this would be too obvious, the exclamation "Oh! Washington!" was used.[33]

On entering the society a member was sworn to absolute secrecy on the penalty of having his "head cut open...brains taken out...and strewn over the ground and...body cast to the beasts of the field."[34] The society neither individually nor collectively was permitted to keep any kind of record and it was very difficult to verify members.[35]

The following were the passwords and signs of the "Heroes of America":

"These are gloomy times."

"Yes, but we are looking for better."

"What are you looking for?"

"A red and white cord."

"Why a cord?"

"Because it is safe for us and our families."

When there was no suspicion, the grip was followed by the word "Three." If the other answered "days" it established his identity as a member.[36] As in the case of the "Peace Society" no records were kept and the penalty for divulging secrets was death.[37]

The purposes of the "Peace Society" and the "Heroes of America" were the same: to bring about peace by submission to the Federal government. However, they had many intermediate objectives, all leading ultimately to the one main purpose. The leaders tried to make use of all shades of disaffection to accomplish their object. A man who was tired of war but loyal was told that the purpose was an "honorable peace" through honorable means. Once a member, such a person would gradually be led through the varying gradations of disaffection until he became disloyal. If a man were dissatisfied with Davis, and most men were, he was told that the organization was formed to put in better men than he and his supporters. If a man were disloyal to the Confederacy, he was immediately put to work upon the main objectives, encouraging desertions, destroying loyalty at home by propaganda and giving any information he possessed with reference to Confederate affairs, to the Federal authorities.[38] The "Peace Society" of Alabama claimed that information furnished by it to the Federal armies resulted in the surrender of Vicksburg and the defeats around Chattanooga.[39] Whether this be true we do not know, but there is full proof that the leaders of the peace societies kept in touch with the Federal authorities, and were busy creating trouble and finding out secrets of the Confederate armies. In North Carolina Horace Dean, W. W. Holden, and Worth were in touch with the enemy;[40] in Alabama, General Roddy, and Major McGoughy were in communication at the last with the Federal authorities, while Jeremiah Clemens, Judge Lane, and L. E. Parsons, prominent leaders, were from the first in constant touch; in Tennessee, Brownlow, Maynard, and Nelson acted as the liaison officers.[41] The same conditions existed in the other states where these societies were organized.

It is difficult to arrive at any exact knowledge of the numbers involved in these peace societies. For the last two years of the war the number of deserters ranged from 90,000 to 136,000,[42] and since early in the war the number had been large.[43] But not every deserter was a member of the peace societies, though he may be put down as belonging to the defeatist element, which, after all, is the main point. The reports of those sent to investigate Alabama indicated that two-thirds of the people in the hill counties of Randolph, Coosa, Talladega, Calhoun, and contiguous counties were disaffected and the southern counties of Pike, Conecuh, Henry, Dale, and Barber, Fayette, Marion, and Blount were overwhelmingly disloyal.[44] The local troops were reported filled with the peace organization. Clanton's brigade, Hilliard's Legion, Bolling Hall's battery, Gracie's brigade were all honeycombed.[45] East Tennessee was under the complete control of the "Heroes of America."[46] Across the line in North Carolina in the counties of Yadkin, Cherokee, Catawba, Ashe, and Randolph likely had a majority of disloyal people. These were the counties where the deserters flocked, and organized themselves into regiments and drilled.[47] Southwest Virginia, according to a report of Brigadier General Echols and others sent to investigate, was completely in the control of the "Heroes of America." Three-fourths of the people of Floyd, Giles, Botetourt, Roanoke, Patrick, Henry, Bedford, Franklin, Montgomery, Washington, Pulaski, Scott, and Pittsylvania were members. The sheriffs, justices, and courts were in their hands. They organized a brigade of deserters and a state government with governor, lieutenant governor, and judges.[48] The strength of the societies must have been just about as great in the other states.[49]

The result of this widespread, and well organized disaffection was the rapid growth of their control of local, state, and Confederate governments, and the attempt to assemble the Southern and Northern states in a convention which would bring about peace. The convention idea was fostered by the states' rights group, which thus found themselves working side by side with the disloyal. There is little doubt that, with this large group of disaffected citizens, the Confederacy, even had it not suffered military defeat at the hands of the North in 1865, would have been defeated in the next state and congressional elections, which would have disintegrated its armies and brought peace.

[1]Frank Owsley, *State Rights in the Confederacy* (Chicago, 1925), pp. 5–24.

[2]For a discussion of this sectionalism see Charles Henry Ambler, *Sectionalism in Virginia from 1776 to 1851* (Chicago, 1918), William A. Schaper, *Sectionalism in South Carolina* (Washington, 1901), and Theodore Jack, *Sectionalism and Party Politics in Alabama, 1819–1842* (Menasha, 1919).

[3]Walter Lynwood Fleming, *Civil War and Reconstruction in Alabama* (New York, 1905), pp. 53, 59; *Harper's Annual Cyclopedia, 1861*, pp. 9, 10. (Cited henceforth as *Ann. Cyc.*)

[4]*Tribune Almanac, 1862*, p. 42; *Ann. Cyc., 1861*, pp. 338–339.

[5]*Ibid.*, pp. 6, 7, 8, 688–689; *Tribune Almanac, 1862*, p. 42; Charles Wilham Ramsdell, *Reconstruction in Texas* (New York, 1910), pp. 14–17.

[6]*Ann. Cyc., 1861*, pp. 473–474.

[7]*Ibid.*, pp. 729–735; Mrs. Roger A. Pryor, *Reminiscences of Peace and War* (New York, 1904), p. 126.

[8]William Woods Holden, *Memoirs of W. H. Holden* (Durham, 1911), p. 15; *Ann. Cyc., 1861*, pp. 337, 537–538.

[9]*Ibid.*, p. 22.

[10]*Ibid.*, pp. 677–678; *War of the Rebellion* (Official Record of the Union and Confederate armies, cited henceforth as O. R.), Ser. I, Vol. LXVI, Pt. I, pp. 674, 678, 691, 808.

[11]For Tennessee see Edward McPherson, *Political History of the United States of America During the Great Rebellion, from November 6, 1860, to July 4, 1864* (Washington, 1864), p. 5; *Ann. Cyc., 1861*, pp. 680–681; Arkansas, *Ibid.*, pp. 22, 231; *Tribune Almanac, 1862*, p. 43; North Carolina, O. R., Ser. I, Vol. I, p. 486; Joseph Gregoire de Roulhac Hamilton, *Reconstruction in North Carolina* (New York, 1914), pp. 26, 27.

[12]For soldier's pay, depreciated currency and high prices see John Christopher Schwab, *Confederate States of America, 1861–1865* (New York, 1901), p. 181; Thomas C. De Leon, *Four Years in Rebel Capitols* (Mobile, 1890), p. 186; *Ann. Cyc., 1863*, pp. 212, 447–448, 829; J. B. Jones, *A Rebel War Clerk's Diary at the Confederate States Capitol* (Philadelphia, 1866), Vol. I, p. 261; O. R., Ser. I, Vol. XV, pp. 928–929, Vol. LII, Pt. II, pp. 256–257; *Ibid.*, Ser. IV, Vol. I, p. 739, Vol. II, p. 774.

[13]For effects of invasion and enemy raids see Nathaniel Wright Stephenson, *Day of the Confederacy: A Chronicle of the Embattled South* (New Haven, 1919), pp. 110, 118; Pryor, p. 247; O. R., Ser. I, Vol. X, Pt. II, p. 204; *Ibid.*, Vol. XXIII, Pt. I, pp. 245–249; *Ibid.*, Vol. LII, Pt. II, p. 312.

[14]On impressment and tax in kind see Schwab, pp. 224–225; Stephenson, p. 99; Ulrich Bonnell Phillips, *Life of Robert Toombs* (New York, 1913), pp. 246–248; Owsley, Chapter V *passim;* O. R., Ser. IV, Vol. II, pp. 559–561; *Ibid.*, Vol. III, pp. 45, 46, 47, *Ibid.*, Ser. I, Vol. XXVI, Pt. II, p. 550.

[15]O. R., Ser. IV, Vol. II, pp. 856–857; *Ibid.*, Vol. III, pp. 1042–1044.

[16]*Ann. Cyc., 1862*, p. 11; Georgia Lee Tatum, *Disloyalty in the Confederacy* (Chapel Hill, 1934), p. 40.

[17]O. R., Ser. I, Vol. XIII, pp. 828–832; *Ibid.*, Ser. IV, Vol. III, pp. 1042–1044.

[18]O. R., Ser. I, Vol. X, Pt. II, p. 431.

[19]For opposition to conscription among these people see Albert Burton Moore, *Conscription and Conflict in the Confederacy* (New York, 1924), *passim.*

[20]O. R., Ser. IV, Vol. I, pp. 1095–1097; Jones, Vol. I, pp. 218–219, Vol. II, p. 30 and *passim;* Schwab, pp. 196; *Ann. Cyc., 1862*, p. 246; De Leon, p. 178.

[21]For the effect of the escape from service of able-bodied men of means and of speculating by these men see O. R., Ser. IV, Vol. II, pp. 85, 86, 214, 856–857, 901–902; Schwab, p. 181; Pryor, p. 293; Jones, Vol. I, p. 250.

[22]O.R., Ser. IV, Vol. I, p. 971, Vol. III, pp. 12, 14.

[23]*Ibid.*, Vol. I, pp. 971, 1087, 1104, Vol. II, pp. 122, 128, 162.

[24]For example of discontent caused by this type of men escaping service see O. R., Ser. IV, Vol. II, pp. 856–857.

[25]O. R., Ser. I, Vol. X, Pt. II, p. 431.

[26]O. R., Ser. I, Vol. X, Pt. II, pp. 161–163, 174–175; Fleming, p. 125.

[27]O. R., Ser. IV, Vol. II, p. 258.

[28]*Ibid.*, pp. 141–142.

[29]O. R., Ser. IV, Vol. II, p. 726; *Ibid.*, Ser. I, Vol. LII, Pt. II, p. 403.

[30]Walter Lynwood Fleming, "The Peace Movement in Alabama During the Civil War. 1. Party Politics, 1861–1864," *South Atlantic Quarterly*, II (1903), 119.

[31]Tatum, pp. 36–101.

[32]*Ibid.*, pp. 107–165; O. R., Ser. I, Vol. LII, Pt. II, pp. 10–32, 209; *Ibid.*, Ser. IV, Vol. II, pp. 783–785, Vol. III, pp. 803, 806, 809, 810–812, 816.

[33]O. R., Ser. IV, Vol. III, p. 397.

[34]*Ibid.*, p. 395.

[35]*Ibid.*, 393.

[36]O. R., Ser. IV, Vol. III, pp. 809–811.

[37]*Ibid.*, p. 810.

[38]O. R., Ser. IV, Vol. III, pp. 393, 803, 807, 813, 814.

[39]*Ibid.*, p. 398.

[40]O. R., Ser. I, Vol. LI, Pt. II, p. 739; *Ibid.*, Ser. IV, Vol. II, p. 784; *Ibid.*, Vol. III, p. 807; Hamilton, pp. 37, 67.

[41]O. R., Ser. I, Vol. XLVI, Pt. I, pp. 656, 678; *Ibid.*, Vol. LII, Pt. II, p. 116.

[42]Moore, p. 202.

[43]*Ann. Cyc.*, *1862*, p. 16; O. R., Ser. I, Vol. XXV, Pt. II, pp. 285, 352, 393, 401, 455, 456; Ibid., Vol. XLVIII, Pt. II, pp. 1309, 1313; *Ibid.*, Ser. IV, Vol. II, pp. 251, 680, 681; Schwab, pp. 198–199.

[44]O. R., Ser. I, Vol. XV, pp. 939–940, 949; *Ibid.*, Vol. LII, Pt. II, p. 403; *Ibid.*, Ser. IV, Vol. II, p. 726; *Ibid.*, Vol. III, pp. 394, 398.

[45]*Ibid.*, Ser. I, Vol. XV, pp. 939–940, 949; *Ibid.*, Vol. XXVI, Pt. II, p. 556.

[46]De Leon, pp. 182–183; O. R., Ser. I, Vol. LXVI, Pt. I, pp. 256–257, 674, 678; Mary Boykin Chestnut, *Diary from Dixie* (New York, 1905), p. 188.

[47]O. R., Ser. IV, Vol. III, pp. 783–785.

[48]O. R., Ser. IV, Vol. III, pp. 712–722, 802–816.

[49]O. R., Ser. I, Vol. XXVI, Pt. II, pp. 241, 285; *Ibid.*, Ser. IV, Vol. II, pp. 360, 770, 772, 774; *Ibid.*, Vol. III, p. 976; *Ann. Cyc.*, *1863*, p. 448.

Why Europe Did Not Intervene

If slavery was the cornerstone of the Confederacy, cotton was its foundation. At home its social and economic institutions rested upon cotton; abroad its diplomacy centered around the well-known dependence of Europe, especially England and France, upon an uninterrupted supply of cotton from the southern states. Until well into the third year of the war the Confederate government and its people relied primarily upon this power of cotton to coerce rather than persuade England and France to interfere in some way with the struggle in America. This interference might take the form of a denunciation and breaking of the blockade on the grounds that it was a paper blockade contrary to international law and especially to the provisions of the Declaration of Paris; it might be in the form of a peaceful mediation or of an outright recognition of the independence of the South; or, finally, it might be armed intervention.

Underlying the diplomacy of the Confederate States in behalf of intervention was the King Cotton doctrine that Europe must have Southern cotton or perish. This King Cotton philosophy was a fairly reasonable one, for about a fourth or fifth of England's population gained its bread from the cotton industry, based principally on the supply from the Southern states, and one-tenth of England's wealth was invested in this industry and nearly half of her export trade was made up of manufactured cotton goods. France was not as involved as England, yet the cotton industry, based largely on American cotton, was her largest and most profitable industry, and there were about a million restless operatives including their families engaged in this industry.

The surplus stocks on hand in England and France in 1861 staved off the cotton famine until 1862. This was a disappointment to the South, for such a contingency had not been anticipated. But by the combination of the Confederate embargo and a Federal blockade a cotton famine was finally produced in England and France in 1862, which threw over half the operatives out of employment and forced them and their families upon charity, amounting to two millions in England and one million in France. The Confederacy was very confident of securing intervention as a result of this famine; and the question was seriously canvassed in both the French and the English cabinets in the fall of 1862, but nothing came of it. Then there was in 1863 another serious effort of the Confederate commissioners and their friends to induce England and France to intervene. During this interval the Confederacy had continued to rely upon the need of Europe for Southern cotton to move England and France into intervention. However, the faith in cotton was rapidly weakened after the fall of 1862 when intervention did not come and the cotton famine began to grow less acute. But two other probable forces which might operate in favor of English and French intervention revealed themselves to the Confederate commissioners in the meantime, and after the approaching failure of King Cotton they began to stake success heavily upon these two motives. These were the extreme hatred and jealousy shown in England against the United States as a powerful rival, and the desire of Napoleon to establish a vassal empire in Mexico. These had operated more than all else to throw the sympathies of Napoleon and of the majority of the English upon the side of the South. The appeals of the commissioners for European aid, whether in the building of a navy or in recognition of armed intervention, took cognizance more and more of the desire of England and Napoleon to divide and weaken the United States.

But neither England nor Napoleon ever raised a hand in aid of the Confederacy, either to get cotton or to divide the country. What are the explanations? Why did King Cotton fail to move these powers as had been anticipated? Why did not the desire for weakening a powerful and hated rival bestir England and Napoleon? The answer as far as Napoleon is concerned is simple and may be disposed of briefly. This despot was always eager from the beginning until the end of the American war to join England in intervention. On the other hand, he was under no circumstances willing to intervene alone or in company with weaker powers. He had been perfectly frank with Slidell and Rost in admitting that he refrained from repudiating the blockade or from recognizing the independence of the Confederacy because of his apprehension that the United States would declare war on him should he do so. While he had a powerful navy of ironclads, he was fearful of the results of a war with America. The reasons for his fear were many: It was not America alone which he feared in case of war, but most of Europe, he thought, would be on his back. There were Prussia, Russia, Austria, Sardinia, and even England who would welcome such a war to close in upon him from the rear, and he knew it and constantly adverted to the subject in his conversations with Slidell and others on the question of intervention. However, there was another force which he feared equally as much—the disapproval of the French people of a war with America. The French people were in sympathy with the North because of the fact that the South was slaveholding and because of the traditional friendship of the French for the United States, and especially because of the universal desire to see the United States grow strong as a counterpoise to England. Napoleon's American policy was diametrically opposed to traditional French policy and sympathies, and he himself was as unpopular with the French as was his policy. Should he bring on a war with America, even with his foreign enemies quiescent, he might lose his throne. He could not hazard a war with America, or if he did it must be in company with England, his chief ally and deadliest enemy. He always stood ready to join England in intervention.

Why, then, did England not bow to the command of King Cotton and break the blockade, or recognize the Confederacy, or meddle in some way with the struggle so as to assure herself of a supply of cotton and the permanent division of a too-powerful rival. How can one explain the spectacle of twenty-six members of Parliament from Lancashire and eight or ten from Lanarkshire, Derbyshire, and Leicestershire—the cotton districts—and especially from Liverpool, sitting silently, apparently bored with all questions of intervention; and of hundreds of thousands of operatives with their families upon charity, losing $200,000,000 in wages without revolting?

How England and especially the industrial population resisted the power of King Cotton has two usual explanations—though other factors are conceded as playing minor parts. The older school has placed England's non-intervention upon a high and idealistic basis: the sympathy of the Lancashire population—and of the common people generally—with the Union as a great experiment in democracy, as a great model which was held up to the English; and their antipathy to slavery. The newer school of economic historians has not been satisfied with such high motives for mere cotton-mill workers; they have insisted that the antidote for one economic impulse is to be found in another and greater economic impulse. This antidote for the King Cotton virus has been found in a simple name which bears no royal trappings like King Cotton. It, in fact, had until 1861 been the scullion in King Cotton's kitchen or at most a buck private in the rear ranks of this sovereign—the name referred to is "wheat." England must have American wheat or perish.

These two motives together or separately are inadequate explanations of why England did not intervene to obtain cotton. The idealistic theory of the sympathy of the Lancashire population with the North as a sole explanation is too good to be true. The agitations and mass meetings held in England by William Forster, John Bright, other less radical Northern propagandists, and the vast multitudes who voted petitions to Parliament and cabinet against intervention, have been taken too much at their face value, while similar agitations and mass meetings and giant petitions got up by James Spence, William Lindsay, Roebuck, Beresford-Hope, and other Southern propagandists have been too much ignored. The fact of the whole business is, that these meetings, whether pro-Northern or pro-Southern, were not spontaneous, but were drummed up by well-subsidized leaders and were frequently packed by the liberal use of small coin. The population of Lancashire and of all industrial England was politically apathetic, sodden, ignorant, and docile, with the exception of a few intelligent and earnest leaders. They wanted bread, they wanted clothes, they needed medicines to give their sick children and aged parents, they wanted pretty clothing for their daughters and sisters who were being forced into prostitution. One is not surprised, therefore, to learn from the correspondence of Mason, Spence, Henry Hotze, and others that the purchasability of these people was a coldly recognized fact of which the pro-Northern and pro-Southern agitators made use. Under these circumstances the public meetings and agitations of the Federal and Confederate sympathizers would be largely determined by the use of slush funds. This gave the edge to the Northern agitation, perhaps. Another factor already noted which would still further give the appearance of greater sympathy for the North than for the South was the fact that Bright and Forster could always with perfect timeliness raise a town meeting, a petition, or a resolution against intervention, while James Spence and his cohorts could hold a mass meeting or pass a resolution favoring intervention only when the military situation was overwhelmingly in favor of the South.

John Watts, connected with the committee for the relief of the Lancashire population and a native of that section, expressed the opinion in his *Facts of the Cotton Famine* that the population of Lancashire was pretty evenly divided in their attitude toward the

Civil War.[1] But be that as it may, whether the population was evenly divided or all on the Northern side, it is doubtful whether they exercised much influence upon the non-intervention policy of the British government. Few of these people wielded the vote, so the government had little to fear from them in a political way; and there is no evidence to show that the government feared that they would refuse to support a possible war with the United States should England decide to intervene. The fear lay in the opposite direction. The government, in fact, was convinced that the only danger lay in this population's forcing England into war with the United States to obtain cotton. This fear was not great, however, as Palmerston knew his docile and submissive British workmen. They required only enough to keep body and soul together, and the wealth of England saw that they had just this much and no more. As John Bright remarked, it would be cheaper to feed these workers on champagne and venison than to have them force England into intervention, but it was found necessary to feed them only with bread and water. These people, then, did not count in a political way, and, as long as they could be kept from insurrection, they would not count in any other respect as far as the government of Palmerston and Russell was concerned.

What about the more recent economic interpretation, the influence of wheat in keeping John Bull on his good behavior with the United States? In this interpretation it is pointed out that England suffered from a very short grain crop in 1860–1861–1862, and that the great deficiency was supplied by the wheat and grain of the United States, just at the time when Parliament and the cabinet were considering the question of intervention to get cotton; and that the probability or certainty of a wheat famine in case England should become involved in a war by intervention prevented the British government from taking action. It is true that William E. Forster, John Bright, and a few others in and out of Parliament conducted a considerable agitation against intervention, based partly on the supposed dependence of England upon American wheat and grain.[2] But outside of the industrial districts this doctrine made no impression. Parliament and the House of Lords did not think enough of it to discuss it, and complete silence on the subject existed in the cabinet circles. No mention has been found in official or private correspondence of these men which would indicate that a wheat famine would accompany a war with the United States.[3]

This silence would not be conclusive were there not other evidence of a more positive character which corroborates this negative evidence. In the first place, the wheat-famine idea can be identified as Federal propaganda emanating from William H. Seward and Abraham Lincoln. In the fall of 1861–1862 Seward wrote several dispatches to Adams and Dayton, at the time when rumors of intervention were causing the American people great alarm, warning England and France that while they might have a cotton famine now, they would suffer both a wheat and a cotton famine if they interfered with the struggle in America. Charles Francis Adams was on intimate terms with William Forster, and there is definite evidence to show that he read or paraphrased some of these dispatches to that gentleman, who in turn passed the good word on to Bright. In the meantime, Seward indoctrinated Charles Sumner and the latter was soon writing about it to Bright and his other British friends.

The British press, however, with few exceptions, sneered at the idea. Both the London *Economist* and the London *Times* touched upon the focal point, namely, that the assumption was made without foundation that Great Britain could not get wheat elsewhere than from the United States, when as a matter of fact, Great Britain's deficiencies could be easily supplied in many other places, including Poland, Russia, and Prussia. The large purchases from the United States during the years 1860, 1861, and 1862, amounting in 1862 to almost half the total importation, were, according to the *Times,* matters of mere convenience of transportation and a slightly cheaper purchase price, not of necessity. Most important of all, it was pointed out that England took this wheat in payment for the countless millions of dollars' worth of rifles, cannon, powder, and other munitions of war which she was selling the United States. In fact, the North, now that cotton could no longer be shipped to England, had no other means by which it could purchase its munitions abroad. No other medium of international exchange existed, and it was pointed out with much truth that the United States would be bankrupt if its wheat were cut off by war, and its munitions of war would be so curtailed that it would have been defeated by the South.[4]

This contention of the *Times* and other papers seems convincing, especially in view of the fact that in 1864 and 1865, after the United States became practically self-sufficient in the production of war supplies and no longer made large purchases from England, the latter country turned abruptly away from America to Russia and East Europe for her wheat supply.[5] Recent researches in the British archives disclose no concern with a wheat famine; the explanation that American wheat was cheaper and served as the chief medium of international exchange for British munitions of war, and the proof of this in the abrupt cessation of purchases of wheat when the munition trade ceased, all tend to demonstrate that wheat had little if anything to do with preventing English intervention in the American Civil War.

What, then, is the answer to the question as to why England did not intervene to obtain cotton? One must admit the correctness of the principle laid down by the economic interpretation group of historians, namely, that in order to counteract one economic impulse another stronger economic motive is necessary. But it is difficult to see that wheat was a strong element in the economic impulse which counteracted the King Cotton impulse. It is proposed to substitute a much more sinister term for wheat—"war profits." Those who are at all familiar with the war profits in the last wars ought not to have any great difficulty in grasping the role England played of war profiteer, and the powerful influence upon government of her war profiteers, especially when all, even the small operatives were prosperous as a result of the war.

Perhaps the most surprising of the war profits was in the cotton industry itself. The warehouses of India, China, and England had a surplus that it would take two years to consume were no other goods manufactured, and England had on hand in her warehouses 700,000 bales more than the normal surplus of raw cotton. The raw cotton had cost around fourteen cents a pound, and the manufactured goods stored in the warehouses could not be sold at the cost of the raw material. The British industry was faced with bankruptcy. The mills were already beginning to slow down before the war, and British financial and economic writers were predicting a long period of unemployment and suffering for the operatives. Then the Civil War came and cut off the supply of cheap cotton. The price of raw cotton rose from fourteen to sixty, and as time passed the surplus manufactured goods followed suit until at length everything was sold at a net profit of not less than $200,000,000. In the meanwhile, the larger and well-financed mills continued to manufacture goods and hold against the rising markets. These larger mills, which Arnold estimates as composing two-thirds of the industry, not merely made a profit out of this vast surplus of cheap pre-war goods, but averaged a neat profit on their output over the four years of war.[6] The only people who went down were the small mill-owners and the cotton operatives. They lost all they had. But the industry was saved from one of the worst panics in history, and impending ruin turned into undreamed-of profits.[7] No wonder the members of Parliament from Lancashire sat silently during the debates on intervention. Instead of desiring intervention these members of Parliament and the industrialists they represented must have been praying the Lord would see fit to let the Civil War continue forever. This attitude is well illustrated by one of the small cotton-buyers who had bought a few-score bales and was holding them against a rising market when the news reached England that Sherman had captured Savannah with perhaps 30,000 bales of cotton. This Englishman, with all his small fortune tied up in these few bales of cotton, on hearing of this news exclaimed, "if that news should come true, some one will ha' to stick to me" lest he commit suicide![8] Every peace rumor or rumor of captured cotton, according to Watts, brought a panic and "good and honorable men spoke of the probable cessation of the most terrible war of modern times as a thing to be dreaded." As paradoxical as it may seem, even the operatives who were working, when at all, on short time, with a total loss of wages almost equal to the war profits of their employers, shared in the apprehension of peace. Each peace rumor, each rumor that the government was discussing intervention, sent the price of cotton down and caused the shutdown of small mills whose owners had been caught on narrow margins or who were unable to manufacture in the hopes of future profits. The operatives were caught in a vicious circle. They could not hope for full-time work during the war but they were afraid that when the war ended they would lose their jobs entirely. Not only were the mill-owners and cotton-buyers involved in this speculation, but the banking interests of England were directly and indirectly concerned. To these men who had made big profits and had refinanced the cotton industry upon the basis of high-priced raw cotton the end of the war meant a flood of cheap cotton, and that meant Judgment Day. James Spence wrote that to these men, though they were in entire sympathy with the South, "the idea of recognition was that of heavy instant loss,—a very formidable obstacle in the way" of recognition.[9]

There is another phase of the cotton profits which must not be overlooked, namely, the development of India as a rival source for raw cotton. England had tried with little success for twenty or more years before 1860 in the face of American rivalry to rehabilitate the Indian cotton industry. The elimination of the American crop was India's opportunity. The London *Times* rejoiced that "American cotton is actually out of the running—and there is no saying how long it may continue so,...and when America appears in the market again India ought to be her match. If this can be accomplished, England will be relieved from any risk of another cotton drought."[10] It would have been difficult, continued the *Times* later, "to beat America out of the market, but America is out of the market by her own act. Before she comes in again, there will be time, in all probability, to organize a new trade, and though we must be sorely straightened in the interval, it may be hoped that the result will finally emancipate us from difficulties which had been foreseen and dreaded."[11] Great hopes were expressed that the American monopoly might be overthrown. Some were optimistic enough to believe that the American staple might be permanently eclipsed; others were of the opinion that as soon as the war ended the cheap American supply would drive all other cotton out; while perhaps the majority thought that if the war lasted long enough India would at least share equally in the world market with American cotton.[12] Certainly the Indian supply made great strides during the war. Before the Civil War from 80 to 85 per cent of the British and European supply of cotton came from America. When the war ended England was getting 85 per cent of her supply from India. Nor did the end of the war bring an immediate end to the increase, for in 1866 England imported 2,000,000 bales, or 6,000,000 hundredweight (the Indian bale weighed 300 pounds) from India, and it was still believed that the American market could never again reduce the Indian supply to less than 2,000,000 bales, or about 50 per cent of the British supply.[13] The failure of this prophecy has no part in Civil War diplomacy.

The next great sources of profits are closely related to the cotton industry—the profits which were reaped from the linen and woolen industries, the old rivals of cotton. These two textile industries, which had languished since the Industrial Revolution, waked to life again and recaptured much of their lost ground and reaped a golden harvest. The linen industry responded instantly to the rise in the price of cotton. In 1858 there were only 91,648 acres in flax in Ireland—the chief source of supply; whereas in 1864 there were 301,942 acres under this crop, or an increase of 229 per cent. The production increased from less than 20,000 tons to above 80,000 tons during this time, or 300 per cent. The importation of flax was increased about 20,000 tons. The importation of yarn increased from 58,866 pounds in 1861 to 3,997,106 pounds in 1863. The output of the mills was increased almost as much as were the exports of certain products. The export of yarns increased from 27,981,042 pounds in 1861 to 40,510,967 pounds in 1864—44 per cent; the export of thread increased from 2,390,461 pounds in 1861 to 4,030,365 pounds in 1864, or about 68 per cent; the export of plain cloth increased from 116,322,469 yards in 1861 to 209,859,714 yards in 1864, or about 80 per cent. The domestic sale of linen was also greatly increased.[14]

It is estimated by John Watts in his *Facts of the Cotton Famine* that during the three years 1862, 1863, and 1864 the linen industry realized £14,500,000 above the normal profits covering an equal period before the Civil War.[15] For 1865 the excess profit continued and carried the figures up above £20,000,000, or nearly $100,000,000.[16] Watts also estimates that 100,000 extra operatives and laborers were employed as a result of this expansion of the industry,[17] thus taking up much of the slack caused by the slump in employment in the cotton industry.

The woolen industry netted a larger profit than did linen, distributed from farmer to manufacturer. In 1861 the export of the chief woolen products was about 160,000,000 yards, while in 1864 it had increased to 240,000,000 yards, or 50 per cent increase.[18] A similar increase in domestic sales took place. Watts estimates the excess profits to the manufacturers in the three years 1862, 1863, and 1864 at £17,000,000, and the profits for 1865 may be put at £5,000,000.[19] The same writer estimated the excess profits the farmers received from raw wool at £8,932,286—carrying the excess profits in the woolen industry above £30,000,000, or $150,000,000.[20] As in the linen industry there was great increase in the number of operatives, estimated at between 50,000 and 100,000.

Another business which prospered mightly during war conditions was the munitions industry. The United States for two years and the Confederacy for the entire war bought most of their small arms, cannon, powder, lead, steel plate, rails, knives, sabers, and bayonets from Europe and especially from England. From 1861 to 1864, $7,027,730 worth of alkali-saltpeter, kanit, etc.; about 3,000,000 small arms, or $25,000,000 worth; 30,000,000 pounds of powder, or

$10,000,000 worth; $3,000,000 worth of lead; $10,000,000 worth of unwrought steel; $3,000,000 worth of boiler plate; $5,000,000 worth of artillery, to mention only the most important war supplies, were recorded as exported to the United States and the Confederacy.[21] It is certainly a conservative estimate based upon the Board of Trade reports to say that the North and the South bought together no less than $100,000,000 worth of war supplies from Great Britain. This is exclusive of clothing, tents, shoes, and leather goods.

Nor does it include the sale of ships and steamers to the Confederacy or the building of steamers for English blockade-runners. This last item is of great importance, for it stimulated very greatly the shipbuilding industry. Altogether about four hundred steamers, many of them iron, and eight hundred sail vessels were sold as blockade-runners. Great numbers of those vessels were constructed during the war. In addition to this, six ironclads and two wooden cruisers were constructed by the shipbuilders of Liverpool and Glasgow for the Confederate government.

Attention is called to the enormous profits which the blockade-running houses made in that business. Between a million and a million and a half bales of cotton were run through the blockade at a net profit of seldom less than 300 per cent. Goods shipped into the Confederacy, exclusive of munitions which formed only a small portion of this trade, netted a profit frequently amounting to 500 per cent. One round trip through the blockade frequently paid for a vessel and its cargo and left a profit. Many of these vessels, it will be recalled, ran scores of times, the "Little Hattie" making about sixty trips.

But the greatest profit of all, one which was so enormous it cannot be measured in dollars and cents, was made possible in the complete destruction of the American merchant marine directly or indirectly by the Confederate privateers and cruisers. This destruction was done without England's lifting her hand, except in a benediction upon the Confederacy for doing her work so thoroughly. In 1860 the United States was and had been for many years England's only serious rival in the world-carrying trade. So successful, in fact, had been the United States that she had largely driven England out of the direct trade between America and Great Britain—the most sensitive point of all. The United States had in this trade, in 1860, 2,245,000 tons and Great Britain had only 946,000,[22] while the total ocean-going tonnage of the American merchant marine was between

5,500,000 and 6,000,000 tons, practically as large as that of Great
Britain and doubling every ten years. Its ships were magnificent.
They could outsail anything afloat. The "Yankee Clipper" had been
the despair and envy of the world.[23] In 1861 England saw this magnificent fleet of seabirds begin to scatter and then disappear, until
when the war ended only a little over a million tons of culls, mostly
coasting vessels which could not be sold, were left.[24] As Admiral
Porter remarked sadly, the American merchant marine was virtually
extinct.[25] The cruisers and privateers had sunk or captured above
two hundred ships, destroying around thirty million dollars' worth
of property.[26] But their greatest havoc was wrought by indirection.
The hazard was so great that marine insurance rose higher than it
was in the war with England in 1812 when that power had our coast
blockaded, and shippers and merchants, American as well as European, were so fearful of the work of the *Alabama* and her sisters that
they could not be induced to ship their merchandise on American
ships.[27]

So the magnificent ships lay in dock swinging idly at their cables,
their crews scattered, and their sails and hulls rotting, while less
worthy craft plied the seas. Nothing was finally left except to sell
them to neutrals whose flag would make them safe. England got the
best and the greatest number. By the first of July 1864, all had been
sold of this great fleet except 1,674,516 tons, and England had
bought over $42,000,000 worth out of a total sale of $64,799,750.[28]
This sale continued until little more than 1,000,000 tons of scraps
were left. England's only rival had been destroyed for an indefinite
span of years. England had fought wars for less than the destruction
of a rival's merchant marine. Surely England could keep the peace
for such a magnificent reward—especially since war would mean the
destruction of her own merchant marine, in a similar fashion.

It is evident, therefore, that England far from being hag-ridden
by poverty during the American Civil War made enormous profits.
Her surplus stock of cotton was sold at a fabulous profit, her linen
and woolen industries reaped unexpected harvests of gold, her munitions and steel industries enriched themselves, her shipbuilding was
enormously stimulated by the demands of the Confederate government and the blockade business, merchant houses made millions out
of blockade-running, and finally the American merchant marine was
driven from the seas and largely transferred to England. An examination of the volume of British imports and exports and the pauper

list during the Civil War is rather eloquent of this profit, despite the fact that much of the imports were the invisible earnings of the greatly enhanced merchant marine which do not appear on the books.

The volume of foreign trade in 1864 was £509,000,000 as against £374,500,000 in 1860, or 34 per cent greater than before the war. There had been a temporary shock in 1861 with the upset of the American markets, but this was largely gained back after that and markets elsewhere, especially in France, greatly expanded.

An examination of the Poor Law Board reports shows that despite the fact that at one time over a half million people were on the dole in Lancashire, the average of those dependent upon charity for all England and Wales was little if any higher during the four years of the American war than during a like period before 1860. For the ten years before 1860 there was an average of about 925,000 people on charity in England and Wales. During the Civil War, despite the increase of the population for these ten years previous, the average number receiving charity was about 975,000, which was little if any larger percentage of the population than before the war in America. This corroborates the statement that the slack caused by cotton operatives being out of work was taken up by the greater productivity of the linen, woolen, munition industries and the expanding merchant marine and the shipbuilding. Even with Lancashire unemployed the labor situation was normal—which meant that outside the cotton districts it was far above normal.[29]

The London *Times* in summing up the situation remarked that "outside of Lancashire it would not be known that anything had occurred to injure the national trade. That is the most extraordinary and surprising incident of the story. An industry which we conceived to be essential to our commercial greatness has been utterly prostrated, without affecting the greatness in any perceptible degree. We are as busy, as rich, and as fortunate in our trade as if the American war had never broken out, and our trade with the States had never been disturbed. Cotton was no king, notwithstanding the prerogatives which had been loudly claimed for him."[30] England could dispense with the cotton industry, so it seemed. John Watts, writing at the same time, remarked that not only could England do without the cotton industry, but "that so far as the people who pay income tax are concerned Lancashire itself seems as if it could almost do without its staple industry," since those incomes seemed unimpaired by the war. *So we may conclude, with regard to the economic motive for intervention: it did not exist.* With the exception of the Lancashire operatives all was well and God was in his heaven!

If the King Cotton basis of diplomacy proved unsound, what about the political motive that England had in desiring a division of the Union? Why did not she intervene to accomplish that greatly desired end? The answer to this is that in the first place England never doubted until it was too late that the South would win its independence and the roast pigeon would thus fly into the open mouth of the British lion without any other effort than the opening of his jaws. It was almost a universal belief. In the second place, had this belief not existed the British government could not have been induced to interfere with the American struggle because of a conviction that it would involve the two countries in a war which, as Bright said, England would be the most vulnerable nation in the world. This is a fear which was constantly expressed by cabinet, Parliament, and press. It was feared that England would lose Canada, and it was absolutely a certainty that she would lose her entire merchant marine, just as the United States was doing. Certainly she would lose all the great war profits. In fact, the economic motive not to intervene outweighed what might be called the political motive of weakening a military and national rival. Finally, there were certain considerations of international laws which would have very strong bearing in preventing England from meddling with the struggle. Had England harbored no fear of war nor loss of her profits she might have refrained from taking any part. She did not wish to help establish a precedent of interfering in the domestic struggle of a first-class power. That privilege was reserved to backward third-rate powers. The Palmerston government hoped to disarm American protests at a later date by allowing that country to establish a paper blockade, and thus vitiate the Declaration of Paris with regard to blockades. The practices of the recent world wars demonstrate the value of this precedent.

[1]London and Manchester, 1866, *passim.*

[2]Louis Bernard Schmidt, "Influence of Wheat and Cotton on Anglo-American Relations During the Civil War," *Iowa Journal of History and Politics,* July 1918, *passim.*

[3]E. D. Adams, *Great Britain and the American Civil War.* 2 vols. (New York, 1925), II, 13n.

[4]London *Times,* Sept. 16, 1862; March 17, 1862; April 17, 1863.

⁵*De Bow's Review and Industrial Resources*, XXXIV (July 1866), 79–80.

⁶R. A. Arnold, *The History of the Cotton Famine* (London, 1864), pp. 48–49.

⁷For profits made in the cotton industry see *ibid.*, pp. 40–47, 79–83, and *passim;* James Scherer, *Cotton as a World Power* (New York, 1916), pp. 264–265; and M. B. Hammond, *The Cotton Industry* (New York, 1897), pp. 254–259.

⁸Watts, pp. 359–361.

⁹James M. Mason Papers (Library of Congress, Washington, D.C.) Spence to Mason, May 4, 1864.

¹⁰London *Times*, October 24, 1861.

¹¹*Ibid.*, January 16, 1862.

¹²See Hammond, p. 275, for the opinion of a prominent ex-government official.

¹³*Ibid.*

¹⁴For these figures see Watts, pp. 384–390; *Economist*, March 1, 1862; February 28, 1863; March 4, 1865; Schmidt, pp. 22–23, n. 37.

¹⁵*Ibid.*

¹⁶See *Economist*, June 3, 1865.

¹⁷*Ibid.*

¹⁸*Ibid.*, February 27, 1864; March 4, 1865; cf. Schmidt, pp. 22–23, n. 37.

¹⁹Watts, pp. 399 ff.

²⁰*Ibid.*

²¹See *Economist*, February 28, 1862; March 1, 1862; February 27, 1864; March 4, 1865; cf. Parliamentary Papers and Accounts, North America, LXIX, No. 4 (1872), 48–66.

²²John Bigelow, *Retrospections of an Active Life*, 5 vols. (New York, 1909–1913), I, 536.

²³New York *World*, July 7, 1864.

²⁴*Ibid.*, for figures of that date.

²⁵New York *Herald*, July 19, 1865.

²⁶Parliamentary Papers and Accounts, North America, LXIX, No. 11 (1872), 69; cf. C. F. Adams, *The Treaty of Washington*, *passim;* J. T. Scharf, *History of the Confederate States Navy* (New York and San Francisco, 1887), *passim;* William Robinson, *The Confederate Privateers* (New Haven, 1928), *passim.*

²⁷New York *World*, October 22, 1864.
October 22, 1864.

²⁸*Ibid.*, July 7, 1864; *ibid.*, October 22, 1864, statement of Reverdy Johnson.

²⁹See fourteenth, fifteenth, sixteenth, seventeenth, and eighteenth annual reports of the Poor Law Board (1861–66) in Parliamentary Papers and Accounts, Vol. XXIV (1862); Vol. XXII (1863); Vol. XXV (1864); Vol. XXII (1865); Vol. XXXV (1866), respectively.

³⁰London *Times*, January 7, 1864.

 *America and the Freedom of the Seas,*
1861-1865

America and the Freedom of the Seas, 1861-1865

When the War of Secession commenced, the position of America regarding the rights of neutrals on the high seas was well known in all the chancelleries of Europe, and in none better than in England. Presidential messages and orders, diplomatic memoranda and correspondence, and, perhaps, most important of all, treaties with many of the principal nations of the world, embodied clearly America's conceptions of international law and most particularly her conception of the rights of neutrals on the high seas. There were exceptions, however, to this clear-cut position: in a few cases the federal courts, having had few opportunities to act as prize courts, had rendered decisions which tended to uphold the position of the British prize courts; and two or three writers on international law had shown some tendency to uphold the British position. These were of a minor nature and had had little influence upon America either in diplomacy, executive or congressional attitudes, or in the minds of the people.[1]

It was, therefore, a shock to continental Europe and a pleasant surprise to Great Britain when the government of the United States during the War of Secession completely reversed its former position on belligerent and neutral maritime rights and stumbled unintentionally but irrevocably upon the side of the Mistress of the Seas.

That the United States had championed the most advanced and latitudinarian doctrines of neutral rights on the high seas before 1861 is a matter which is too well known to need repetition. From 1793 to 1815 especially, the chief object of American diplomacy had been to induce or force foreign powers, and especially England, to recognize the doctrine of maritime neutral rights. This American doctrine of neutral rights was essentially that of continental Europe as expressed in the League of Armed Neutrality of 1780 and 1800. The efforts of the United States at this time were directed at England, who not only refused to recognize any such doctrine but who gave the most extreme extensions to maritime belligerent rights.[2] The fundamental principles involved during the period 1793–1815 concerned contraband, visit and search of merchant vessels, enemy goods on neutral ships, neutral goods on enemy ships, and—most important of all—the blockade, which, it was insisted, must be effective in order to be binding. The famous decisions of Sir William Grant and Sir William Scott (Lord Stowell) gave the highest judicial sanction to the British conception of international maritime law. Against this definition and practice America, as well as most of continental Europe, protested earnestly; and finally, after wars had been fought and others threatened, England reluctantly accepted, to a large degree, the American and continental definition of maritime law in the Declaration of Paris of 1856. The United States, while not signing the declaration, for reasons which cannot be discussed here, nevertheless, saw the chief principles for which she had always stood embodied in this famous agreement.

When Lincoln declared the entire coast of the Southern states from the Potomac to the Rio Grande under blockade, he crossed the Rubicon, for he laid down a paper blockade, destined to remain so for a good portion of the war and which was never really effective. It was out of this ineffective paper blockade that most of the measures arose which cut America off from her historic position as the champion of neutral rights on the seas. The methods adopted to enforce this blockade were the same as those made use of by England in the past, but which, presumably, she had agreed to forego in the future by signing the Declaration of Paris. The British government, while elated at America's adoption of the paper blockade and many of the methods used in its enforcement, and the doctrine of ultimate destination of contraband, was, nevertheless, almost constantly exasperated; and the British people were at times greatly aroused at the spirit which seemed to animate the American naval officers and the excesses which these officers committed in enforcing the blockade or in seizing vessels carrying contraband. In fact, it can hardly be doubted when the matter is examined closely that, despite England's approval of America's reversal of position with reference to neutral maritime rights, the irritation of the English people and government over the treatment of British commerce and subjects was frequently as great as that of the American people and government over the destruction wrought by the *Alabama* and other Confederate cruisers built in England. Strange, then, is the silence which reigns on this subject. The *Alabama* claims have been the subject of much historical writing; but the laying of a paper blockade and the seizure of British commerce hundreds of miles away from the coast, on the basis of the doctrine of ultimate destination, and the attitude of the British government and public toward these acts have been eloquently ignored.

In April 1861 when Lincoln declared the existence of the blockade, covering 3,549 miles, 189 rivers, bays, and inlets, not to mention
hundreds of miles of double-line seacoast and inner channels not
exposed to the open sea, there were 40 steamers in the navy and 50
sailing vessels. However, 37 of these steamers were on foreign stations
or in dry dock; only 3 were available for active service. The sailing
vessels were useless against blockade runners propelled by steam.[3]
Though the navy bought and built vessels as rapidly as possible, it
had, by the end of 1861, only 79 steamers, ranging from 800 tons to
ferry boats, and 81 sailing craft.[4] By October 1862 the navy had 256
ships of all kinds;[5] and when the war ended, there were 600. When
Lincoln first declared the coast blockaded in 1861, there was only 1
vessel for about each 66 miles of outer coast; in December 1861,
when the navy possessed 160 vessels, there would have been only 1
ship for each 22 miles; in October 1862, when there were 256 vessels,
there would have been about 15 miles for each ship; and even at the
end of the war, there was only 1 vessel for each 6 miles of coast.

Despite the fact that the entire coast of the Southern states was
declared blockaded, only the ports were ever actually blockaded,
while the remainder of the coast was patrolled irregularly by cruisers. The swiftest and most effective ships were sent cruising in the
Gulf Stream or in the West Indies, and sometimes as far east as the
Madeira Islands, in search of ships whose cargo, papers, or reputa-
tion indicated that the vessels or goods were ultimately destined to
run the blockade or enter the Confederacy by way of Mexico as
contraband. It is hardly to be doubted that the "flying squadrons"
under Wilkes and Lardner which patrolled the waters of the West
Indies and the Gulf Stream contributed more to the destruction of
Confederate foreign trade than did those other squadrons which
formed cordons about the principal ports or cruised up and down
the coast occasionally. But the point must not be overlooked that it
was just this feature of the old British paper blockade to which
America had offered the most objections.[6]

Just how far the blockade came, aside from the method of its
enforcement, from meeting the old American specifications of an
effective blockade may be seen from the reports of the British consuls
who were stationed in the Confederacy, the American consuls in the
West Indies and England, especially Dudley and Morse, the Confederate port records, and the correspondence of the Confederate agents
in the West Indies and in England. Only a few of the most significant of these reports can be presented here: On September 4, 1861,

British Consul Bunch, of Charleston, whose jurisdiction extended over North and South Carolina, reported to Lord John Russell, British Secretary of Foreign Affairs, that, as usual,[7] "the blockade of the coast of both North and South Carolina continues to be totally ineffective. No difficulty whatever seems to be experienced by vessels either in entering or sailing from even this port of Charleston which is supposed to be fully blockaded."[8] In the spring of 1862 Bunch saw no appreciable change in the situation. "The blockade runners," he wrote British Minister Lyons at Washington, "are doing a great business.... Everything is brought in abundance. Not a day passes without an arrival or departure...passengers come and go freely and no one seems to think that there is the slightest risk—which, indeed, there is not."[9] On April 22, 1863, Consul Walker, Bunch's successor, informed Russell that "the trade of the port has been most active during the past year, notwithstanding the increased number of blockading vessels which have been maintained on the coast during that interval and...during the last quarter the cotton exports and custom receipts have been much heavier than any other quarter."[10] Several months later he reported that "the inefficiency of the blockade of the port of Wilmington continued."[11]

The British consular reports from Mobile, New Orleans (before its capture), Galveston, Matamoras, Vera Cruz, and other Gulf ports in the Confederacy and Mexico were in agreement with those from Charleston and Wilmington: the blockade was not effective, except at times, even at the most important ports; while hundreds of miles of open seacoast were left unguarded and open to small craft and vessels of shallow draft.[12]

The Confederate port records, kept and reported carefully until the spring of 1862, but sent in only occasionally after that, tell the same story. Frequently these reports were published by Henry Hotze in the British-Confederate *Index* in London. It was, of course, Hotze's business to minimize the dangers of blockade-running so as to encourage the traffic, and one would be inclined to take his reports with a grain of salt, unless they were corroborated by more disinterested witnesses. As a matter of fact, as far as checking has been possible, the *Index* reports have proved surprisingly accurate: they tally often with reports of the American consuls whose business would be to minimize the blockade business. On May 5, 1864, the *Index* gave a complete list of vessels which had been using the port of Nassau, New Providence, as a blockade-running base from November 1, 1861, to March 10, 1864—about two and one-half years. There had been 84 such vessels running between Nassau and Wilmington or Charleston. They had made 425 attempts to run the blockade from Nassau, and 363 had been successful. In short, only 1 out of 6 had failed. However, the *Index* pointed out, these same vessels during this period had run the blockade from Cuba and Bermuda and had brought the average of failure down to 1 in 8. The same journal later[13] published a list of vessels running the blockade at these two ports, and 498 had been successful, that is, only 1 in 6 had failed. Earl Russell might consider it "an effective blockade," complained the *Index*, "which lets five vessels go through and apprehends or destroys the sixth, but it hardly comes up to the requisition of international law."[14]

The reports of the American consuls stationed at Bermuda, Nassau, Havanna, Matamoras, Tampico, and Vera Cruz corroborate the version of the blockade given by the Confederate agents and the British consuls. Consul Hawley summed up the situation in May 1863 in a report to Secretary of State Seward. Since March 10 of that year, he wrote, there had been 28 vessels using Nassau as a base for blockade-running. These vessels "have passed our blockading squadron say 112 times in less than 90 days," he complained, and only 13 captures or wrecks had been made.

> Suppose a foreigner should allege that our blockade is null and void for want of force or vigilance, claiming that successful voyages are the rule and failure the exception, would a reply that our squadron had defeated or captured one in 10 or 12 of the venture satisfy the requirements of the blockade.[15]

As late as November 1864 the consul at Nassau wrote Seward: "there appears to be no interruption from that end of the line."[16] The dispatches of Consul General Shufeldt, at Havana, and his successor, Thomas Savage, indicate considerable uneasiness on the part of these officials at the ineffectiveness of the blockade on the east coast as well as in the Gulf.[17] Consul Chase, stationed at Tampico, Mexico, felt that the dignity of the American government was badly compromised by the haphazard blockade. He informed F. W. Seward in December 1863:

> This traffic so successfully carried on impresses the people of this country [Mexico] with the belief that our navy is too impotent to enforce a blockade, and that our government has no control over any of the Southern ports, which emboldens them to give our enemies all the aid

and comfort in their power. Hence the power and influence of our government, and its agents are daily losing ground in this distracted part of the Mexican Republic.[18]

A more complete view of the blockade can be gained by considering the volume of trade which was carried on through the blockade. The writer has estimated elsewhere[19] that the blockade-runners made 8,250 successful trips through the blockade; that, in 1861, 9 out of 10 vessels were successful; in 1862, 7 out of 8; in 1863, 3 out of 4; in 1864, 2 out of 3; and in 1865, 1 out of 2.[20] That is, the average of successful voyages for the period of the war was about 5 out of 6. It is estimated that 1,250,000 bales of cotton were carried through the blockade in the period from the spring of 1862 until the end of the war—which was about half the cotton crop raised during that time. Not less than 600,000 stand of small arms, a good portion of the artillery, and much of the other supplies of food and clothing came through the blockade.[21]

But as the writer has attempted to bring out elsewhere,[22] the British were far from offended at an American paper blockade. Both the government and the public press were quite frank in their approval. They reminded those who were inclined to be impatient and resentful that England's usual role was that of the belligerent, America's that of the neutral; and that it was to their ultimate, though not immediate, interest to have America extend belligerent rights as far as possible at the expense of neutral rights on the sea: only America would suffer for that in the future. The London *Times,* paraphrasing Lord Palmerston's speech in the House of Lords of recent date, reminded its impatient readers that

> if in a future war America is neutral, English squadrons may watch New York and Boston, and in a contingency of a contest between the two countries, neutral commerce with the Northern States may be justly and consistently impeded by every lawful method.[23]

Later, the *Times* admitted that America had pushed the rights of belligerents on the high seas, especially with reference to the ultimate destination of blockade-runners and contraband, "beyond anything that has ever been claimed in their behalf" in modern times. But, continued the *Times,* "if the Americans are determined to rivet this patch upon the hard old international law, we of all people in the world are the least interested in opposing the innovation." The Americans say they have the authority of Sir William Grant and

Lord Stowell for what they are doing, and these "principles now in course of recognition and extension in the American Prize Courts may be very precious to England at some future crisis."[24]

II

In attempting to enforce the blockade, the American federal government adopted the British method and pattern of the days of the Orders in Council and the Berlin and Milan decrees. Flying squadrons were sent out to cruise the Atlantic and dog the tracks of commerce, or to lie in the neutral ports of the West Indies, Mexico, and even Central and South American ports, from which ships suspected of the intention of violating the blockade would be pursued and taken. The blockade of neutral ports was, indeed, the most effective means of enforcing the blockade of the Confederate coast; and, as has been stated, the flying squadrons of Wilkes and Lardner did more to cut off commerce from the Confederacy than the fleets lying off the ports of Charleston, Wilmington, Mobile, or Galveston. Not only did the federal cruisers blockade neutral ports and seize ships apparently plying from one neutral port to the other, but they frequently captured the ships' crews and apparently dealt with them as prisoners of war.

It must be pointed out, too, that these flying squadrons of Wilkes and Lardner and others cruising in neutral waters were not just enforcing the blockade. Without doubt the blockade was their most important business; but had there been no blockade, there would have still been the contraband trade, either directly with the Confederacy or indirectly through Mexico. An examination of the prize cases discloses the fact that the charge of carrying contraband was coupled, wherever possible, with the charge of an intent to violate the blockade; or, where no intent to violate the blockade was disclosed, the charge of carrying contraband directly or indirectly to the Confederacy was made. So, in dealing in detail with the seizure of neutral commerce—which was, with few exceptions, British—by the American cruisers, it should always be kept in mind that the ultimate destination of contraband for the Confederacy or vessel to the blockaded coast were the two grounds on which captures were made.

It has been said that England accepted America's reversal of her doctrine of international maritime law with pleasure, but that the methods and spirit of enforcing American belligerent rights on the

high seas frequently appeared obnoxious and created great resentment. It must be further observed, too, that disagreement arose not
so much over the principles of law involved as over the facts. The
story of the owners and crew of a merchant vessel seized in mid-
ocean on the charges of ultimate intention of violating the blockade
or of carrying contraband to the Confederacy would invariably differ
from the version of the seizure given by the captors.

It has been observed that one of the most effective methods of
enforcing the blockade and of capturing contraband was the blockade and use of neutral ports as bases of operation. This had been
England's chief weapon during the Napoleonic wars. The school
child of the day must have been as familiar with this as with the impressment of seamen by the British navy. All were familiar with the
tale of how the British fleet lay outside of New York and Boston,
using these harbors as bases of supply and at the same time effectually blockading them by seizing neutral American vessels as they
came out. However, the knowledge was not so general that England
had been careful in the days of her greatest arrogance *not to claim
the practice as a right.*

It is, therefore, not surprising that England quickly objected
when Lardner and Wilkes anchored their cruisers just outside, and
sometimes inside, the harbors of Nassau, Bermuda, Cuba, St.
Thomas, Matamoras, and even Madeira, and lay in wait for British
merchantmen which might be headed for the blockade or might
have goods on board which were ultimately destined for the Confederacy. Nor is it surprising that in the face of British protests the
American federal government disclaimed the right to blockade neutral ports, and thus kept the records clear, but nevertheless continued the practice, just as the English had done, as long as it was
possible to do so and avoid war. Thus the principle of blockading
neutral ports which was basic in the doctrine of ultimate destination
was constantly denied as a belligerent right, but always practiced—
not infrequently in the most reckless fashion—by the American
naval officers.

The trouble over the blockade of neutral ports or the use of such
ports as bases of operation seems to have started in the summer of
1862, when Rear Admiral Wilkes was dispatched to the West Indies
in command of a squadron and Commodore Craven was sent further
east to cruise in the neighborhood of the Madeira Islands. Wilkes,
who had taken Mason and Slidell off the *Trent,* was regarded with

complete disfavor by the British people and government; and his promotion and appointment to the important West Indian station was considered a retort discourteous to Britain's vigorous stand in the Trent affair of the fall and winter previous.[25] Naturally, the inhabitants of the West Indies—especially the British—and the British fleet stationed there under the command of Vice-Admiral Sir Alexander Milne were critical and unfriendly toward Wilkes, and they expected the worst of him; nor did Wilkes greatly disappoint their expectation. He soon created a sensation by his activities off the Bahamas, and especially at the port of Nassau. About the first of August, forty shipowners of Liverpool protested to Lord Russell that "the Federal cruisers are now blockading Nassau...seizing vessels sailing from one British port to another with British goods..., that the confidence of mercantile men in the sanctity of the British flag is thoroughly shaken."[26] Russell promised to "urge the Federal Government to enjoin upon their naval officers greater caution in the exercise of their belligerent rights";[27] while Palmerston, who had his eye on the future, urged patience upon Parliament where Wilkes's conduct had aroused protest. "The House must be aware," Palmerston said, "that there is no nation more interested than the British nation in maintaining to the utmost extent belligerent rights at sea."[28]

The activity of the squadron under Wilkes was next noted graphically by a correspondent of the *Index* at St. George's, Bermuda, on September 27, 1862. Apparently, the yellow fever had caused the blockade-runners to shift their base from Nassau to Bermuda, whereupon Wilkes, at the urgent request of the American consul, followed with his flagship, the *Wachusett*, the *Sonoma*, the *Tioga*, and others. He anchored the three vessels named above in the harbor and for five days took on supplies and informed himself "concerning every vessel in the port."

> The flag ship [reported this correspondent] has disappeared from British waters, but the two others are still plainly visible in the offing steaming slowly to and fro across the entrance of this harbor exactly like sentries, and frequently not more than two miles distant. From the telegraph station of St. Georges other Federal cruisers are constantly seen; and it is said that there are about twenty of them on the track hence to Charleston.

Wilkes was soon in a quarrel with the governor of Bermuda over his abuse of the use of the harbor, and he confided to Welles that the governor and all the people of the island were "rank secessionists."[29]

The ubiquitous Rear Admiral Wilkes was soon heard from in another quarter. With part of his squadron he left Bermuda and steamed over to Havana, Cuba.[30] Here in October, one of his steamers, the *Montgomery* chased the British ship *Blanche* aground within 60 yards of the shore, fired into her, and, despite the fact that the Spanish alcalde ran up a Spanish flag above the British flag, the crew boarded and set fire to her.[31] United States Consul General Shufeldt and Admiral Wilkes hurried to the governor, General Serrano, and assured him, without waiting for instructions from Washington, that the captain of the *Montgomery* had acted without orders.[32]

The British public were indignant at what appeared to be an arrogant disregard of both British and Spanish neutrality. The London *Times,* usually midway between public sentiment and official caution, was acid. It had heard, so it thought, on good authority, that the captain of the *Montgomery* had stated that the protection of the Spanish flag which had been raised meant nothing to him, nor did the Spanish officials. The *Times* asserted that

> his orders were to take possession of the vessel wherever he found it; and that he would do so and send the crew as prisoners on board the Montgomery....
>
> Here, everything—ship, flag, destination, place of capture and burning —all were neutral, and more international rights were violated in broad day light than a casuist would have thought of combining in a single hypothetical case. To justify such a proceeding would indeed be...to reverse the whole tenor of American policy in the interpretation of maritime law, and leave the United States without an answer to the most extravagant pretension of belligerents in the event of their being neutral in any future war.[33]

By November, 1862, Wilkes was back at Nassau with his squadron, and ill will between the American cruisers and the British fleet and colonials had almost grown to the breaking point. On November 23, United States Consul Whiting reported a situation that was ominous. Admiral Wilkes in the *Wachusett,* together with another cruiser, had anchored near by and then moved out, whereupon Captain Malcolm of H.M.S. *Baracouta,* according to Whiting's account,

> came to my rooms and informed me that on the approach of the U.S. ships, he had sent his boat, with an officer to communicate with the admiral, but that greatly to his mortification the ship did not slacken her speed, but passed his boat without deigning to notice his presence in the least. Captain Malcolm also stated that a pilot named Lloyd who had

gone off to the flag ship had told him that when he informed the admiral that he could not anchor without first obtaining the governor's permission to do so, the admiral or executive officer of the ship had replied "that he should anchor if he saw fit without reference to the governor's prohibition."

Capt. Malcolm further said "that he considered it due to me, that he should inform me of his determination, if either of the U.S. vessels should anchor without the governor's permission he should fire upon them at once; and that he had put his ship in readiness for action before leaving her to come on shore."[34]

III

Hardly had the British government and public ceased to discuss the burning of the *Blanche,* when Commodore Craven, whose ship, the *Tuscarora,* had been lying near the harbor of Madeira, going in and out and inspecting the merchant vessels anchored there, boarded the *Thistle* as it left port, and created another diplomatic incident and stirred the British public to fresh anger. Craven, in boarding the *Thistle,* had done so on the authority of a "black list" of vessels supposed to be blockade-runners or carriers of contraband. This list had been furnished by Charles Francis Adams, who, with the aid of Consuls Wilding, Dudley, and Morse, of Liverpool and London, and a corps of detectives and spies, had been able to collect much evidence as to the movements of British merchant vessels and munitions of war.[35] The affair created a sharp public reaction in England, in which Lord Russell seemed to share. He instructed Lord Lyons at Washington to make a strong protest against the use of Madeira as a base of operation. Lyons accordingly told Seward that

> Her Majesty's government were of opinion that it was competent to the Tuscarora to stop and visit the "Thistle" upon the high seas, but that Her Majesty's government considered that it was never competent to the U.S. cruisers to make a belligerent use of the port of a neutral State and that a more unneutral use of a port could not be well conceived than by lying in wait in it for the vessels of another neutral state as they entered and left it.[36]

Seward conceded that Commodore Craven's conduct had been "censurable"; but just about the time when Seward was making reassuring promises that neutral harbors would not be blockaded or used as bases of operation, Rear Admiral Wilkes and his flying squadron were pursuing a course off the island of St. Thomas which was calculated to stir the British government and public opinion deeper than anything which had thus far occurred, with the exception of the *Trent* affair, and to renew the deep-grounded suspicion of the sincerity of the professions and promises of the United States government, particularly as voiced either by Secretary of State Seward, or Secretary of Navy Welles. Apparently using the neutral harbor of St. Thomas as an ambuscade, Wilkes and his subordinates captured the British steamers *Peterhoff* and *Dolphin* on February 25 and March 24, 1863, respectively, while ostensibly en route to Nassau and Matamoras, two other neutral ports. On April 13, W. M. Grazebrook, owner of the *Dolphin,* notified Lord Russell that the *Dolphin* had been captured just as it left the neutral port of St. Thomas, nearly a thousand miles from the blockaded coast, en route to Nassau. Grazebrook was caustic: "As Nassau is a part of the British possessions, and no notification of the blockade of Nassau or of the Danish Island of St. Thomas has yet been issued, I have to claim the protection of the British Government." He continued, a few days later:

> As the foregoing capture occurred nearly one thousand miles from the blockaded ports, I have to request from Her Majesty's Government some exact information as to the limits of the laws within which we may demand protection, as at present it seems to be left to the acquisitiveness of each American Captain who can catch a British vessel going toward our West Indian possessions.[37]

He and his firm had another ship which they had loaded and ready to sail, but they wished "to know before despatching her what protection we have to expect on her legitimate voyage."[38]

The British fleet stationed in the West Indies was making observations and reporting to the admiralty and the Foreign Office at the same time. Captain E. H. Barnard, of the royal navy, who visited the port of St. Thomas at about the time that the *Dolphin* was captured, reported that "it appears that the United States ships of war are using the harbor of St. Thomas as a rendezvous for intercepting vessels supposed to be engaged in trading with the Southern ports of the United States." There was at the time of his visit there the *Wachusett, R. D. Shepherd,* and *Gemsbok* in the harbor, while Admiral Wilkes was expected in momentarily with the *Vanderbilt.* He reported that the *Wachusett* had waylaid the *Dolphin* at this harbor. It was further rumored that the United States fleet was establishing a coaling station at that place.[39]

On April 24, 1863, Russell instructed Lyons to renew the protest of the British government against the unneutral use of St. Thomas and other neutral ports;[40] but it was the alarming report and earnest warning of Vice-Admiral Milne, who had made a careful investigation of the seizures of the *Peterhoff* and *Dolphin*, which reached Lyons before Russell's instructions and sent him in haste to the Secretary of State. Milne, in whom the British government relied implicitly and who had a very delicate situation to deal with, was obviously stirred out of his usually calm and judicious attitude.[41] He confessed that it was becoming more and more difficult to avoid a conflict with the American squadron in the West Indies. It was difficult to lie idly by and actually see the American cruisers dart out of a neutral port and seize "bona fide British vessels bound from one neutral port to another merely because their names are included in a list of suspected vessels and therefore characterized and dealt with as contraband...." The seizure of the *Peterhoff* under such circumstances, he continued, had aroused great indignation in the British fleet; and, unless the United States would put a check on such practice, "it can hardly fail to give rise to very serious complications."[42]

IV

Lyons hastened to take up with Seward the special questions involved in the seizure of the *Peterhoff* and *Dolphin*, which will be discussed later, and the general question of the use of neutral ports as bases of operation against neutral commerce. He discussed Milne's report and assured Seward of the implicit confidence of the British government in Milne's judgment and opinion; he warned Seward, just as Milne had warned him, that serious trouble could be avoided only by putting an immediate stop to the unneutral use of St. Thomas and other neutral harbors; he reminded Seward of Commodore Craven's seizure of the *Thistle* and of Seward's disavowal of that act in the previous winter; and he committed the discussion to paper, so that Seward might lay it before Secretary of Navy Welles.[43] After a conversation with the hard-headed, anti-British Secretary of the Navy, Seward obtained a note from the former which stated, for the benefit of the English government, that instructions had been sent the navy that St. Thomas should not be used in an unneutral way.[44] Welles, as a matter of fact, denied that Wilkes or any of the American naval officers had made any such use of that port as that described by Milne or Lyons. On the other hand, he assured Seward, for the benefit of the British government, that Wilkes was doing all in his power to avoid the violation of Danish neutrality.[45]

Lyons transmitted Seward's and Welles's notes to Russell with the observation that they did not satisfactorily explain the conduct of the *Wachusett* in lying in wait for the *Dolphin* and beginning pursuit from the neutral harbor of St. Thomas.[46] Russell strongly approved of Lyons' protest against the "improper use made by the United States cruisers of the port of St. Thomas," and instructed him to renew his representations in "stronger terms" unless he received "an assurance from Mr. Seward that fresh orders have been issued to put a stop to the practice complained of. . . ."[47]

But, apparently, the protest of the British Vice-Admiral Milne and Lord Lyons had had no effect upon the conduct of Admiral Wilkes, for within a few weeks after Lyons' spirited conversation with Seward, Lloyd's reported to the Foreign Office that "the intention of the United States government of making this port a regular naval station for their vessels in these waters now seems quite certain." There were seven United States vessels in St. Thomas harbor at one time: the *Vanderbilt* (Admiral Wilkes), *Wachusett*, *Oneida*, *Alabama*, *Chippewa*, *Gemsbok*, and the *R. D. Shepherd*. "These proceedings on the part of the United States government will of course materially injure the trade of this place, although a strictly neutral port."[48]

Near the middle of June, Lyons, acting on Russell's vigorous instructions of May 23, made another remonstrance to Seward "against the use made by its [the United States] cruisers of the neutral port of St. Thomas."[49] Seward, thus crowded for a specific answer, consulted Welles again, who once more assured Seward, for the benefit of the British minister, that Wilkes, from whom he had had recent reports about this very matter, had committed no breach of neutrality at St. Thomas.[50] Welles, in what seemed to Lyons equivocating terms, assured Seward, who in turn promised Lyons in the same language, that the harbor of St. Thomas would not be used as a naval base in the future. Since the United States government completely denied that St. Thomas had ever been used in any such capacity, Lyons placed very little credence in this fresh, but ambiguous, pledge made by Seward and Welles. He tried a different tack by bringing pressure to bear on Count Piper, minister of Sweden and acting minister of Denmark at Washington;[51] but Piper could only get just such assurances of neutrality from Seward as the latter had given to Lyons, that St. Thomas had not been and would not be used as a rendezvous for the American naval vessels cruising in West Indian waters. The acting minister of Denmark gave Lyons a copy of the correspondence, and Lyons submitted it to Russell. But the British Foreign Secretary, having fresh reports from Lloyd's and Vice-Admiral Milne, found very little comfort in Seward's bland but vague assurance that the United States navy would not make unneutral use of St. Thomas. In fact, Russell thought that the attitude of Seward and Welles—not to mention Wilkes—was so equivocating that nothing had really been promised with regard to the future conduct of the American fleet. Russell complained to Lyons:

> Her Majesty's Government cannot perceive that Mr. Seward or Mr. Welles or Vice Admiral Wilkes give any assurance that the use of the port of St. Thomas to watch neutral merchant vessels, and then dart out and seize them on their departure, is disapproved or that such conduct will not be repeated.
> There are abundant expressions of civility toward the Danish government, but of regret and promise of observing the law of nations in future there is not a word. Your Lordship will ask Mr. Seward to state explicitly whether the law of nations is to be violated in the instance of the port of St. Thomas during the continuance of the war or whether a different conduct is to be followed.[52]

On July 18, 1863, Lyons embodied Russell's caustic letter in a note to Seward.[53] Apparently, Seward and Lincoln had reached the conclusion that the American navy had gone about as far as was wise in this direction; so Admiral Wilkes was recalled from St. Thomas, and Rear Admiral Lardner was stationed there with instructions to be cautious in his use of the harbor of St. Thomas—and of any other neutral ports on his station. But Welles always insisted that he had recalled Wilkes for violating orders in commandeering the steamer *Vanderbilt* and that he had not been recalled because of his violation of neutrality.[54] Seward apprised Lyons of the action of the United States government. "It is presumed," he wrote Lyons, "that the information thus conveyed is a sufficient answer to your note upon the subject."[55]

While assurances were at last given of past good intentions and future good conduct on the part of the American navy in the port of St. Thomas, and the Foreign Office could let the question drop, the law officers of the crown left a parting word with Russell—for the record:

> A conclusion still exists in our mind (both from the reports of the British naval officers, and from the very manner in which question of fact has been avoided in Mr. Seward's communications with Lord Lyons) that the Vanderbilt and Wachusett did really commence these proceedings,

with a view to the visitation and capture of the Peterhoff and Dolphin respectively within Danish waters.[56]

While the controversy over the unneutral use of St. Thomas raged, another incident occurred which spurred on the British Foreign Office to a more determined stand against the blockade of neutral ports where British commerce was involved. This incident was the capture in June 1863 of the British steamer *Victor* by the United States war vessel *Juaniata,* just off the coast of Cuba. The Spanish officials, who were still smarting from the disregard of their neutrality in the case of the *Blanche* the previous fall, contended that the vessel had been pursued from the harbor of Havana by the *Juaniata* and captured two and one-half miles off shore.[57] It was reported to the British Foreign Office at the same time that the commander of the *Juaniata,* in an unguarded moment, had quoted an order from Admiral Wilkes "to capture every British vessel bound to the westward from Havana"[58] and the commander had further confessed that he had indeed captured the *Victor* within Cuban waters but that he had reported the capture as having been made ten miles from shore in order to avoid trouble with Spain.[59]

Spain now joined her voice with that of England, which had already been raised so often. Senor Tassara wrote Seward July 7 that the seizure of the *Victor* in Cuban waters was an "outrage against every maritime law" and that it had been "committed with the coolest and most deliberate intention and with the smallest extenuating circumstance. . . . It is necessary," continued Tassara, "that such outrages should be put an end to, and that the responsibility of any conflict which might arise out of them would not rest with the Spanish."[60]

Seward quickly assured Tassara that, should the circumstances attending the capture of the *Victor* prove to be as the latter had described, the vessel would be released at once. At the same time, however, Seward expressed serious doubts as to the correctness of Tassara's version of the incident: he had had a report from Admiral Wilkes, who denied that orders had been given to seize British vessels bound west from Havana or that other acts of doubtful legality had been committed.[61]

Copies of the correspondence of the Spanish officials among themselves and with the United States were placed in the hands of Lord Lyons, and he in turn transmitted them to Lord Russell.[62] This strengthened the position of the British government, which was already deeply involved in the St. Thomas controversy. On July 27, Lyons instructed Acting Consul General Crawford, of Havana, to send him any authentic information as to whether or not the commander of the United States naval vessel *Juaniata* took "undue advantage of his presence in a neutral port, either to obtain information about the Victor or to facilitate the capture."[63] The next day Lyons wrote Lord Russell that he was convinced that the "*Juaniata* followed the *Victor* out of the harbor of Havana for the purpose of capturing her," but that, because of the

> gravity which the discussion between the two governments on the question of pursuing British vessels from neutral harbours has assumed in the case of the port of St. Thomas, I have not thought it prudent to bring a new case before the United States Government, without being sure of the facts.[64]

Seward, however, did not wait for the British government to prepare its case, but hastened to assure Lyons that the commander of the *Juaniata* had satisfied the United States government that he had captured the *Victor* outside of Cuban waters.[65] But Lyons was still of the opinion, so he informed Russell, that while the *Victor* had possibly been captured outside the three-mile limit, the statement of the commander of the *Juaniata* showed that the "following of the *Victor* out of the neutral port of Havana was for the purpose of seizing her."[66] At this time Vice-Admiral Milne made his report to the admiralty, which sustained Lyons' position thoroughly.[67] With the information in hand from the Spanish authorities in Cuba, Consul General Crawford, of Havana, and Vice-Admiral Milne, Russell consulted the law officers of the crown; and he immediately instructed Chargé d'affaires Stuart to express the protest of the British government against the capture of the *Victor* and the principle involved and to demand prompt redress. He considered that it was a "case of a most serious character." From all the evidence, including the statement of the commander of the *Juaniata,* it appeared certain "that the *Juaniata* lay in wait for the *Victor* in a neutral harbor, and followed her from thence with the intention of capturing her." There was little doubt, too, that the *Victor* had been taken in Spanish waters. It was

> difficult not to believe that whatever may be the intentions entertained and orders issued by Mr. Seward for respecting neutral rights and observing generally the rules of International Law those orders have been practically disregarded by the United States Cruisers under the command of Admiral Wilkes.[68]

Lord Lyons, now in Washington, incorporated Russell's instructions to Stuart in a note to Seward.[69]

In the meanwhile the district prize court released the vessel, and the attorney-general had the case appealed to the Supreme Court. Lyons urged Seward, in an informal and confidential interview, to have the appeal dropped; but, according to Lyons' statement to Russell, Seward said "confidentially, that with the strong feeling of the secretary of the navy on the subject of not interfering with legal procedure in prize cases it would be useless to propose to him to release the *Victor* in the present state of the case."[70] Russell, already nettled by the appeal to the Supreme Court of other cases in which the legality of the capture seemed very doubtful, instructed Lyons on December 9, 1863, to make a formal demand of the United States government for the release of the *Victor,* in view of the illegal circumstances surrounding its capture.

> The making use of a neutral port as a place from whence to sally forth and pursue the captured vessel appears to H.M.'s Government to be an incontrovertible fact in this case; within one hour (whatever was the distance) from the time of leaving the harbour of Havana the "Victor" was seized by the "Juaniata" coming out of the same port; and H.M.'s Government conceive that such a fact alone ought to induce the Government of the U.S. to abide by the decision of its own prize court and not to seek its reversal by appeal...."[71]

When Lyons presented Russell's demand that the vessel be released,[72] Seward consulted President Lincoln. The president upheld the position of the secretary of the navy that all captured vessels, regardless of the circumstances of the capture, must go through the courts until condemned or released by the Supreme Court. "The power," Seward told Lyons, "to restore prizes without trial can, in the president's opinion, only be justifiably exercised in extraordinary, clear and unquestionable cases." As the case of the *Victor* was not considered as being of such character, it must be allowed to go through the regular routine of court procedure.[73] In this status the *Victor* was permitted in the winter of 1864 to drop from the annals of diplomacy.

During the spring and summer of 1863, when the British public and the government were exasperated over the use of Cuba and St. Thomas as bases of operation against British commerce, Wilkes increased the tension by transferring his attention back to Nassau, which had been somewhat relinquished in favor of St. Thomas. Bagley, the governor of the Bahamas, complained to United States

Consul Hawley at Nassau that United States vessels were slipping in and out of the harbor at that place without observing the twenty-four-hour rule or the harbor regulations in general. The *Rhode Island,* in particular, had been guilty of this coming and going without notice, in the pursuit of alleged blockade-runners or vessels carrying contraband. Bagley informed Hawley about the middle of May that the matter would be referred to Admiral Milne, who would, presumably, put a stop to such conduct.[74] Two weeks later the American consul reported that several federal cruisers had anchored in the harbor at Nassau without permission and that Governor Bagley was now threatening to refuse permission to any American vessels to use the anchorage.[75] Hawley feared that trouble with England would be precipitated by the American navy unless more caution was practiced; and soon after his warning, the *Rhode Island* almost fulfilled his worst fears. While lying in the harbor, the *Rhode Island* sighted the famous blockade-runner *Margaret and Jessie* and, according to the reports of the British officials, began chase from that place, firing shells at the vessel, which fell in a fishing village. Finally, it was reported, the *Rhode Island* sent a shot through the hull of the *Margaret and Jessie* while within 100 yards of the coast.[76]

The British Foreign Office protested against the violation of neutrality involved in firing on a British vessel within the three-mile limit of British territorial waters and in the use of Nassau as a naval base.[77] But Seward's reply was to challenge all the facts on the basis of the statement made by the officers in command of the *Rhode Island.*[78] Public excitement in the island was intense, and the affair precipitated a debate in the British Parliament.[79] Some conceded that the vessel might have been fired on outside the three-mile limit —though shots fell on the shore—but at the same time all were of the opinion that the *Rhode Island* and its companion cruisers were virtually using Nassau as a base just as St. Thomas was being used.

V

The seizure of merchant vessels at the mouth of the Rio Grande, known in diplomatic history as the "Matamoras seizures," in actual fact belongs in the same category as the blockade of St. Thomas, Havana, Nassau, Madeira, or other neutral ports. The United States squadron which lay in wait for merchantmen bringing contraband to Matamoras or using the Mexican port as a blockade-running base was at the same time carrying on a legitimate blockade of the Texas coast and, for the reason that the American cruisers on the Texan station had legitimate business here and an unchallenged right to lie near Matamoras, England—or any other neutral whose commerce was injured—had no legal grounds on which to protest the actual blockading of the neutral port of Matamoras. However, the blockading squadron at this point soon furnished other grounds on which to base a first-class controversy. When the seizure of the *Magicienne,* the *Peterhoff,* and the *Dolphin*—the former two actually, and the latter ostensibly, destined for Matamoras—and Charles Francis Adams' granting of immunity from capture by the American navy to certain parties shipping arms to Matamoras for the Juarez faction are added, it may be said that Matamoras was the focal point of as sharp a public reaction and diplomatic controversy as grew out of America's exercise of belligerent rights on the high seas.

The Matamoras seizures occurred in 1862 and 1863—chiefly in the latter year. The *Labuan* and the *Will-o'-the-Wisp* were seized on February 4 and May 3, 1862, respectively. Then on September 11, 1863, the *Sir William Peel* was captured; and on November 4 the *Volante, Science, Dashing Wave,* and *Matamoras* were taken as prizes.

When Captain Swartout of the United States steamer *Portsmouth* captured the *Labuan* on February 4, 1862, the latter vessel was, according to its captain, lying in Mexican waters. It was taking on a load of cotton from Matamoras. British Consul Blacker, according to his report of the matter, visited Captain Swartout aboard the United States steamer *Portsmouth* and asked for an explanation of the seizure, which, he thought, seemed to have been made without justification. Captain Swartout, at first, seemed irritable and informed Blacker "that he had no explanation to give..., that he had seized the Labuan and that the reasons would be made known before the proper competent tribunal." But he at length, according to Blacker's version, told the British consul that the *Labuan* had been taken for violating the blockade in loading cotton from Texas by means of rebel steamers. Blacker replied that the cotton was being loaded from Matamoras and not from the Texas side, and that the *Labuan* lay in Mexican waters. Swartout, however, insisted that while the cotton came immediately from Matamoras its ultimate source was Texas, and that he was prepared to seize every vessel along the Mexican coast even as far west as Tampico, should it have cotton on board.[80]

Consul General Crawford, at Havana, on receipt of Blacker's report, wrote Lyons that the seizure of the *Labuan* on the new doctrine that cotton shipped from Matamoras was contraband had paralyzed all commerce for the time being at the mouth of the Rio Grande. None of the half-dozen or more British vessels which were loading at the time would venture out of Mexican waters.[81]

Lyons laid the matter before Seward about March 10 in a confidential interview. He told the latter that the capture of the *Labuan*, as reported, had been a flagrant violation of neutral rights; and he urged that the vessel be released. Seward promised to have the *Labuan* released if the capture had been made in the manner described.[82] On March 13 Seward informed Lyons that, on examination of the papers relating to the *Labuan*, he had been convinced that the seizure was illegal; but he advised that redress could be more quickly obtained if the vessel were permitted to go through prize court. He assured Lyons that orders had been issued against seizures under circumstances similar to that of the *Labuan*.[83]

Lord John Russell, on receipt of the details of the capture of the *Labuan* was too indignant to await possible explanations from Washington. On March 28 he instructed Lyons to demand the release of the *Labuan* on the grounds that she carried a cargo to a neutral port, that she was loading from a neutral port, and that she was seized in neutral waters. There could not have been any violation of blockade at that point, for he had full information, he said, that there had been no blockade of that part of the coast. The case was

> one of serious aspect, both as regards the interests of the British owners of the Labuan and of the position of the cargo; and as regards the principles involved with a view to similar cases, which in consequence of the conduct and declarations of Captain Swartout may be expected to recur at Matamoras.[84]

On the same day, Russell, still in a rage, asked the admiralty to order Vice-Admiral Milne to send one or two more war vessels to Matamoras "to protect numerous British vessels at that port from similar acts of violence which the commander of the *Portsmouth* has announced as his determination to commit."[85]

At this time Russell received Lyons' dispatch containing Seward's promise that orders would be given forbidding any future seizures similar to that of the *Labuan*.[86] Russell turned to the American minister, Charles Francis Adams, and urged that the *Labuan* be promptly released. Adams, however, either was instructed to pay no heed to any British grievance or was temperamentally incapable of doing so, for, instead of discussing the *Labuan* case, he countered, as nearly always, with a complaint against the concerted efforts of the British to violate the blockade and the shipment of arms from England to the Confederacy. Forced from a discussion of the *Labuan* case, Russell reminded Adams that

> the arms and munitions received from Great Britain as well as from other neutral countries, have enabled the United States to fit out the formidable armies now engaged in carrying on the war against the Southern States; while by means established by the Federal Government, the Southern States have been deprived of similar advantages;[87]

so that England's neutrality had operated in favor of the North.

While Russell was engaging in this futile correspondence with Adams, Lyons received fresh evidence that satisfied him that Captain Swartout had been both arrogant and careless of neutral rights on the Rio Grande, and he asked for the release of the *Labuan* without further court procedure.[88] When Lyons received Russell's sharp note of March 28, he presented its substance to Seward and again asked that the *Labuan* be released.[89]

In an interview about May 8, Seward informed Lyons that he had evidence which seemed to prove that the *Labuan* had been seized in Texas waters and that it must, therefore, go through prize court. Lyons replied that the evidence in his possession all pointed to the conclusion that the vessel had been captured in Mexican waters; but. even if it should be proved that the *Labuan* had been taken in Texas waters, the act would still be without legal foundation because of the absence of a blockade.[90]

Soon after this, however, the court released the *Labuan* and awarded damages on the grounds, as put forth by the British government, that there had been no blockade at the place of capture before February 1, 1862, and that the *Labuan* had been in the vicinity since January 1.[91] However, the Congress of the United States refused to appropriate the money until many years later, when the settlement of the *Alabama* claims seemed assured; and there were recurrent exchanges of sharp notes between the two governments.[92]

Before the release of the *Labuan,* the captain of the steamer *Montgomery* captured the *Will-o'-the-Wisp* lying just across the bar outside of Mexican waters. The vessel had brought a shipment of munitions and was in the process of unloading in Matamoras by means of lighters at the time of the capture. Captain Hunter of the *Montgomery* made his seizure on the grounds of ultimate destination of contraband; that is, he contended that the arms were ultimately destined to the Confederacy by way of Matamoras. But it seems that he announced to British Captain Tatham that he would seize vessels loaded with munitions anywhere in Mexican waters. This, of course, was not acceptable; and Tatham protested to United States Admiral Farragut that "the doctrine of the commander of the *Montgomery* that 'powder landed in Mexico may reach Texas' cannot be admitted as a reason for capturing neutral property landed in a neutral port." On July 12, 1862, Chargé d'affaires Stuart brought the case up for discussion in an interview with Seward. Seward dodged the question of contraband but repudiated Hunter's doctrine that the United States claimed the right to make seizures in neutral waters. However, Judge Marvin ended the discussion soon by releasing the vessel on the grounds that there was no evidence of an intention ultimately to deliver the munitions in the Confederacy. Therefore, the trade was bona fide neutral; "and in a trade carried on between neutral nations there can be no such thing as contraband of war, but the trade of neutrals is unaffected by the war."[93]

While the capture of these two vessels in the spring of 1862 had the effect of putting a serious check on commerce between Matamoras and Great Britain, their release quieted, somewhat, the British public mind and ended, for the time being, the diplomatic discussion of the question. But the strong revival of the British trade with Matamoras which, according to Seward, sprang up as "suddenly and quickly as palaces, cities, States or Empires" and the *Arabian Nights,* caused the American government to put another serious check on the trade in the spring of 1863 by the seizure of the *Magicienne, Peterhoff,* and *Dolphin,* supposedly destined for Matamoras, and, in the fall of 1863, the *William Peel, Dashing Wave, Science, Volante,* and *Matamoras* lying in the mouth of the Rio Grande. It will be recalled that the last four were all captured on the same day. A consideration of these several cases will show how near to blows Great Britain and America came over the seizure of British commerce destined to a neutral port.

The *Sir William Peel* was taken upon a sort of shotgun charge in the apparent hopes that something would hit the mark. The captain of the *Seminole,* which made a prize of the *Sir William Peel,* offered as the grounds for his action the belief that the British merchantman was actually owned by the Confederacy, that she lay in Texas waters, that she had on board a cargo of cotton, loaded from Matamoras but in actual fact belonging to the Confederate government, and, finally, that there was believed to be artillery on board with which to equip her as a privateer.[94] The answer of the British government to these charges was that the ship's papers proved British ownership, that the cargo had been discharged at Matamoras and a load of cotton belonging to neutral parties had been taken on, and, finally, that the vessel had been seized without search, on suspicion, and in Mexican waters.[95]

The British government decided to allow the case to go through the prize court without further discussion;[96] but, just as this decision was made, information reached both Russell and Lyons that four other vessels had been seized on November 4 at the same place and under similarly doubtful circumstances. The owner of the *Dashing Wave* wrote Lord Russell that he was "wholly at a loss to know on what grounds the ship had been captured. She has never been engaged in any blockade running or contraband trade and the vessel was loaded...in the ordinary course of her cruising." It was especially desired "to bring before your lordship the injury done to the regular trade between this country and Mexico, if without any justifiable cause vessels are to be seized and carried to an American port simply on suspicion."[97] The proprietors of the *Volante* informed Russell that their vessel had been captured in neutral waters on the grounds that it had contraband of war on board intended for the Confederacy.[98] In a similar fashion it was represented to Russell that the *Matamoras* and *Science* were taken in Mexican waters.[99] The complaint was reiterated that "it seems now, that the Federals are determined to capture all vessels sailing to Mexican ports on the Rio Grande."[100]

At the same time Lord Lyons was receiving information which seemed to throw grave doubts on the legality of the capture of these ships. It appeared that they had been trading with Matamoras, delivering shoes, cloth, and supplies which might be used for military or private purposes, and some definitely intended for military use; and they all either were taking on cotton from Matamoras or were preparing to do so. The *Matamoras,* according to Lyons' information, was in Mexican waters; the *Science,* north of the channel; while the positions of the *Volante* and *Dashing Wave* were uncertain, since the ships' masters had not been permitted to take their bearings at the time of the capture.[101]

Russell assured the indignant proprietors "that the seizure of the

Dashing Wave and the other vessels at Matamoras is under the consideration of H.M.'s Government" and that proper steps would be taken to obtain redress. But, as usual, it was information furnished by naval officers on the spot and by Vice-Admiral Milne which stirred the British government to take a strong stand. On January 8, 1864, Milne wrote the Lords Commissioners of the Admiralty an indignant report, concerning the Matamoras seizures, on what he considered new principles of international law. These new doctrines were that a neutral vessel could be seized in Mexican waters *after* it had discharged contraband in a neutral port, that capture could be made on suspicion without search in the hopes of uncovering *ex post facto* evidence which would incriminate the vessel, and that trade with the Confederacy was sufficient grounds for capture without any reference to blockade or contraband.[102] The letters of Milne and the other British naval officers were referred to Russell, who immediately instructed Lyons to make a strong protest against the Matamoras seizures and the introduction of new principles of international law. The *Sir William Peel,* said Russell, following Milne's report, was captured in neutral waters, on suspicion without preliminary search; the cotton taken on from Matamoras had been treated as contraband; the capture was made after the discharge of contraband; and, finally, according to the statement of United States Captain Rolando, one of the motives of capture was to obtain the vessel for the United States Navy. "H.M.'s Government fully expect that the United States Government will direct the immediate restoration of the vessel with proper indemnification to the owners and will cause a proper rebuke to be administered to the captor." The contention that the case was already in prize court and therefore beyond the interference of the executive was not a satisfactory justification for refusing to release the ship. Nor could the *Science,* which had discharged munitions at Matamoras and taken on cotton from that port, be legally captured for such action. The case should "be made the subject of an immediate application for release and redress...." The *Volante* should be allowed to go through prize court, unless she had been taken in neutral waters, because she had Confederate cloth on board. The *Dashing Wave,* he said, should be released at once, regardless of the charges against her, because she had been taken without search.[103]

Lyons delivered Russell's instructions to Seward practically verbatim, with the comment that Captain Rolando's statement showed that the seizure was made upon a wrong principle in the case of the

Sir William Peel, a principle "acted upon in a similar manner by
other U.S. cruisers in the Rio Grande—in open defiance of neutral
rights."[104] Again, a day or two later, Lyons sent another note to
Seward in which he discussed sharply the principles on which the
United States cruisers had acted. The letter of Rolando and particularly the one of United States Commander Woolsey to the British
vice-consul at Matamoras seemed particularly clear, said Lyons, in
their statement of the principles on which the American navy was
acting in making prizes of British vessels in the mouth of the Rio
Grande. The inference from these documents, he continued,

> while they remain without disavowal or explanation, is that it is the
> intention of the U.S. government to direct its cruisers to seize neutral
> vessels in U.S. waters for having traded *simpliciter* with the so called
> Confederacy, apart from all consideration connected with questions of
> contraband or blockade.
>
>   Again it would appear from Commander Woolsey's letter that he
> considers himself to be instructed to seize neutral vessels carrying foods
> bona fide destined to Mexico.[105]

On March 14, 1864, Seward, though he did not promise to release
the vessels, made the explanation which Lyons had demanded. His
explanation consisted of a letter from Welles. "I do not understand
our government," wrote Welles, "to claim the right of capturing
ships for having carried contraband of war, after the contraband has
been landed, unless the contraband has been landed in a blockaded
port, and they are on the return voyage from such a port; nor the
right of capturing ships in Mexican waters, or any neutral waters;
nor the right to capture neutral ships on a bona fide voyage from
one neutral port to another," though laden with contraband, "nor
the right to capture neutral ships bound to an enemy's port not
blockaded unless such ships have contraband on board; nor the right
to exercise exclusive jurisdiction to the extent of more than a marine
league from our coast."[106]

About this time it looked as if the court would put an end to the
dispute by releasing all the vessels except the *Volante,* which was
condemned. First released was the *Matamoras*[107] and then the *Sir
William Peel,* on the grounds that the seizure had been made in
neutral waters.[108] In a few days the *Science* and the *Dashing Wave*
were freed on the same grounds.[109]

But the United States government decided to appeal. This, of
course, would delay the cases for years and without doubt would

exercise a restraining influence on the commerce of the Rio Grande. The appeal aroused a blast of fury in British quarters. On July 1, Acting Consul Scales, of New Orleans, where the cases had been tried, wrote Lyons that this "appears to be adding insult to injury. Can nothing be done to avert this vindictive appeal? The whole case from beginning to end can only be characterized as a piratical outrage...."[110] Lyons wrote Seward that he hoped that the appeal would be dropped and "the serious diplomatic questions involved" in the Matamoras seizures "will not be kept alive and embittered...." by the proposed appeal.[111] Seward assured Lyons that the case was being considered "with every disposition towards a just respect for the rights of all parties concerned under the law of nations."[112]

But the appeal went forward and added to that suspicion which Russell had expressed after the seizure of the *Magicienne, Peterhoff,* and *Dolphin,* that it is the intention of the American Government, by capture without cause, by delays of adjudication, by wanton imprisonment of the master and part of the crew of the captured vessels to put a stop to British trade to Matamoras altogether."[113] Russell promptly instructed Chargé d'affaires Burnley to protest against the condemnation of the *Volante* on the grounds that it had been anchored in "interdicted waters": the term "interdicted waters" must be explained, as it was a new term in international law. He was to make a strong remonstrance against the appeal of the other cases, because the seizures had been made under "no recognized principles of Prize law." In fact, it seemed all "too clear for any reasonable controversy, that the seizure of all these vessels was made upon a false principle, contrary to International Law, in which (even if it were to receive the sanction of the American prize court) H. M.'s Government could not acquiesce."[114] Burnley presented to Seward, practically as received, Lord Russell's instructions.[115] Seward did not commit himself: he laconically replied that the matter "will receive attentive consideration."[116] When Lyons returned to his duty, he renewed the protest against the appeal of these cases; but Seward unctuously assured him that the executive could not interfere with judicial proceedings.[117]

Russell felt that Seward was not frank, and reminded him that the executive had interfered in the case of the mails of the *Peterhoff* and that the British government made it a rule to interfere, where necessary, in prize cases. It was suggested that Seward was confusing the ordinary courts with prize courts.[118] Seward's reply in January, 1865, was curt and ironic. He refused to discuss the issue. He acknowledged the receipt "of your note...giving me the impression of H. M.'s Government in regard to the powers of the Executive Government of the U.S. concerning the adjudication upon captured vessels in certain waters."[119] All danger of intervention had passed, the Confederacy was doomed, the United States Navy was powerful, and its victorious armies prepared for any eventuality. One might indulge in sarcasm now to his heart's content.

The cases were finally disposed of by the United States Supreme Court, as has been suggested, in 1866. The *Dashing Wave* was released subject to payment of cost.[120] The *Science* was released under similar conditions.[121] The decision of the lower court was reversed in the case of the *Volante,* and this ship was released on the payment of costs and damages;[122] and the *Sir William Peel* was released without costs or damages being paid the owners.[123] The Supreme Court could find no ground on which to condemn these vessels, but justified the refusal to pay costs or damages because the vessels were lying in positions near enough the blockaded coast to arouse suspicion. The *Dashing Wave* and the *Volante* had been sold *pendente lite,* so that they could not be restored to the owners; nor did Congress appropriate the money to reimburse the proprietors until 1870. These cases were linked, as most of the prize cases were where the court had awarded damages or had released the vessels, with the *Alabama* claims.[124]

As it has already been suggested, the capture of the *Magicienne, Peterhoff,* and the *Dolphin* was identified in the minds of the British public and government with the intention of the United States to put a stop to the trade with Matamoras.

The *Magicienne* was taken in the late winter of 1863, before the seizure of the *Peterhoff,* en route via St. Thomas to Matamoras. It was claimed by the British that no search was made before capture but that the vessel was taken into Key West for search and part of the crew taken off and sent to Boston as prisoners.[125] A careful search failed to disclose any evidence of intention either to violate the blockade or to deliver contraband to the Confederacy directly or indirectly. The vessel was released; but no damages were paid the owners for the delay, loss of part of the crew, or other losses entailed upon them by the capture.[126]

Russell instructed Lyons to proceed at once to inform the United

States government of the displeasure of the British government at the unjustifiable seizure of the *Magicienne* and other vessels under similar circumstances. "There can be no question now as to the capture of this vessel being illegal. It is admitted by the district attorney of the U.S. to have been so." The destination, cargo, and habits of the vessel were all neutral; her papers were all correct; and "there was, therefore, no plausible excuse for her detention." Lord Lyons was to "point out to Mr. Seward with reference to this case that the habit of the United States cruisers of seizing vessels on the chance that something may probably be discovered *ex post facto*" which would help to prove an unneutral purpose "renders the practical fulfillment of the obligation of a neutral state to respect the abstract rights of the belligerent a task of daily increasing difficulty."[127]

The seizure of the *Magicienne* was obviously a violation of neutral rights; and the fact that it seemed to be another blow at the Matamoras trade, as well as another case too near St. Thomas, made Seward unusually quick to agree to do something about the matter at once. A commission was appointed and damages assessed.[128] But Congress, as in all other cases of damages arising from seizure of British commerce, was intransigent. It was not until 1869—six years later—that the British minister at Washington could report that the claims had been paid.[129]

The seizure of the *Peterhoff* on February 25, soon followed by that of the *Dolphin,* brought public opinion close to the pitch it had reached at the capture of Mason and Slidell off the British steamer *Trent,* and precipitated a series of debates in Parliament which lasted for several weeks. Seymour Fitzgerald in the Commons expressed the belief that Admiral Wilkes, who had captured the *Peterhoff* and was responsible for the seizure of the *Dolphin* and for many other irritating seizures in the West Indies, was acting under orders to seize all vessels on the black list furnished through Charles Francis Adams; in other words, that the captures had all been made on suspicion without search. Crawford indorsed Fitzgerald's opinion that the North was deliberately, and with much success, attempting to drive British commerce away from Mexico.[130] The *Times* took the position that the United States was deliberately attacking British commerce to gain the carrying trade of the world,[131] and the *Economist* pronounced the capture of the *Peterhoff* a more flagrant violation of international law than the seizure of Mason and Slidell off the *Trent* in 1861.[132]

On April 3 Russell wrote Lyons that "the seizures by Admiral Wilkes seem like a plan to embroil our two countries. He always protests that such is not his object, but his acts do not agree with his words."[133] Russell instructed Lyons to require the release of the *Peterhoff* unless legal grounds for seizure had been definitely established. Before Lyons received instructions from Russell, he wrote a vigorous remonstrance against the seizure of the *Peterhoff;* but Seward's reply was evasive.[134]

On April 6, Lyons received the report that the royal mails had been taken from the *Peterhoff* and opened, and he hastened to lay the matter before Seward and asked that the mails be restored.[135] Seward evidently considered the opening of British mails a more serious matter than the capture of a British merchant vessel. In the fall of 1862 he and Lincoln had overridden Welles in the case of the *Adela* and issued orders against the opening of foreign mails. He hastened now, as in the case of the *Adela* the year before,[136] to confer with Secretary Welles and to urge the release of the mails. But Welles, as in the case of the mails of the *Adela,* was not willing to budge an inch; he insisted—correctly, so it appears—that the seizure of mails was not covered by international law and that the right should be insisted on as an essential means of obtaining evidence as to the true character and destination of captured vessels. Seward, thus checkmated in a serious diplomatic move, laid the case before President Lincoln. He again pointed out that the seizure of mails was fraught with present and future danger. Lincoln once more sustained the Secretary of State, and the latter informed Lyons that the mails of the *Peterhoff* would be forwarded to their proper destination—as a concession and not as a right.[137]

Admiral Milne's report on the capture of the *Peterhoff* added to the indignation of the British government against the alleged seizure of British vessels without search. Milne thought that Welles's recent order issued after the seizure of the *Adela*[138] would have put an effective stop "to this reckless practice of seizing British vessels bound from one neutral port to another, apparently on the sole ground of their names being included in a list of suspected vessels"; but the order had not been obeyed. He forwarded a letter from Captain Tatham which asserted that the United States naval officers "have extended the operation of belligerent rights without reference to necessary evidence for condemnation" and that such practices could not continue without "rupture between the two countries."[139]

But the representations of Lord Lyons[140] had no effect on the United States government—except in the case of the mails,—and the *Peterhoff* went through prize court and was condemned in the late summer of 1863 on the grounds that it was carrying contraband ultimately destined to the Confederacy by way of Matamoras.[141] Judge Betts's decision in the case of the *Peterhoff* is worthy of careful examination as a typical decision of the United States district prize courts, and later the Supreme Court. It upheld to the fullest extent, just as Judge Marvin had done in the case of the *Dolphin,* to be discussed later, the doctrine of continuous voyage which had been the subject of so many diplomatic protests in the early days of our government when we were neutral and England was at war.[142] In the decisions of Judge Betts and Judge Marvin there is no indication of squeamishness in taking on the new doctrine or in shuffling off the old. The decision in the case of the *Peterhoff,* like those in the case of the *Hart* and *Dolphin,* was able, couched in clear, incisive English, and destined, like Judge Betts's other decisions and those of Judge Marvin, to furnish the pattern and the citation of English precedents for the Supreme Court when it came to pass on many of these cases of seizure on the grounds of ultimate destination either to deliver contraband or violate the blockade. British precedents upon which the main points of the decision were based will be readily seen by quoting from the decision:

> If the Peterhoff had on board goods contraband of war [said Judge Betts] which were destined, when they left England, for the use of the enemy, and not for sale or consumption in Mexico, the mere destination of the vessel to Mexican waters, and even the mere intended landing of the goods at Matamoras, on their way to the enemy's country, would not exempt the vessel or her contraband cargo from lawful capture as prize of war.... It is equally well settled, that the ulterior destination of contraband determines the character of the trade no matter how circuitous the route by which they are to reach that destination; that, even though the Peterhoff was destined to Mexican waters, and the goods were there to be unladen, yet if they were to be transported thence, by any mode of conveyance to the enemy's country, the trade was unlawful; that the trade in contraband goods with the enemy's country, though through neutral territory, is likewise unlawful; that the goods so shipped through neutral territory, even though they may be unladen and transshipped, are liable to condemnation; that, if the voyage of the Peterhoff was of such a character, it was an attempt to carry on trade with the enemy by the circuitous route of Mexican waters or a Mexican port, which the law will not countenance; that under such circumstances her voyage was illegal at its inception; and that she and her goods were liable to seizure at the

instant it commenced.... So also, the inception of the voyage completes the offense; and from the moment that the vessel, with the contraband articles on board, quit her port on the hostile demonstration, she may be legally captured. It is not necessary to wait until the goods are actually entering the enemy's country, but the voyage, being illegal at its commencement, the penalty immediately attaches, and continues so long as the illegality exists.[143]

One cannot fail to see that implicit in this and other decisions of its type was the legal justification for the blockade of neutral ports.

The Supreme Court later upheld the condemnation of the contraband, but released the vessel on the condition that costs be assessed on it. The principle of continuous voyage, however, was fully sustained; and the British authorities and decisions on which Judge Betts rested his decision were the mainstays of the Supreme Court's decision.[144]

Judge Betts especially cited in support of his decision the British cases: the *Yonge Pieter* (4 Rob. 79), the *Richmond* (5 Rob. 325), the *Neptune* (2 Rob. 110), the *Nancy* (3 Rob. 122), the *William* (5 Rob. 385), the *Zelden Rust* (6 Rob. 93), the *Maria* (6 Rob. 201), and the *Columbia* (1 Rob. 154). These decisions were chiefly, if not entirely, Lord Stowell's and Sir William Grant's and fell within the period 1793–1815, when the United States, under the leadership of Jefferson and Madison, was making a dogged stand against the principles involved.

When, therefore, the decision was placed before Russell and the law officers of the crown, they could find no fault with it. In fact, despite the great irritation involved in the method and spirit of the seizure, the Foreign Office and the British government were greatly pleased.[145]

Just as excitement over the *Peterhoff* case was beginning to abate somewhat, news of the capture of the *Dolphin* came in and Charles Francis Adams issued his "maritime passport" granting immunity to certain merchants who were shipping arms to the Juarez government in Mexico. Presently the whole transaction leaked out and the newspapers and Parliament and the public at large were aroused anew. Adams, in granting the license of immunity—from interference by the United States fleet—was unfortunate in the accompanying remarks:

Amid the multitude of fraudulent and dishonest enterprises from this Kingdom [he said] to furnish supplies to the rebels in the United States, through the pretense of a destination to some port in Mexico, it gives me pleasure to distinguish one which has a different, and a creditable purpose.[146]

Bentinck considered that the United States was surreptitiously waging war against Great Britain. The *Times* was of the opinion that the blockade had been extended to England by Adams' "ticket of leave," to which, of course, England would not submit.[147] Adams' black list, "maritime passport," and the indiscriminate seizure of British vessels in Mexican waters or en route there left England practically no freedom, should she submit.

Russell made a lengthy speech in the House of Lords concerning the "Matamoras seizures," the *Peterhoff* and *Dolphin,* Adams' letter, and the unneutral use of St. Thomas as an ambuscade. All these except Adams' letter he had already had under serious discussion, and the prize cases were in court. As for the American minister, said Russell, "there is no doubt...that the conduct of Mr. Adams was entirely unwarrantable; but I should not think of complaining to Mr. Adams. I should bring that conduct under the consideration of the United States government."[148] The *Times* remarked the next day

> that from the debates which took place in both houses last night the American government and their more zealous than wise representative, Mr. Adams, may learn the feeling that their acts have produced among all classes of the English people. It cannot be denied that very great irritation exists.[149]

William Dayton, American minister to France, was very pessimistic at this time. On April 27 he wrote Seward that

> the chances of peace with England seem to me growing less and less daily; that the exasperation upon that side of the channel growing out of the seizures, searches, etc., of British vessels fully keeps pace with that in the United States growing out of the depredation of rebel privateers. The two together may drive these two countries into war in despite of the rulers or diplomatists of both.[150]

He could have more easily said because of the rulers of each.

But diplomacy soon smoothed over the Adams' blunder; and Russell received confidential information from a Scotch firm of underwriters that the *Dolphin* had attempted to obtain insurance from them for the purpose, not of going to Matamoras, as was generally thought, but of running the blockade, and this case quickly dropped out of diplomatic, as well as public, discussions.[151]

But the general question of the interference of the United States with the British trade to Matamoras still remained unsettled; and

Lyons, acting on Russell's instructions of an earlier date, brought the matter before Seward in a personal interview. He reminded Seward that there was an "impression which prevails in England that it is the intention of the United States Government to put a stop, by vexatious proceedings, to the British trade with Matamoras," and that some decided "practical steps were necessary to do away with the impression which the recent proceedings of the United States cruisers had produced." Lyons warned Seward that he should "regard another questionable seizure of a British vessel in the neighborhood of St. Thomas or another questionable seizure made anywhere of a British vessel bound to Matamoras, as little short of a calamity." If, through jealousy or suspicion of contraband,

> this British trade were deliberately and systematically made subject to vexatious interference it is obvious that Great Britain must interfere to protect her flag. While submitting to the most severe interpretation of the Law of Nations she cannot allow that under pretense of that law hostilities should be carried on against a lawful branch of her commerce.[152]

In the interview and the note to Seward which covered it, Lyons had practically demanded the release of the *Dolphin*. But that vessel was in prize court; and in a few weeks Judge Marvin, of the District Court at Key West, condemned her on the grounds of ultimate destination of vessels and contraband cargo to a blockaded port.[153]

Though the manner of seizure—on the basis of Adams' black list and apparently without preliminary search—was objectionable, the evidence in the case of the *Dolphin* proved beyond reasonable doubt that the vessel was destined to the blockaded coast. On the basis of this evidence Judge Marvin delivered his decision, which preceded the decision of the *Peterhoff*, already discussed, by several weeks and without doubt influenced it. If

> it was the intention of the owner [said Marvin] that the vessel should simply touch at Nassau, and should proceed thence to Charleston or some other port of the enemy, then the voyage was not a voyage prosecuted by a neutral from one neutral port to another, but to a port of the enemy— begun and carried on in violation of the belligerent rights of the United States to blockade the enemy's ports and to prevent the introduction of munitions of war. The act of sailing for a blockaded port, with a knowledge of the existence of the blockade and with an intention to enter, is itself an attempt to break it, which subjects the vessel and cargo to capture in any part of the voyage.

Judge Marvin cited particularly the British cases of the *Columbia* (1

Rob. 154) and the *Neptune* (2 Rob. 110) in support of the doctrine of ultimate destination to a blockaded port and the right to capture from the inception of the voyage. The same principle was applied to the contraband ultimately destined for the Confederacy.

> The offence of attempting to carry articles contraband of war to the enemy is complete, and the vessel liable to capture the moment she enters upon her voyage.... The offence consists in the act of sailing coupled with the illegal intent. The cutting up of a continuous voyage into several parts by the intervention or proposed intervention of several intermediate ports may render it the more difficult for cruisers and Prize courts to determine where the ultimate terminus is intended to be; but it cannot make a voyage nor make any of the parts of one entire voyage to become legal which would be illegal if not so divided.

In support of the doctrine of the right of seizure of contraband ultimately destined to the enemy, Judge Marvin cited as his chief authority the famous British cases of the *Imina* (3 Rob. 168), the *Maria* (5 Rob. 365), the *William* (5 Rob. 385), and the *Richmond* (5 Rob. 325). The shades of Lord Stowell and Grant, against whom Washington, Jefferson, and Madison had attempted to defend the freedom of the seas, were called up to testify in support of American efforts to sweep British commerce from the ocean and curtail the freedom of the seas. But the British government expressed entire satisfaction at Judge Marvin's decision and his liberal use of British authorities.[154]

Of all the vessels seized in the mouth of the Rio Grande—known as the "Matamoras seizures"—or en route, not a single one was finally condemned; and in all but the *Peterhoff*, the cargoes were conditionally released. This fact gives strong support to the contention that the United States had set out to break up this trade without reference to international law. The resistance of the British, however, caused a cessation of such seizures as had occurred in 1862–1863. Nor is it difficult to avoid the conclusion that, had Seward and Welles, supported by Lincoln, persisted in such flagrant abuse of neutral rights as interpreted by England, the latter would have declared war on the United States.

VI

Let us turn now to the examination of a few typical examples of the seizure of neutral commerce—almost invariably British—whose ultimate destination was the blockaded coast of the Confederacy. We have already noted the friction over the blockade of the neutral ports, especially those of Nassau, St. Thomas, St. George's, Bermuda, and Havana, Cuba. Most of the vessels captured by the squadrons blockading these neutral ports were destined for the blockaded ports. After all, the Matamoras trade was relatively unimportant. The chief trade with the Confederacy went on through the blockaded Confederate ports and coast. It has been estimated that there were perhaps over 8,000 successful trips through the blockade and about 1,500 unsuccessful ones. That is, about 1,500 were captured during the four years of war. So many of these vessels were caught, red-handed, violating the blockade, that their capture or destruction was not contested by the owners and therefore did not give rise to a diplomatic discussion or involve the doctrine of ultimate destination. On the other hand, a fairly large number were captured while plying between Nassau and Bermuda, or St. Thomas and Nassau, or Nassau and Cuba—that is, between neutral ports—on the doctrine of ultimate destination to the blockaded coast, and almost invariably were captured on suspicion and without a bona fide preliminary search because their names were on Adams' black list. It must, however, be said that, while it was a violation of international law to seize ships on suspicion and without search, nevertheless Adams' black list was weirdly accurate. He had spies and detectives in every port, every munitions factory, every shipyard, and in every important source of supply for the Confederacy.[155] These vessels, captured when apparently engaged in trading between neutral ports, and especially their manner of capture, gave rise to numerous diplomatic discussions, sometimes sharp in tone, and helped to add fuel to the blaze already well stoked in England. The cases of the *Bermuda, Gladiator, Adela, Springbok, Victor* (already noted), *Circassian, Stephen Hart, Pearl,* and *Gertrude* were all subject to considerable diplomatic controversy; and the decision rendered illustrated the American acceptance of the British doctrines. However, an examination of the cases of the *Stephen Hart* and the *Springbok* will furnish sufficient illustration of this particular type of case.

The *Stephen Hart* was captured about the first of March 1862 on the charge that, while the vessel was ostensibly booked for Cardenas, Cuba, her actual destination was a blockaded port. There were some exchanges of notes over the case; but the owners of the vessel, Isaac, Campbell and Company, were so well known as special agents for the Confederate War Department that Russell and Lyons decided to

allow the case to go through prize court without making any protest.[156]

The case was decided by Judge Betts of the Federal District
Court of New York in the summer of 1863. The case is important as
one of the early decisions upholding the principle of ultimate desti-
nation. Judge Betts followed very closely the opinion of Judge
Marvin, of the Southern District Court of Florida, in the case of the
Dolphin.

> If it was the intention of the owner of the Stephen Hart, or the
> owners of her cargo, having control of the movement of the vessel, that
> she should simply touch at Cardenas, and should proceed thence to
> Charleston, or some other port of the enemy, her voyage was not a
> voyage prosecuted by a neutral vessel from one neutral port to another
> neutral port; but a voyage which was at the time of her seizure, in course
> of prosecution to a port of the enemy, although she had not as yet
> reached Cardenas, and although her regular papers documented her for a
> voyage from London to Cuba. Such a voyage was one begun and carried
> on in violation of the belligerent rights of the United States to blockade
> the ports of the enemy, and prevent the introduction into these ports of
> arms and munitions of war. The division of a continuous transportation
> of contraband goods into several intermediate transportations, by means
> of intermediate voyages of different vessels carrying such goods, cannot
> make a transportation which is in fact a unit, to become several transpor-
> tations, although to effect the entire transportation of the goods requires
> several voyages of different vessels, each of which may, in a certain sense
> and for certain purposes, be said to have its own voyage, and although
> each of such voyages except the last one in the circuit may be between
> neutral ports. Nor can such actions make any of the parts of the entire
> transportation of the contraband cargo a lawful transportation, when the
> transportation would not have been lawful if it had not been
> divided.... If the guilty intention, that the cargo of contraband goods
> should reach a port of the enemy, existed when such goods left their
> English port, that guilty intention cannot be obliterated by the innocent
> intention of stopping at a neutral port on the way

or by transshipping in other vessels at neutral ports.

> This court holds that, in all such cases, the transportation or voyage of
> the contraband goods is considered as a unit, from the port of lading to the
> port of delivery in the enemy's country; that if any part of such voyage or
> transportation be unlawful, it is unlawful throughout; and that the vessel
> and her cargo are subject to capture, as well before arriving at the first
> neutral port at which she touches after her departure from England, as on
> the voyage or transportation by sea from such neutral port to the port of
> the enemy.

The same principle was applied to the vessel whose voyage had been broken into parts but whose ultimate intention from the beginning had been to violate the blockade.

In support of the condemnation of contraband and vessels ultimately destined to the Confederacy, Betts, just as Judge Marvin had done in the case of the *Dolphin* (and later the *Pearl*), summoned as his chief precedents the decisions of Stowell and Grant. He cited the *Yonge Pieter*, the *Richmond*, the *Maria* (from which he quoted at length), the *William*, the *Columbia*, the *Imina*, the *Trende Sostre*, and the *Neptune*.[157]

The owners appealed the case to the Supreme Court, but in 1865 that body affirmed the decision of the lower court in condemning vessel and cargo on the doctrine of continuous voyage or ultimate destination.[158]

The British merchantman the *Springbok* was captured near the Bahama banks ostensibly en route to Nassau on the grounds that the actual destination of vessel and cargo was a Confederate port.[159] The owner of the vessel, T. S. Begbie, protested almost incessantly, until the vessel was finally released in 1866, that the steamer was pursuing a bona fide voyage from one neutral port to another. On February 27, 1863, Begbie wrote Under Secretary for Foreign Affairs Hammond that the capture of his vessel on such a flimsy pretext "was a monstrous proceeding" which "surely cannot be permitted."[160] A few days later, Begbie's agent informed Lord Russell that the ship's crew had been thrown in jail and held incommunicado, while their personal belongings and the chronometer had been stolen.[161]

On March 14, 1863, Russell forwarded to Lyons the copies of the ship's papers and statements of the owner and master of the ship.

> There does not [he told Lyons] appear to be any justification for the seizure of this vessel and her cargo. The supposed reason, namely, that there were articles in the manifest not accounted for by the captain, certainly does not warrant the seizure, more especially as the destination of the vessel appears to have been bona fide neutral.[162]

However, since the case was probably before the prize court, Lyons was instructed simply to watch the proceedings in the case.

The case of the *Springbok* was disposed of by the end of July 1863. The vessel and cargo were condemned on the grounds of ultimate destination to a blockaded port.[163]

Though at first inclined to believe that the *Springbok* and her cargo were innocent of the charges on which the condemnation had rested,[164] Russell quickly changed his mind when he had read the trial proceedings and the decision of Judge Betts. "A careful perusal of this elaborate and able judgment," he wrote Lyons, "containing the reasons of the Judge's, the authorities cited by him in support of it and the important evidence properly invoked from the cases of the *Stephen Hart* and *Gertrude*," which showed that the cargoes of all three vessels belonged to the well-known British-Confederate agents, Isaac, Campbell and Company, proved that the ultimate destination for the *Springbok* was a "blockaded port" and that the condemnation of the vessel and cargo for violation of blockade and transportation of contraband to the enemy was just.[165]

The principles, said Judge Betts, on which the *Springbok* and her cargo were condemned were the same as those applied in the case of the *Stephen Hart* and *Peterhoff.*

> Those principles, as established by the highest authorities in England as well as in this country are that articles contraband of war destined for the aid and use of the enemy, and transported by sea to the enemy's country, are liable to capture as lawful prize of war, if seized while being transshipped; that if a cargo be despatched from a neutral port, with an intention, on the part of the person despatching it, that in violation of a blockade known to exist, it should enter a port of the enemy, it may be captured as lawful prize; that contraband articles destined on their departure from a neutral port to be delivered to the enemy, either by being carried directly into a port of the enemy in the vessel in which they leave the neutral port or by being transshipped, at another neutral port, into another vessel are subject to capture; that, if the contraband articles are really intended to be delivered to the enemy at some other place than the neutral port named in the papers of the vessel as the destination of the cargo, and that neutral port is to be used merely as a port of call or transshipment, and the goods are not to be delivered there for discharge and general consumption or sale there, and if, in that way, the representations contained in the papers of the vessel are false and fraudulent as to the real destination of the goods, they are liable to capture; that no principles of law of nations, and no consideration of the rights and interests of lawful neutral commerce requires that the mere touching at a neutral port, either for the purpose of making it a new point of departure of a vessel to a port of the enemy, or for the purpose of transshipping the contraband goods into another vessel, which may carry them to the destination which was intended for them when they left their port of departure, can exempt the goods from capture, that the division of a continuous transportation of contraband goods into several intermediate voyages by different vessels carrying such goods, cannot cause a transportation which is, in fact, a unit to become several transportations although to effect the entire transportation of the goods requires several voyages by different vessels. . .and although each such voyage, except the last one in the circuit, may be between neutral ports; that such a transaction cannot

make any of the parts of the entire transportation of the contraband goods a lawful transaction, when the transportation would not have been lawful if it had not been thus divided;... And that the contraband goods are subject to capture, as well before arriving at the neutral port, as during their transportation by sea from such to the port of the enemy.

The same doctrine of continuous voyage thus applied to goods destined for a blockaded coast or contraband destined to violate the blockade or be delivered to the Confederacy by some other means— provided the first port of the transportation was by sea—was applied to the vessel carrying the goods or contraband. Judge Betts continued:

It is well settled that, from the moment a vessel having on board contraband articles which have a destination to a port of the enemy, leaves her port of departure, she may be legally captured; that it is not necessary to wait until the goods are actually endeavoring to enter the enemy's port and that, the transportation being illegal, at its commencement, the penalty immediately attaches.

Betts cited the usual British cases as his chief authorities—notably the *Trende Sostre*, the *Columbia*, the *Neptune*, and the *Imina*.[166]

In 1866 the Supreme Court upheld the decision of the district court with reference to the cargo, but released the vessel because there was no evidence that the owner of the vessel was cognizant of the intention of the owners of the cargo to violate the blockade to deliver contraband to the enemy.[167]

VII

While there were other controversies over the seizure of British vessels for the violation of the blockade or the transportation of contraband to the enemy, only one was of a serious nature: the treatment of British subjects as prisoners of war. Some friction had arisen in 1862–1863 over this subject, but it was not until the fall of 1863 that the subject became one of the chief irritations which disturbed the relationship between the United States and Great Britain.[168] Word reached Lyons in the latter part of 1863 that James O'Neil, member of the crew of the *Nicolai I*, had been held prisoner since the beginning of 1863. First, O'Neil had been shot for an alleged attempt to blow up the captured ship; then he had been held on board first one and then another United States cruiser. Lyons wrote Seward:

You are well aware that I am positively instructed by Her Majesty's

Government to press in the strongest manner upon the attention of the Government of the United States the rule that neutrals found on board neutral vessels are not in the category of prisoners of war; that they are not to be subjected to indignities; that the authority of the belligerent over them extends only to the detention of the witnesses necessary to establish the truth of the case; and it is the duty of the belligerent to afford every reasonable facility for their early release.

He was bound, he told Seward, "to lose no time in asking for further explanations concerning his protracted imprisonment."[169]

Seward promptly investigated the imprisonment of O'Neil and had an order issued to free him at once.[170] But over a month later the prisoner was reported as still held,[171] and Lord Lyons again demanded his release.[172] On receipt of Lyons' dispatch of January 26, Russell consulted the law officers of the crown and wrote Lyons to obtain redress in the case of O'Neil and demanded that such practices be stopped. "It would really seem," he wrote Lyons, "from these papers as if the U.S. had secretly determined to treat the crews of all prize vessels as prisoners of war in order thereby to stop the continued violation of the blockade."[173] Lyons presented Russell's instructions to Seward, and told the latter most emphatically that the continued treatment of British subjects as prisoners of war as a penalty for blockade-running would endanger the good relations between the two countries.[174]

Not only had O'Neil been held as prisoner of war, but, as we have said, he had been shot by one of his captors, who had been freed on his own statement that the prisoner was attempting to blow up the ship. Russell demanded of the United States government that the officer who had thus wounded the prisoner be tried.[175] Seward complied with the request of the British government and had the officer tried, and he was convicted.[176]

The imprisonment of the crew of the *Banshee,* which occurred in the fall of 1863, appeared without justification and very harsh. Watson, one of the crew, wrote Consul Archibald that "the living is not a bit better than what the Federal prisoners get in Southern jails, about which so much has been written." Lyons took the matter up with Seward, but the latter was vague and noncommittal. At length he notified the secretary of state that he would be forced to refer the matter back to Russell, inasmuch as Seward had failed to act or to make any commitments. He wrote that it was impossible to "acquiesce in this exercise of power by the Government of the United States." At length Seward explained that the crew was being held on suspicion that the *Banshee* was a Confederate ship; but Lyons replied that it had already been condemned and that the decision of the case would show the nationality of the vessel.[177]

In a few days Seward notified Lyons that the nationality of the crew and vessel had been established and that all but one of the crew—presumably an American—would be released. But Seward warned Lyons that the greatest scrutiny would henceforth be exercised by determining the character and nationality of the crew of blockade-runners.[178]

On March 8, 1864, Lyons notified Russell that the British crew of the *Sylvanus,* which had been sunk by a federal cruiser, were being held as prisoners of war without examination. He had written Seward, he reported, and reminded him again that "British subjects belonging to neutral captured vessels ought not to be detained indefinitely as prisoners, or to be treated with indignity"; and he had pressed for immediate information as to the grounds on which the men were held prisoners.[179] On the same day Lyons reported that part of the crew of the British vessel *Sallie* had been held as prisoners of war since December of the previous year[180] and that he had likewise asked for their release unless proper grounds for their imprisonment could be furnished. In a few days orders were issued for the release of both crews.[181] But no sooner had these prisoners been set free than Lyons received information that the crews of the *Don* and the *Marianne* were being held in Fort Warren under strict conditions.[182] Next it was the crew of the *Minnie,*[183] and the *Alliance,*[184] and so on until the end of the war.

Seward and Adams both announced to the British government that it was the intention of the United States government to look with suspicion upon the crew of every ship that ran the blockade. Adams finally went so far as to announce to Russell that all British subjects engaged in the violation of the blockade "must incur a suspicion" that they were actually in the services of the Confederacy "strong enough to make them liable to be treated as enemies, and if taken to be reckoned as prisoners of war,"[185] and that it was now, under present conditions, necessary for the United States to presume the guilt of the captured crew of a blockade-runner "until they can show the contrary."[186]

Adams' justification—Seward was too canny to commit himself in such a way—was that, owing to the requirement of the Confederate government that every blockade-runner devote half of the cargo to

Confederate government account, every member of the crew of a blockade-runner was in the service of the Confederacy.[187] To Adams' extension of belligerent rights Russell replied that Great Britain was not prepared,

> on account of the exigencies or distress of either belligerent, to assent to the introduction to the injury of the neutral states, of any alteration in the well established practice of international law.... You are no doubt aware as every American jurist must be aware, that it is not competent to a belligerent government to treat as prisoners of war the subjects of neutral states taken on board vessels (not being ships of war of the enemy) endeavoring or alleged to be endeavoring to break a blockade, and it would be impossible for H.M.'s government to permit British subjects to be excepted to the general rules and practices of international law on this or any other subject.[188]

But Adams, far from receding from his position, held it and fortified it;[189] and while Seward wiggled through most any tight place in which Lord Lyons got him, he and Secretary of Navy Welles nevertheless continued apparently to act on the new principle which Adams had been unwise enough to announce to the British government.

Lyons, despite fair words from Seward, found it increasingly difficult to obtain information concerning the crews which were held—some in irons—in prison. On May 9, 1864, he wrote Lord Russell:

> I have not only addressed to Mr. Seward written communications...but have repeatedly remonstrated with him verbally against the continued enforcement of the order of the Secretary of the Navy to detain as prisoners of war British subjects captured on board vessels seized for breach of blockade. I have not concealed from him my opinion, that whatever may be the motives of the United States government, the system which that government has adopted is in fact neither more nor less than an attempt to increase the efficacy of the blockade, by inflicting penalties not warranted by international law on neutrals concerned in violating it.[190]

Lyons continued to press Seward and tell him emphatically that the British government could not "acquiesce in a practice which has no warrant in the principles of international law";[191] and at last he seems to have convinced Seward and the president that they had best make a gesture against the extreme doctrines of Adams and the extreme practices of the navy under Welles's orders. The result was that Welles issued a new set of orders to the navy that neutral citizens on neutral vessels, even when violating the blockade, were not to be treated as prisoners of war.[192] However, as with the other orders of Welles, this one was honored more in the breach than in its enforcement. In fact, a close scrutiny of the order leaves the impression that loopholes aplenty had been left, or—more properly—opened in it after the main concession against the treatment of neutrals as prisoners of war had been made, to permit the naval officers and United States marshals to use their own judgment and discretion as to the correct meaning of the order.

VIII

Perhaps the question has constantly arisen in the mind of the reader as to why the United States reversed itself with reference to the rights of neutrals on the high seas. Immediately, of course, there arises the explanation that the United States was fighting for its existence and that any practice which strengthened the possibilities of success was justifiable. This, of course, is always the justification of any nation for violating international law or reversing its position with reference to international law. Such was the justification of England and France in the Napoleonic era, when American commerce was subjected to such great oppression; and such was Germany's justification of her submarine warfare in the last two world wars. If the justification is sound, then there is no such thing as "international law," for in any war a nation is fighting for its existence, and therefore international law would be in abeyance—at the only time when it is needed. However that may be, there is little doubt that America reversed herself during the War of Secession partly because she was fighting for national existence, whether that be justifiable or not. But one must not forget that Lincoln had practically no knowledge of diplomatic history and of international law, and that Secretary of State Seward and Secretary of Navy Welles were almost as innocent of a knowledge of either history or international law as Lincoln. This lack of understanding of our historic past must help account for the new position taken by the United States government in 1861–1865. True, there was a body of highly trained lawyers and jurists in the United States, learned in both American and British case law, whose advice was at the disposal of the federal government; but, like the administration, they knew little and cared less, apparently, about the historic position of America in international law. Familiar with the great British decisions, whether in criminal, civil, or prize cases, their advice as attorneys at law and their decisions as jurists were rendered on the basis of *stare decisis*. The most famous prize cases with which they were familiar were those decided by Lord Stowell and Sir William Grant during the Napoleonic wars, which upheld the doctrine of ultimate destination and the most extreme definition of contraband of war. Hence, in default of an executive and cabinet learned in diplomacy and the history of international law, America's position on the freedom of the seas was, to a considerable degree, reshaped by her lawyers.

As for the abuse of these principles, which gave rise to much bad feeling in England, such as the use of neutral ports as bases and the seizure without a bona fide search, there are three explanations: In the first place, these so-called "abuses" are implicit in the doctrine of ultimate destination or continuous voyage. The doctrine could not be practiced without the blockade of neutral ports or the use of a black list or the use of neutral ports as bases of operation and coaling stations. In the second place, the resentment of the American naval officers against England, and especially the English navy, for their secession sympathies, manifested in the building of the Confederate cruisers and ironclads in English ports, gave rise to arrogant conduct and a desire to get revenge. Finally, as an examination of the reports and correspondence of the American naval officers will show, lieutenants, captains, commanders, commodores, and admirals shared the administration's lack of a broad grounding in international law and diplomacy.[193]

[1]See, for example, Henry Wager Halleck, *International Law; or Rules Regulating the Intercourse of States in Peace and War* (New York, 1861).

[2]James Brown Scott (ed.), *The Armed Neutralities of 1780 and 1800* (New York, 1918).

[3]See Frank L. Owsley, *King Cotton Diplomacy: Foreign Relations of the Confederate States of America* (Chicago, 1931), pp. 250–251; cf. James R. Soley, *The Blockade and the Cruisers* (New York, 1883), pp. 11–12.

[4]Soley, pp. 16–17; London *Times*, December 4, 1861; Owsley, pp. 250–251.

[5]Owsley, p. 252.

[6]For description of the blockade and blockade running see James Sprunt, *Tales of the Cape Fear Blockade* (Raleigh, 1902), I, No. 10, 6–9; Thomas E. Taylor, *Running the Blockade* (London, 1897); Soley; John Wilkinson, *The Narrative of a Blockade-runner* (New York, 1877); Francis B. C. Bradlee, *Blockade Running During the Civil War and the Effect of Land and Water Transportation on the Confederacy* (Salem, 1925).

[7]See previous reports of British Foreign Office, America (cited as F.O. 5), Vol. 781, Bunch to Russell, August 6, 1861, No. 94; *ibid.*, August 7, 1865, No. 95; *ibid.*, September 4, 1861, No. 105.

[8]*Ibid.*, September 14, 1861, No. 108.

[9]Ephraim Douglas Adams, *Great Britain and the American Civil War* (New York, 1925), I, 368–369, n. 2.

[10]F.O. 5, Walker to Russell, April 22, 1863, Vol. 906, No. 59.

[11]*Ibid.*, August 1, 1863, Vol. 907, Pt. II, No. 107.

[12]*Ibid.*, Vols. 848, 908, 909, *passim*.

[13]London *Index*, June 20, 1864.

[14]*Ibid*.

[15]United States Consular Despatches (cited as U. S. Con. Des.), Nassau, Vol. 12, Hawley to Seward, May 30, 1863.

[16]*Ibid.*, Vol. 13, Kirkpatrick to Seward, November 1, 1864, No. 37.

[17]*Ibid.*, Havana, Vols. 45, 46, *passim*.

[18]*Ibid.*, Tampico, Vol. 7, Chase to Seward, December 17, 1863, No. 40.

[19]Owsley, pp. 283–286.

[20]*Ibid.*, p. 285.

[21]*Ibid.*, pp. 286–290.

[22]*Ibid.*, *passim*.

[23]August 9, 1862.

[24]June 30, 1863.

[25]The *Trent* affair, which involved certain aspects of the freedom of the seas, has been so thoroughly discussed that no space will be devoted to it here. The principle involved is closely akin to the old British custom of the impressment of British subjects on American ships and never claimed as a right by America during the Civil War.

[26]*Index*, August 7, 1862.

[27]*Ibid.*, August 14, 1862.

[28]*Ibid.*, *Official Records of the Union and Confederate Navies*, 31 vols. (Washington, 1894–1927; cited hereafter as O.R.N.), Ser. I, Vol. I, 470–471, gives Welles's order to Wilkes, September 8, 1862, to proceed to cruise in the West Indies and Bahamas. Welles cautioned Wilkes to be careful of neutral rights.

[29]U. S. Con. Des., Bermuda, Vol. 6, Allen to Seward, August 19, 1862, No. 36; *ibid.*, September 10, 1862, No. 40.

[30]*Index*, October 30, 1862, correspondence dated September 27; O.R.N., Ser. I, Vol. I, 493–496, 502–504, 569–570.

[31]U. S. Con. Des., Havana, Vol. 45, Shufeldt to Seward, October 9, 1862, No. 97; London *Times*, November 12, 1862.

[32]U. S. Con. Des., Havana, Vol. 45, Shufeldt to Seward, October 12, 1862, No. 99.

[33]London *Times*, November 12, 1862.

[34]U. S. Con. Des., Nassau, Vol. 12, Whiting to Seward, No. 88; O.R.N., Ser. I, Vol. I, 571–572, Wilkes to Welles, December 4, 1862.

[35]See, for example, U.S. State Department Consular Letters, Liverpool, Vols. 19ff, January 1861–June 1865; Parliamentary Accounts and Papers, United States, 1863, LXXII, 34.

[36]F.O. 5, Vol. 973, Lyons to Russell with enclosures, May 5, 1863, No. 370, which quotes the former letter on a later occasion in another similar case; see also O.R.N., Ser. I, Vol. I, 564–565, Welles to Craven, November 29, 1862.

[37]F.O. 5, Vol. 935.

[38]*Ibid.*, April 21, 1863.

[39]*Ibid.*, Vol. 937, Paget to Hammond, April 28, 1863, encloses Barnard's letter; O.R.N., Ser. I, Vol. II, 127–128. Wilkes reported on April 24, 1863, that he had established coaling stations in several ports of the West Indies.

[40]F.O. 5, Vol. 935, April 24, 1863, No. 211.

[41]See J. P. Baxter, 3rd, "The British Government and Neutral Rights, 1861–1865," *American Historical Review*, XXXIV (1928), 9–29, for a discussion of Milne's role in keeping the peace during the Civil War.

[42]F.O. 5, Vol. 937, Lyons to Russell, May 5, 1863, No. 370, enclosing Milne to Lyons.

[43]*Ibid.*

[44]*Ibid.*

[45]*Ibid.*

[46]*Ibid.;* cf. *ibid.,* Vol. 1235 A, Lyons to Russell, May 6, 1863, No. 384.

[47]*Ibid.,* Vol. 937, May 23, 1863, No. 299.

[48]*Ibid.,* Lloyd's to Hammond, May 29, 1863.

[49]*Ibid.,* Lyons to Russell, June 16, 1863, No. 547, with enclosures of correspondence of Seward and Welles.

[50]*Ibid.;* O.R.N., Ser. I, Vol. II, 7–9, 11–15, Wilkes to Welles, January 2, 24, 1863. Wilkes complains of not having sufficient vessels to "guard every outlet" of the harbors of the Indies. He was frank in his purpose of blockading neutral ports.

[51]F.O. 5, Vol. 937, Lyons to Russell, June 16, 1863, No. 547.

[52]*Ibid.,* July 3, 1863, No. 378.

[53]*Ibid.,* Lyons to Russell, July 20, 1863, No. 660, enclosing correspondence with Seward.

[54]*Ibid.,* August 3, 1863, No. 690, with enclosures; O.R.N., Ser. I, Vol. II, 358, 569–571.

[55]F.O. 5, Vol. 937, Seward to Lyons, July 29, 1863.

[56]F.O. 97, Vol. 42, September 9, 1863, reports of the law officers of the crown.

[57]F.O. 5, Vol. 1005, Lyons to Russell, June 15, 1863, No. 650.

[58]*Ibid.,* enclosure of Butterfield to Archibald.

[59]*Ibid.,* Lyons to Russell, June 18, 1863, with enclosures.

[60]*Ibid.,* Lyons to Russell, July 17, 1863, No. 650, enclosing Tassara to Seward.

[61]*Ibid.,* enclosing Seward's note to Tassara, July 10, 1863.

[62]*Ibid.,* Lyons to Russell, July 17, 1863, No. 650, with enclosures.

[63]*Ibid.,* Lyons to Russell, July 28, 1863, No. 676, enclosing Lyons to Crawford.

[64]*Ibid.*

[65]*Ibid.,* Lyons to Russell, August 3, 1863, No. 687, enclosing Seward's note, etc.

[66]*Ibid.*

[67]*Ibid.,* Milne to Secretary of the Admiralty, August 3, 1863, No. 504.

[68]*Ibid.,* September 11, 1863, No. 501.

[69]*Ibid.,* Lyons to Russell, November 3, 1863, No. 772, enclosing Lyons to Seward, October 31, 1863.

[70]*Ibid.,* November 3, 1863, No. 773, confidential.

[71]*Ibid.,* No. 614.

[72]*Ibid.,* Lyons to Russell, December 30, 1863, No. 926, enclosing Lyons to Seward.

[73]*Ibid.,* Lyons to Russell, No. 95, enclosing Seward to Lyons, February 2, 1864.

[74]U.S. Con. Des., Nassau, Vol. 12, Hawley to Seward, May 16, 1863, No. 28.

[75]*Ibid.,* Hawley to Seward, May 30, 1863, No. 30.

[76]Parliamentary Debates, Lords, 3rd Ser., Vol. 172, pp. 728–738; Hon. Augustus Charles Hobart-Hampden, *Sketches from My Life* (New York, 1887), p. 122; *Index,* July 2, 1863.

[77]Parl. Deb., Lords, 3rd Ser., Vol. 172, pp. 728–738.

[78]*Ibid.*

[79]*Ibid.*

[80]F.O. 97, Vol. 42, Lyons to Russell, March 10, 1862, No. 171, enclosing letter from Blacker to Crawford, etc.

[81]*Ibid.,* February 28, 1863, No. 7.

[82]*Ibid.,* Lyons to Russell, March 10, 1862, No. 171, with enclosures.

[83]*Ibid.,* Lyons to Russell, March 15, 1862, No. 104, enclosing Seward's note to Lyons.

[84]*Ibid.,* No. 143.

[85]*Ibid.,* Russell to Lords Commissioners of the Admiralty, March 28, 1862.

[86]*Ibid.*, Russell to Admiralty, April 1, 1862.

[87]Parl. Accounts and Papers, U.S., 1863, LXXII, 1–6.

[88]F.O. 97, Vol. 42, Lyons to Russell, April 21, 1862, No. 257; April 26, 1862.

[89]*Ibid.*, Lyons to Russell, April 24, 1862, No. 269, enclosing note to Seward of April 23, 1862.

[90]*Ibid.*, Lyons to Russell, May 8, 1862, No. 310.

[91]*Ibid.*, Lyons to Russell, June 2, 1862, No. 382.

[92]See, for example, *ibid.*, Atherton, Palmer, Phillmore to Russell, February 25, 1863; *ibid.*, Vol. 1211, Thornton to Clarendon, March 9, 1869, April 23, 1870.

[93]The account of the seizure of the *Will o' the Wisp* is based on the correspondence concerning the matter published in the Parl. Accts. and Papers, North America, 1863, LXXII, 1–46; see also F.O. 97, Vol. 47, Phillmore to Russell, September 15, 1862.

[94]F.O. 5, Vol. 1181, Part I, Lyons to Russell, enclosing copies of correspondence of the American officials, November 17, 1863, No. 822.

[95]*Ibid.*, Lyons to Russell, November 3, 1863, No. 781, with enclosures of papers bearing on seizure.

[96]*Ibid.*, Russell to Lyons, December 4, 1863, No. 610.

[97]*Ibid.*, Bateson and Robinson to Russell, December 18, 1863.

[98]*Ibid.*, Gallichan to Russell, December 17, 1863.

[99]*Ibid.*, Vol. 1181, Part II, Lyons to Russell, December 29, 1863, No. 917.

[100]*Ibid.*, Part I, Bishoff and sons to Russell, December 18, 1863.

[101]*Ibid.*, Part II, Lyons to Russell, December 29, 1863, No. 917.

[102]*Ibid.*

[103]*Ibid.*, Russell to Lyons, February 5, 1864, No. 50.

[104]*Ibid.*, Lyons to Russell, March 4, 1864, No. 157, enclosing note to Seward.

[105]*Ibid.*

[106]*Ibid.*, Vol. 1183, Lyons to Russell, March 14, 1864, No. 191, enclosing Seward's and Welles's notes.

[107]*Ibid.*, Lyons to Russell, March 11, 1864, No. 183.

[108]*Ibid.*, Lyons to Russell, June 20, 1864, No. 410.

[109]*Ibid.*, Lyons to Russell, June 28, 1864.

[110]*Ibid.*, Lyons to Russell, July 15, 1864, No. 489, enclosing Scales to Lyons. These cases were finally decided in 1866 and the decision of the lower court upheld, except in the case of the *Volante*, which had been condemned but was now released.

[111]*Ibid.*, enclosing note to Seward of July 11, 1864.

[112]*Ibid.*, enclosing Seward's note to Lyons.

[113]Parl: Accts. and Papers, North America, 1863, LXXII, 1–5.

[114]F.O. 5, Vol. 1184, September 13, 1864, No. 433.

[115]*Ibid.*, Burnley to Russell, October 7 1864, No. 94.

[116]*Ibid.*, Burnley to Russell, October 21, 1864, No. 114, enclosing Seward to Burnley.

[117]*Ibid.*, Lyons to Russell, November 1, 1864, No. 636, enclosing Seward's note to Lyons.

[118]*Ibid.*, Russell to Lyons, December 2, 1864, No. 534, Burnley to Russell, December 27, 1864, No. 173.

[119]*Ibid.*, Burnley to Russell, January 13, 1865, No. 24, enclosing Seward's note.

[120]James B. Scott (ed.), *Prize Cases Decided in United States Supreme Court, 1789–1917* (Carnegie Endowment for International Peace, Oxford, 1923), III, 1662–1667.

[121]*Ibid.*, pp. 1167–1168.

[122]*Ibid.*, pp. 1168–1169.

[123]*Ibid.*, pp. 1725–1738.

[124]See F.O. 5, Vol. 1185, Thornton to Foreign Office, June 11, 1870.

[125]*Ibid.*, Vol. 1180, Butterfield to Archibald, March 6, 1863, No. 23.

[126]*Ibid.*

[127]*Ibid.*, Russell to Lyons, April 3, 1863.

[128]*Ibid.*, Lyons to Russell, April 24, 1863, No. 343, with note from Seward; *ibid.*, Lyons to Russell, June 22, 1863, No. 579.

[129]*Ibid.*, Vol. 1185, Thornton to Clarendon, August 30, 1869.

[130]London *Times,* April 2, 1863.

[131]*Ibid.*

[132]*London Economist,* April 4, 1863.

[133]Lord Newton, *Lord Lyons: A Record of British Diplomacy,* 2 vols. (London, 1913); F.O. 5, Vol. 1235A, No. 171.

[134]*Ibid.*, Lyons to Russell, March 30, 1863, No. 275, enclosing Seward's note.

[135]*Ibid.*, Archibald to Lyons, April 6, 1863, No. 107; Lyons to Russell, April 13, 1863, No. 311, with enclosure of note to Seward.

[136]See below.

[137]F.O. 5, Vol. 1235A, Lyons to Russell, April 17, 1863, Nos. 321, 322; J. P. Baxter 3rd, "Papers Relating to Belligerent and Neutral Rights [Seward to the President, April 24, 1863]," *American Historical Review,* XXXIV (1928).

[138]See below.

[139]F.O. 5, Vol. 1235A, Padget to F.O., May 11, 1863, with enclosures.

[140]See *ibid.*, Lyons to Russell, April 21, No. 334.

[141]*Ibid.*, Vol. 1235C, Edwards to Lyons, August 1, 1863, No. 256.

[142]For the case of the *Dolphin,* see below.

[143]Decision of *Peterhoff* case in pamphlet form, New York, 1863; also in British F.O. 5, Vol. 1235C, March 11, 1864.

[144]*Prize Cases, etc.,* pp. 1629–1653.

[145]See, for example, F.O. 5, Vol. 1235C, Russell to Lyons, April 27, 1864.

[146]Quoted by Bentinck in Parliament, April 23, 1863, Parl. Deb., Commons, 3rd Ser., Vol. 170, pp. 580–660.

[147]London *Times,* April 18, 1863.

[148]Parl. Deb., Lords, 3rd Ser., Vol. 170, pp. 554–600, April 23, 1863.

[149]London *Times,* April 24, 1863.

[150]U.S. Des., France, Vol. 53, Dayton to Seward, April 27, 1863, No. 302.

[151]F.O. 5, Vol. 1235, Burns, McBayne, and Wigan to Russell, April 23, 1863.

[152]F.O. 5, Vol. 935, Lyons to Russell, May 8, 1863, No. 388, enclosing note to Seward.

[153]*Ibid.*, Lyons to Russell, June 12, 1863, No. 527, enclosing printed copy of court proceedings and decision in the case of the *Dolphin.*

[154]F.O. 5, Vol. 935, Russell to Lyons, August 8, 1863, No. 442.

[155]See Owsley, *op. cit., passim.*

[156]See F.O. 5, Vol. 995, Isaac Campbell and Company, to Russell, March 6, 1862; *ibid.*, Lyons to Russell, March 24, 1862, No. 204; *ibid.*, Russell to Isaac Campbell and Company, May 26, 1862.

[157]The *U.S. vs. the Schooner, Stephen Hart and Her Cargo, etc.,* New York, 1863; F.O. 5, Vol. 995, Lyons to Russell, August 3, 1863, No. 150, enclosure.

[158]*Prize Cases, etc.,* p. 1588.

[159]F.O. 5, Vol. 994, Archibald to Russell, February 12, 1863, No. 36; *ibid.*, Vol. 1186, No. 2, Lyons to Seward, February 25, 1863; *ibid.*, Vol. 994, Begbie to Russell, February 27, 1863; *ibid.*, Begbie to Hammond, February 27, 1863.

[160]*Ibid.*

[161]*Ibid.*, Partout to Russell, March 9, 1863.

[162]*Ibid.*, No. 134.

[163]*Ibid.*, Edwards to Russell, August 1, 1863, No. 147.

[164]*Ibid.*, Russell to Lyons, December 29, 1863, No. 640.

[165]*Ibid.*, February 20, 1864, No. 84.

[166]*Ibid.*, Vol. 994, Archibald to Russell, January 22, 1864, enclosing printed decision in the case of the *Springbok*.

[167]*Prize Cases, etc.*, pp. 1609–1629.

[168]For previous examples see F.O. 5, Vol. 1235B, Lyons to Russell, May 8, 1863, No. 387, case of Redgate and Elsworth taken from *Peterhoff; ibid.*, Lyons to Russell, May 11, 1863, No. 409; *ibid.*, Lyons to Russell, May 19, 1863, No. 443; *ibid.*, Lyons to Russell, July 17, 1863.

[169]*Ibid.*, Vol. 996, Lyons to Russell, January 26, 1864, No. 52, enclosing note to Seward, etc.

[170]*Ibid.*, Seward to Lyons, January 11, 1864.

[171]*Ibid.*, Lyons to Russell, February 27, 1864, No. 140, enclosing Archibald to Lyons, February 26, 1864.

[172]*Ibid.*

[173]*Ibid.*, Russell to Lyons, March 9, 1864, No. 107.

[174]*Ibid.*, Lyons to Russell, No. 233, enclosing Lyons to Seward, April 5, 1864.

[175]*Ibid.*, Russell to Lyons, April 15, 1864, No. 175.

[176]*Ibid.*, Lyons to Russell, June 28, 1864, No. 440; Lyons to Russell, No. 109, enclosing Seward to Burnley, October 15, 1864.

[177]*Ibid.*, Vol. 1149, Lyons to Russell, January 26, 1864, No. 54, with enclosures.

[178]*Ibid.*, Lyons to Russell, February 1, 1864, No. 73.

[179]*Ibid.*, Vol. 1150, No. 170.

[180]*Ibid.*, Lyons to Russell, No. 171.

[181]*Ibid.*, Lyons to Russell, March 22, 1864, No. 206.

[182]*Ibid.*, Lyons to Russell, April 5, 1864, No. 232.

[183]*Ibid.*, Vol. 1153, Lyons to Russell, May 31, 1864, No. 343.

[184]*Ibid.*, Vol. 1152, Lyons to Russell, May 23, 1864, No. 331.

[185]*Ibid.*, Vol. 1149, January 25, 1864.

[186]*Ibid.*, Vol. 1150, March 15, 1864.

[187]*Ibid.*

[188]*Ibid.*, Vol. 1149, Russell to Adams, March 9, 1864; cf. *ibid.*, Vol. 1150, Russell to Adams, April 11, 1864.

[189]See, *ibid.*, Adams to Russell, April 16, 1864.

[190]*Ibid.*, Vol. 1152, May 9, 1864, No. 302.

[191]For example, *ibid.*, Vol. 1153, Lyons to Russell, May 31, 1864, No. 345.

[192]*Ibid.*, Vol. 1153, Lyons to Russell, June 17, 1864, No. 399, enclosing Welles's order, etc.

[193]See, for example, *O.R.N.*, Ser. I, Vol. I, 470–471, 493–496, 502–504, 569–570, 571–572; *ibid.*, II, 7–9, 12–15, 97–98, 127–128, 188–189.

IV

The Pillars of Agrarianism

Democracy Unlimited

The Pillars of Agrarianism*

Since the appearance of *I'll Take My Stand* in 1930, the Agrarians have been subjected to a fusillade of criticism. I suspect that our philosophy as set forth in that book and in later essays, published in certain periodicals, especially in the Distributist-Agrarian *American Review,* has irked the devotees of our technological civilization. Venturing an even stronger word, it begins to appear that the doctrines announced in *I'll Take My Stand* have actually *infuriated* these people. Just recently, on an important examination for a certain scholarship, it seems that the committee inquired of each candidate what he thought of agrarianism. It was noteworthy that the successful candidate summed up his opinion by saying that the advocates of such a system were "cock-eyed." One of the candidates who was not only rejected, but was urged not to apply again on the grounds of age (he has just celebrated his twenty-second birthday, and the age limit of the scholarship is several years above this age) answered that as far as he understood it he heartily approved of agrarianism. The most recent and, perhaps, the most violent attack upon the advocates of an agrarian state is that of H. L. Mencken. While Mencken's attack is so violent and lacking in restraint that it does not fall far short of libel, I have no desire to single him out as a critic worthy of an answer. However, I must confess that Mencken's attack, because it is typical—outside of the billingsgate—of those coming from the pillars of Industrialism, has prompted, to a certain extent, this essay. Such essays as his, appearing with amazing regularity, have without doubt troubled the mind of the neophyte, and, in many cases, have utterly confused him and made him lose sight of the principles and specific objectives of agrarianism.

Few if any of the Agrarians have expended any effort in answering the criticism of those who attack our principles. From the beginning we have pursued the attack rather than the defence; nor have

*In the summer of 1952 Mr. Owsley said to the editor of *Shenandoah* that this essay was "an attempt to state some of the basic principles of agrarianism" which were agreed upon by the contributors of *I'll Take My Stand.* "In writing that, I was attempting to establish a picture of a balanced economy—a balance between agriculture and industry" (III, 23). [Ed.]

we—if I may continue the military figure of speech—seen fit to consolidate our positions. However, it seems to me very proper, at the present time, for the sake of those who have been confused, or those whom we hope to draw into our way of thinking, to restate and elaborate the fundamental economic and political principles on which an agrarian society will probably have to rest in the United States, and most particularly in the South.

I shall not attempt to restate and discuss all the principles and programs of our hoped-for agrarian society, for this, as John Crowe Ransom has said in another connection, would indeed institute an infinite series. My purpose is to confine my discussion to the five great pillars upon which this society will have to rest. Before going into an exposition of the foundation of a restored agrarianism in the South (or other regions), it will be well to restate our definition of an agrarian state as set forth in the introduction of *I'll Take My Stand:*

> Opposed to the industrial society is the agrarian, which does not stand in particular need of definition. An agrarian society is hardly one that has no use at all for industries, professional vocations, for scholars and artists and for the life of the cities. Technically, perhaps, an agrarian society is one in which agriculture is the leading vocation, whether for wealth, for pleasure, or prestige—a form of labour that is pursued with intelligence and leisure, and that becomes the model to which the other forms approach as well as they may.

I shall edit this definition. We had in mind a society in which, indeed, agriculture was the leading vocation; but the implication was more than this. We meant that the agrarian population and the people of the agricultural market towns must dominate the social, cultural, economic, and political life of the state and give tone to it. Today, the Scandinavian countries are fair examples of such a state. France before the world war was a most beautiful example, where 30,000,000 people lived on the land and 10,000,000 lived in the towns and cities engaging in commerce and industry. Even today, after the disastrous war and its effects upon mechanization of industry, France presents the best balanced economic system of any first-class nation in the world. The ownership of property is more widely distributed there than in any nation comparable in wealth and population. Governments may rise and fall, but the French peasant and farmer seems eternal when compared to those of the United

States. Today there are about 350,000 persons unemployed in France as against hardly less than 12,000,000 in the United States. Yet the United States has less than three times as large a population as France.

Before entering into the details of our fundamental program, let me say that we are not exotics, nor a peculiar sect living in a vacuum, untouched by public affairs, merely irked by the noise of factory wheels and machinery. We fully realize that our program cannot be put into operation until matters affecting the nation as a whole are set aright. Everything which affects the agrarian interests also touches industry, finance, and commerce. Our program, therefore, intimately involves national problems. We are on the side of those who know that the common enemy of the people, of their government, their liberty, and their property, must be abated. This enemy is a system which allows a relatively few men to control most of the nation's wealth and to regiment virtually the whole population under their anonymous holding companies and corporations, and to control government by bribery or intimidation. Just how these giant organizations should be brought under the control of law and ethics we are not agreed. We are, however, agreed with the English Distributists that the most desirable objective is to break them down into small units owned and · controlled by real people. We want to see property restored and the proletariat thus abolished and communism made impossible. The more widespread is the ownership of property, the more happy and secure will be the people and the nation. But is such a decentralization in physical property as well as in ownership possible? We are confident that it is, however much we may differ among ourselves as to the degree of decentralization that will prove desirable in any given industry. We are all convinced, though we hold no doctrinaire principles as to method, that these robber barons of the twentieth century will have to be reduced and civilized in some form or other before any program can be realized by our state and federal governments.

While we are deeply interested in the whole nation, yet, as Agrarians and Southerners, we are not desirous of launching a crusade to convert or coerce the other sections of the country into our way of thinking. We therefore, while inviting all who wish, to go with us, have a fundamental program for the South to which I have referred as the five pillars of agrarianism.

II

The first item in our agrarian program is to rehabilitate the population actually living on the soil. This farming population falls into several categories: large and small planters; large and small farmers, both black and white; black and white tenants who own their stock and tools, and rent land; black and white tenants who own no stock or tools, but are furnished everything and get a share of the crop for their labour. Finally, there is the wage-hand either coloured or white who is furnished a house, and perhaps food and a certain cash wage.

Today the farm population in the South whether wage-hand or large planter is in a precarious and often miserable state. The exploitations by the industrial interests through high tariffs and other special favours from the federal government, which force the farmer to buy in a protected market and sell in a world market, and the periodic industrial depressions following in close order since the Civil War, have greatly oppressed the Southern agricultural population. The majority of the planters do not really own their lands; the real owners are the life insurance companies or the banks. The payment of the interest on his mortgage leaves the almost mythical landowner little on which to subsist. Repayment of the principal is out of the question. Actually, most of the planters are without credit, and are no better off than the tenant or share-cropper. In fact the renter and share-cropper frequently come out of debt with some cash, their corn, sorghum, potatoes, pigs, cows, and other live stock above the board. The fate of the small or large farmer is much better. As a rule he is thrifty, owes less than the other classes, and lives to a great extent off his farm. Sometimes he sends his children to college, especially the agricultural college. His house is usually comfortable and sometimes painted. For the farmer as a class, there is less need of state intervention in his affairs than in the affairs of the tenant and planter classes. Yet a new political economy is necessary for him as well as the planters and tenants, or he will eventually lose his land and status. This new political economy will be discussed later. As for the planter class, there are many whom even the new political economy cannot save. Their equity in the once broad acres which they held in fee simple is too small. It will be best for them to liquidate and begin over as small farmers under the plan which I shall presently offer in connection with the tenant farmers.

The most serious problem, however, is not the bankrupt planters but the tenant-farmers, black or white, because of their great number. I do not know the exact ratio between the tenant-farmer class and the landholding class; but I have heard it said that 75% of the population living on the land in the South are tenants. If this estimate is too high, it will not long remain so unless strong measures are taken, for the tenant class has been increasing so rapidly in recent years that it threatens to engulf the entire agricultural population of the South. Most of the white tenants were once landowners, but have been thrust near to the bottom of the economic and social order by the loss of their lands through industrial exploitation, depression, and, frequently, through high pressure salesmanship of radio, automobile, and farm machinery agents. Industrialism has persuaded, or created a public opinion which has virtually driven, the farmer to accept industrial tastes and standards of living and forced him to mortgage and then to lose his farm. Battered old cars, dangling radio aerials, rust-eaten tractors, and abandoned threshing machines and hay balers scattered forlornly about are mute witnesses to the tragedy of industrialism's attempt to industrialize the farmer and planter.

A portion of the lower class of white tenants, especially the adults, are beyond redemption. Through diseased tonsils, adenoids, unbalanced rations, tuberculosis, hook worm, malaria, and the social diseases, many have been made into irresponsible, sometimes—but not often—vicious people who are lacking in mental alertness and the constancy of will to enable them to till the soil without close supervision. Such people would not be able to make a living on land which might be granted or sold to them on easy terms by the government. However, the county and state public health departments should be enabled to take the steps necessary to salvage the children of such families in order that they may become owners of small farms and good citizens when of proper age. It is this class of whites in particular, who own no stock, plant no gardens, raise no chickens, who are frequently and perhaps accurately described as the "po' white trash."

The higher class white tenants, those who own their stock and cattle and have their gardens and truck patches, are ready to become the proprietors of farms. Frequently they are good farmers and send their children through the high schools. They are probably in the majority in most of the Southern states and, as I have suggested,

their families have been landowners: they were, in short, once a part
of the Southern yeomanry; and for a nation or section to allow these
people to sink lower and lower in the social and economic scale is to
destroy itself.

As for the Negro tenant class, the majority of the Agrarians agree
that the really responsible farmers among them who know how to
take care of the soil and who own their own stock and cattle, should
be made proprietors of small farms.

The planters and large farmers who are left after liquidating
their debts will still have an abundance of tenants who work well
under supervision, but who are irresponsible and incapable of taking
care of themselves without supervision. In the South, the wagehand
is usually the son of a tenant. He is frequently young and more
intelligent than the lower tenant class. He should, where his intelligence and sense of responsibility permit, be homesteaded like the
better-class tenant. Otherwise, he should be kept where he is, under
the supervision of one who has good judgement and a sense of responsibility.

Now, instead of the federal or state government spending $2500
in building a house for the homesteaders, with whom they are very
gingerly experimenting, and several hundred dollars on small tracts
of land, let the national and state governments buy up all the lands
owned by insurance companies and absentee landlords—which are
being destroyed rapidly by erosion—and part of the land owned by
the large planters who are struggling to save a portion of their lands,
and give every landless tenant who can qualify, 80 acres of land,
build him a substantial hewn log house and barn, fence him off
twenty acres for a pasture, give him two mules and two milk cows
and advance him $300 for his living expenses for one year. By this
means 500,000 persons can be rehabilitated in one year at $1,500 a
family or $300 per person. An outright gift of the land is advocated
to the homesteader with one condition attached: the land must
never be sold or mortgaged, and when abandoned it should auto-
matically escheat to the state which should be under immediate
obligation to rehabilitate another worthy family.

The next step would be to bring the technologically unemployed,
intelligent city people back to the country. First, those who have had
experience as farmers should be rehabilitated; next, but relatively
few at a time, those without experience should be permitted to become tenants on plantations, whereupon, if such tenants and their

families should feel that they would like to go on, the government should grant them a homestead with sufficient stock and cattle and enough cash to subsist them one year. It seems quite clear to the Agrarians that technological unemployment is destined to increase with rapid acceleration until the majority of the population once employed in industry will be thrown out of the system. The government will be faced with perhaps three alternatives: it could put these permanently unemployed on a dole—until the government becomes bankrupt or an orderly slave state is established; it could refuse the dole and have a revolution; or it could rehabilitate the unemployed by giving them small farms. We, as interested citizens of the United States, urge this last policy upon the government as the only permanent relief from permanent technological unemployment. As Agrarians we urge it as an opportunity to restore the healthy balance of population between city and country, which will aid in the restoration of agrarianism and in the restoration and preservation of civilization.

Next in order of importance but simultaneous with the first step should be the rehabilitation of the soil. We, in common with the agricultural colleges of the country, urge that small and large farmer, small and large planter, regard the enrichment and preservation of the soil as a first duty. Those who own the soil must be held accountable in some way for their stewardship. Undrained, unterraced, single-cropped land, and lack of reforestation, should be *prima facie* evidence that the homesteader is not a responsible person and his land should, after fair warning and action in chancery court, escheat to the state. As for those farmers and planters who acquire their land by purchase or inheritance, a heavy suspended fine should be imposed upon them; and unless the planter or farmer remedies the abuses within a reasonable time or gives good reason why he has not been able to do so, the fine should be collected. The county agent and three men appointed by the state department of agriculture, should serve in each county as a kind of court to pass on such matters, and appeal from their decision should be allowed to go to chancery court. In short, land must be conserved for future generations and not exploited, as has too often been the practice, by the present owners. Another drastic proposal which would aid in conserving the land as well as preventing its being alienated or becoming encumbered with debt, is that by state constitutional amendment, no land could be mortgaged, except by consent of a court of equity; nor should any kind of speculative sale be permitted. It must become impossible for land to be sold to real estate and insurance companies or banks. In thus making alienation of the soil difficult and its proper management necessary, I am suggesting a modified form of feudal tenure where, in theory, the king or state has a paramount interest in the land.

When the rehabilitation and conservation of the soil and stability of tenure have been provided for, the next consideration must be the products of the soil.

Subsistence farming must be the first objective of every man who controls a farm or plantation. The land must first support the people who till it; then it must support their stock. In the olden days when there were no money taxes or mortgages to meet, nor automobiles and fine carriages to buy, nor life and fire insurance to keep up, and when the priest and the teacher were paid in kind, this type of farming, if carried on with the scientific knowledge available today, would have supported the grandest of establishments. But today, a minimum outlay of cash is necessary even for those fortunate souls who are without debts: taxes, insurance, clothing, certain articles of luxury, and medical attention require cash.

After subsistence come the money crops. In the South these crops, too often planted at the expense of the subsistence crops, are peanuts, rice, sugar cane, tobacco, and cotton. Cotton and tobacco, the two leading staples, can be raised in the South in almost limitless quantities and must always depend, to a large extent, upon the foreign or world market. Considerable talk has been going its rounds concerning the danger of losing the foreign market because of crop limitation. Crop limitation, however, has no bearing at the present time, at least, upon the problem of cotton and tobacco. There are between nine and twelve million surplus bales of cotton and large quantities of tobacco above current crops, stored in the United States and there can hardly be any question about loss of world markets because of crop limitation when we are unable to dispose of this terrific surplus. Further, considerable alarm has been expressed concerning the inability of American cotton growers to compete with Russia, Egypt, Brazil, Turkey, China, and India. This is a groundless fear, for even in the days when the South produced the scrub variety of cotton, the world depended largely upon American cotton, because, with the exception of limited areas in Egypt, the Sudan, and South Africa, no part of the world could raise as much cotton per acre or as good a fibre as the American South. Now that Coker of South Carolina and other plant breeders have produced an upland staple with a fibre about two inches in length, which will grow on any soil in the South, and which is being rapidly introduced everywhere, there can hardly be any serious competition with the South, as far as cheapness of production, quality, and quantity are concerned.

Everything being equal in the world markets, the South could soon drive its competitors out, as it did until past the turn of the century when other factors entered. These factors will have to be dealt with intelligently by the government of the United States or by the regional governments to be discussed later, else the South will be wiped out economically. One factor is that within the last twenty years America has ceased to be a debtor nation and become a creditor. As a debtor we shipped cotton to England, France, or Germany which created foreign exchange with which to pay the principal and interest on our debts and purchase foreign goods. The South could raise large cotton and tobacco crops and be sure that the world markets would take all. As soon as we became a creditor we could no longer ship our cotton and tobacco with the assurances of a sale. England and Germany and France and even Japan, wherever possible, have bought cotton from those countries which owed them money. This loss of a foreign market was seemingly made permanent by the rising tariff scale in America, which effectually cut off foreign goods from our markets, and thereby destroyed the chief sources of foreign exchange in this country with which Southern staples could be bought. The tariff, which was a guarantee of the home markets for the industrial interests of the country, principally located in the East and a belt following the Great Lakes, has been the greatest permanent factor in destroying the foreign market on which the South chiefly depended.

It must be said, at this point, that such a situation was envisaged in 1833 when South Carolina nullified the tariff law of 1832, and again when the Southern states seceded from the Union in 1861. The belief that industrialism, as soon as it got control of the federal government, would not only exploit agriculture but would destroy the South was behind the whole secession movement. Today, we Agrarians witness the fulfillment of the jeremiads of Robert Barnwell Rhett and John C. Calhoun. We, however, are not hoping for or advocating another break-up of the Union; but we are demanding a fair hearing for the fundamental cause of the South—now that slavery can no longer befog the real issue. If the industrial interests continue the monopoly of the home market and thereby cause the agricultural South (and West) to pay a much higher price for goods than the world price level, we must have a *quid pro quo:* a subsidy on every bale of cotton and pound of tobacco or other important agricultural products shipped abroad, based on the difference between world and domestic prices. In order that foreign countries shall have sufficient American exchange with which to purchase our staple farm exports we further insist that all farm products and raw material shipped into the United States be used in creating foreign exchange with which cotton and tobacco may be purchased and exported. (James Waller in *A New Deal for the South* suggests this technique of establishing parity between agriculture and industry.) In short, the South—and, if I may be so bold as to speak for the agrarian interests of another section, the West—must have agriculture put upon the same basis as industry.

III

With such political economy the South would soon become one of the most important parts of the world, and it would add much to the prosperity of the other sections of the country. It is doubtful, however, whether such intelligent legislation is possible under a government so dominated by particular sectional interests.

For that reason—which is founded upon the history of the last one hundred and forty-six years—we are striving for a new constitutional deal which will help put the several sections on equal footing and prevent the exploitation of one by the other. We are in the front ranks of those who insist that the United States is less a nation than an empire made up of a congeries of regions marked off by geographic, climatic, and racial characteristics. It has been suggested that New England would form a distinct region, the Middle States another, the Middle West another, the Rocky Mountain and Pacific States another, perhaps, and the South another. Of course the region to which a state wished to affiliate would be determined by a plebiscite. W. Y. Elliott of Harvard suggests that the regional governments be granted the present powers of the states, and that the states themselves be deprived of anything save administrative functions. He further suggests that one set of courts should serve both as federal and state courts, thus eliminating the maze of courts by which justice is delayed and defeated and encouragement thereby given to lynch law.

Mr. Elliott suggests that in the new set-up the federal government retain its present powers much more clearly defined. He further urges that all concurrent powers be eliminated. As far as I know, Mr. Elliott is not an agrarian; but his plan is essentially what the Agrarians have urged constantly, except in the matter of division of power between federal and regional governments. His plan seems very reasonable and conservative. Something like it will have to be adopted if the United States is to endure. The Agrarians, I believe, advocate that, in the redivision of powers in a new constitutional convention, the regional governments should have much more autonomy than the states have ever had. The federal government should have supreme control over war and peace, the army and navy, interregional or even interstate commerce, banking, currency, and foreign affairs. On the other hand, the sections should have equal representation in the federal legislative body and in the election of the president and in the cabinet. The legislative body should be composed of a senate only and should be elected by the regional congresses. Finally, the regions should have control of the tariff: that is, the several regions should have an equal share in making the tariff, which would be in the form of a treaty or agreement between all the sections, somewhat in the fashion of the late Austro-Hungarian tariff treaties. In case one region, say the South, failed to agree to the tariff treaty, then the South should be exempted from the operation of the law until an agreement could be reached. Such an arrangement does not mean that there would be interregional tariffs; it does mean that, if the South should have a lower tariff than the other regions, goods imported through the South from abroad would have to pay an extra duty on entering the other regions operating under the treaty. There would be some smuggling across the Potomac and Ohio, but not any more than through Mexico and Canada.

The Supreme Court, like the proposed Senate, should have equal representation from all the sections, regardless of political parties, and the members of the Supreme Court should not be the creatures of the Senate or the president, but, like the Senate, should be appointed by the regional governors subject to the ratification of the regional legislature, which also should be only a senate. The courts

—that is, courts of appeal and circuit courts—should be constituted regionally, but should be considered both federal and regional, sitting one time as federal and one time as regional.

In our agrarian program, not only does it seem necessary to grant more local autonomy because of differences of economic interest, but because of differences on social and racial interests as well. Under such a government, the Civil War would not have been possible, nor would Reconstruction and the ensuing difficulties and hatreds have arisen. And what is more to the point at the present time, Communist interference in the Southern courts, and even conservative interference from other sections, would hardly take place. In other words, the Agrarians—who come nearer representing the opinion of Southern people than do newspapers largely subsidized by Northern-owned power companies and Wall-Street-owned banks, or the Southern liberals fawning for the favour of these corporations or of other powerful Northern groups—believe that under regional government each section will find it less difficult to attend to its own social and economic problems, and thereby will be encouraged to restore the old friendships which were crippled or destroyed under our present system.

Let me sum up. The five pillars on which it would appear that an agrarian society must rest are: (1) the restoration of the people to the land and the land to the people by the government purchasing lands held by loan companies, insurance companies, banks, absentee landlords, and planters whose estates are hopelessly incumbered with debt, and granting to the landless tenants, who are sufficiently able and responsible to own and conserve the land, a homestead of 80 acres with sufficient stock to cultivate the farm, and cash enough to feed and clothe the family one year; (2) the preservation and restoration of the soil by the use of fines and escheat, and by making land practically inalienable and non-mortgageable—that is by restoring a modified feudal tenure where the state had a paramount interest in the land and could exact certain services and duties from those who possessed the land; (3) the establishment of a balanced agriculture where subsistence crops are the first consideration and the money crops are of secondary importance; (4) the establishment of a just political economy, where agriculture is placed upon an equal basis with industry, finance, and commerce; (5) the creation of regional governments possessed of more autonomy than the states, which will sustain the political economy fitted for each region, and which will prevent much sectional friction and sectional exploitation.

Once this foundation is securely built, the agrarian society will grow upon it spontaneously and with no further state intervention beyond that to which an agricultural population is accustomed. The old communities, the old churches, the old songs would arise from their moribund slumbers. Art, music, and literature could emerge into the sunlight from the dark cramped holes where industrial insecurity and industrial insensitiveness have often driven them. There would be a sound basis for statesmanship to take the place of demagoguery and corrupt politics. Leisure, good manners, and the good way of life might again become ours.

Democracy Unlimited*

The United States Government was founded upon two great concepts of free government: first, the theory of the natural rights of man; and second, the doctrine of a tangible, written constitution expressing the sovereign will of the people, which embodied the natural rights and other rights agreed upon and which specified clearly the structure of government. These concepts were thoroughly developed in the seventeenth and eighteenth centuries, in both continental Europe and Britain. The spokesman who most clearly stated the basic philosophy of free constitutional government and who most profoundly influenced the builders of the American government was John Locke in his essays on human understanding and especially his *Two Treatises of Government.*

According to the doctrine of natural rights, man is endowed by the Creator with certain rights which neither individual nor government can take from him except by violence and usurpation. Such rights were in our early history spoken of as inalienable or inherent rights. The term inherent rights seems to mean that man as *man* has certain rights and obligations that are as much a part of him as his skin and that without these inherent attributes he is stripped of those characteristics that differentiate him from the lower animals. Locke in his *Second Treatise of Government* specified very broad categories of natural rights; life, liberty, property. Out of these, when he discussed the necessity of government and the social compact or constitution, he derived popular sovereignty or the right of a people to choose their own government. From the right of the people to rule, he derived the principle that the legislature, the representative of the popular will, had the sole right to legislate. From the principle that the representatives of the people were the sole possessors of the right to legislate, Locke derived the doctrine of the right of revolution—when such legislative power was usurped by other departments of government or when the legislature overstepped repeatedly the social compact or constitution.

Our revolutionary forbears followed Locke very closely. The

*This essay by Mr. Owsley was originally the Blazer Lecture for 1955 at the University of Kentucky, and it was given at the Phi Beta Kappa meeting of the University of Alabama chapter in the spring of 1956. [Ed.]

Declaration of Independence practically quotes portions of the *Second Treatise of Government*. A corollary doctrine of natural rights was the theory of limited sovereignty of government. In other words, under the natural rights theory, government has limitations placed upon its operations. If man was endowed with certain rights, there was the unavoidable implication that there were reserved to him certain private areas into which government could not rightfully enter except in the capacity of protector. Without the corollary principle of limited sovereignty the doctrine of natural rights becomes an abstraction and ceases to have any real meaning.

The natural rights theory has been under severe criticism for overemphasizing rights and not emphasizing the duties that form the other half of each right. Nor is there any denial that the greatest national sin from the very beginning until the present day has been our incessant screaming for our rights, whether natural or constitutional, but not the rights of others whose screaming we try to drown out. It should not be forgotten, however, that the natural rights doctrine was not developed in a vacuum or as a beautiful abstraction. It was perfected as a weapon to fight oppression and to justify revolution against tyranny.

But the doctrine of natural rights, especially, as elaborated by John Locke and his American disciples carried always the reciprocal duty of every individual to respect the rights of others. Another criticism is that the doctrine of natural rights when reduced to its ultimate terms is a doctrine of moral license in that it permits a person to indulge all his animal appetites and passions without restraints. Such criticism sets up a straw man, for the old American doctrine of natural rights that forms one of the basic concepts of the American system of government, state and national, carries no such implications. The revolutionary fathers such as Thomas Jefferson, Patrick Henry, Sam Adams, John Adams, George Washington, and their political father, John Locke, always referred to natural rights as a special endowment of man from the Divine Creator. That is, the doctrine of natural rights which is the basic political theory of our government was considered of divine origin. Consequently, although the eighteenth-century philosophers were usually deists, they constructed their theory of human rights and duties chiefly from the concepts of justice and ethics of two great humane sources: the Greek and Roman philosophers and statesmen, and the Judaeo-Christian Bible and religions. In other words, the criticism of the natural rights theory is obviously

directed at a current perversion of the doctrine in which people are
reduced to the same level as the rabbits, white rats, and frogs of the
psychological laboratories.

The theory of natural rights was the springboard to our independence. Of even greater importance, perhaps, it was the frame of
reference for our constitutional system of government. In keeping
with the doctrine of natural rights and limited sovereignty in fram-
ing the United States Constitution, there were many limitations
placed upon the operation of government. In other words, our
political system, contrary to an ever-widening and uninformed opinion, is not intended to be an unlimited democracy. The majority
under our system has neither the constitutional nor moral right to
work its unhampered will upon the individual and the numerical
minority. Certain important restraints were placed upon the federal
government.

The first great self-imposed limitation upon our political system
was the formalizing of the federal principle in the structure of our
government. The federal principle, of course, is the division of powers between two systems of government within the nation. In the
United States it is the division of powers between the state and the
central government. In establishing our system of government during
and after the revolution, those matters which closely affected the
lives of the people and which by custom if not law had remained
under the jurisdiction of the colony were retained under the jurisdiction of the state. Those of a general nature were assigned to the
national government. So concerned were our political leaders over
the permanence of the principle underlying this division of power
that the Tenth Amendment to the federal Constitution was added as
soon as possible after the original constitution was adopted. This
amendment stated that "The powers not delegated to the United
States by the Constitution, nor prohibited by it to the States, are
reserved to the States respectively, or the people." Chief Justice Marshall—among other statesmen of the early republic—characterized
this division of powers as divided sovereignty. Such division of powers was inevitable in a union in which the states were the creators of
the union. But there was also a great element of deliberate purpose
in this structural division of powers. The founding fathers were convinced that a large country with so many divergent interests as the
United States could not be justly or democratically governed except
by leaving the control of local matters to those who understood them

at first hand and who would be most affected by laws relating to such matters. Furthermore, these men lived in an age of centralized government and despotism. Centralization was synonymous with despotism, for America had just been the recipient of the abuses of centralization at the hands of the British Imperial Government, which had asserted the right of unrestrained power over the colonies in legislation and administration. These men of the early republic had seen how power corrupts government and how absolute power corrupts absolutely. They were also fully aware of man's love of power and how in government every man from bureau clerk to chief executive was a potential empire builder and aggrandizer. The division of powers between state and national governments checks this struggle for power, this tendency of entrenched government to overleap the barriers of natural rights and constitutional restraints and brush aside the principle of limited sovereignty.

The equal representation of the states in the Senate, a feature of the federal principle, is a powerful structural check on a majority swayed by impulse and purely local or sectional interest. So, too, is the method of selecting the president in cases where no candidate receives a majority—that is, by the House of Representatives voting by states, each state having one vote.

The establishment in state and national government of three coequal and theoretically independent departments was also intended as a restraint on the concentration and abuse of power. It was thought that the three departments would not be able to conspire together to gain power, but that they would counteract one another. It was certainly assumed that it would be virtually impossible for one department to gain control of the others and thus gain control of the government. The development of political parties was not fully comprehended, where one party gains control of all departments of government, both state and national, from county sheriff to chief executive, and is thereby able to ignore many of the self-imposed restraints of the Constitution and the political theory of natural rights that lies behind the Constitution.

In addition to the structural checks, there were very specific provisions in the Constitution devised for the purpose of protecting individuals and minorities from the transgressions of a heedless majority. The founders of our political system were fully aware that untrammeled power, whether wielded by king or by the masses was, in the long run, destructive of freedom. Thus were incorporated in both state and national constitutions bills of rights, which institutionalized and legalized much of the political theory of natural rights, and in this way placed protecting walls about the individual. Furthermore, four principal restraints were embodied in the federal Constitution for the purpose of preventing the headlong majority from overrunning minority rights. These were: first, the establishment of a slow-moving and complex amendment procedure, requiring a three-fourths affirmative vote of the states to amend the Constitution; second, the requirement of a two-thirds vote of the Senate to remove an official in impeachment proceedings; third, the presidential veto; and fourth, the two-thirds majority vote of the Senate necessary to ratify a treaty.

In explanation of the history and motives behind these constitutional checks upon the acts of the majority, let us begin with the amending process. A two-thirds vote of Congress is necessary to propose an amendment, or two-thirds of the states could request Congress to call a national convention to amend or rewrite the Constitution, and Congress is instructed by the Constitution to call such a convention when thus requested. Finally, when a proposed amendment is submitted to the states, a three-fourths affirmative vote is required for its ratification.

This slow process of amending the Constitution, always requiring a large majority vote at each stage, was based upon two important concepts of the nature of the Constitution: first, that the Constitution embodied most of the fundamental principles of a free central government and that, therefore, whatever changes or amendments were made should not contradict or weaken any of these basic principles; second, that the Constitution also contained numerous compromises between economic groups and geographical sections. For clarity an example of constitutional compromises between groups is cited: equal representation in the United States Senate and representation based upon population in the House of Representatives and the electoral college were a compromise between the large and small states and a further guarantee of the federal principle.

The amending process was slow but not meant to make constitutional change excessively burdensome and practically impossible— something the Supreme Court has of late years done, by its decision that the provision of the Constitution instructing Congress to call a constitutional convention is permissive and not mandatory. The purpose of the slow procedure in amendment was to afford time for serious study and reflection to determine whether the proposed amendment conflicted with the fundamental principles of the Constitution, or violated any of the great compromises which had been the basis of agreement in the constitutional convention, and which were the price of ratification by the states and, perhaps, the price of union. It was believed to be vital to the perpetuation of the union and free government to protect these fundamental principles and compromises from a majority, often misinformed, and swept by emotion, impulse, and immediate interests. The intent was to obtain unanimity if possible. It was believed to be unwise, under certain conditions—even where three-fourths affirmative vote could be obtained—to change the Constitution against the opposition of a large minority, especially if it were an economic minority existing in a geographical section. Perhaps the best modern example of the unwisdom of adopting an amendment in the face of strong sectional and class opposition was the late and not much lamented Eighteenth, or Prohibition, Amendment.

The two-thirds vote needed to remove a federal official in impeachment proceedings has obviously protected both the Supreme Court and the Chief Executive from the domination of the legislative branch of the government. In thus protecting the independence of the judiciary and the executive branches, the concentration and abuse of power, so much feared by the founding fathers, was checked and a minority protected.

The presidential veto is a check upon the legislative branch, just as the senatorial power of removal is a check on the courts and executive. The veto forces upon the congressional majority a serious reconsideration of hasty, hysterical, or unconstitutional measures, by the requirement of a two-thirds vote of both houses to pass a measure over the opposition of the president.

The two-thirds vote of the Senate necessary to ratify a treaty—which has been under serious attack for many years—has a very rational history, which should be understood before any drastic change is undertaken. In 1785 John Jay, United States Secretary of Foreign Affairs, proposed a treaty with Spain in which the United States would agree to suspend for twenty-five or thirty years its claims to the right to navigate the Mississippi River and surrender its claims to the thirty-first parallel as the southern boundary, all in return for a treaty of commerce favorable to the Eastern states. This would have cut off much of the export trade of the Southern states and surrendered to Spain the bulk of the present states of Alabama and Mississippi. The Southern members of the Confederation Congress who defeated this proposal were convinced that the Eastern states in return for commercial favors from Spain would figuratively sell the South down the river, and literally sell the river itself. It was this Jay-Gardoqui treaty, more than any other consideration that was responsible for the adoption of the constitutional provision requiring a two-thirds affirmative vote for the ratification of a treaty.

The provisions in the federal Constitution requiring a two-thirds and three-fourths majority vote were intended to protect the individual and the numerical, racial, and sectional minority against a self-centered majority which so quickly loses sight of the rights of those whom they outnumber. In other words, we are by theory and by the Constitution a limited democracy—limited by many restrictions which were self-imposed.

These restraints have been seriously weakened or rejected over the years. The meaning of this weakening process, which at first appears to be in the interest of more democracy and freedom, is in the long run destructive of both. Consider first, the decline of the theory of natural rights; and then partly as a result of this decline and partly as the result of other factors, the weakening of constitutional government.

During the time since Thomas Jefferson penned the Declaration of Independence—which should have been immortal—we as a people have been losing sight of the doctrine of the natural rights of man, which forms the premise of the Declaration and from which the contents flow as a stream from a spring. It is a decided trend in our modern political and pragmatic thought and legal opinion to reject the validity of the doctrine of natural rights or treat it as a beautiful abstraction and certainly to deny the corollary doctrine of the limited sovereignty of government. The only rights to which we may lay claim according to this trend of thought are those legal rights defined in the constitutions of the states and the nation and interpreted by the Supreme Court. As for the rank and file, the folk tradition of natural rights has virtually disappeared. The only rights of which the people have any knowledge are those they can wring out of the government by block-vote pressure or those which they can obtain in a court of law through the aid of high-priced lawyers —and usually at the expense of the natural and constitutional rights of fellow citizens.

To eliminate the theory of natural rights from our political and legal thought and action has serious implications. To begin with it destroys the theory of limited sovereignty and paves the way for a totalitarian theory—first, total and unrestrained power in the sacred name of democracy for those who have the greatest number and then total power by entrenched government by whatever name one calls it.

Perhaps the least considered but most ominous result of discarding the doctrine of natural rights is that it removes the divine sanction to man's freedom and well being. The Creator, whom the natural rights philosophers—though many claimed to be atheists—were unable to omit from a logical and rational philosophy of government, is thus purged from our system. Man, heretofore responsible to God and his fellow man as a special creature of the Supreme Being, is thus relieved of such moral responsibility or any permanent foundation and sanction for a civilized code of ethics when the doctrine of natural rights is no longer considered to be valid. Man is thus removed from any special category presumed to have been established by divine authority with special rights and for special treatment.

Finally, and of great practical and long-range importance in discarding the theory of the natural rights of man, we discard the political theory on which our government was founded and which teaches the purpose of all government and marks the path of free government with guideposts. We are thus removing the most powerful and ultimate restraint upon ourselves and upon the government which we have established.

In thus taking lightly, habitually neglecting, and in certain schools of thought rejecting the theory of natural rights, which for so long has guided us, we are fast losing our sense of direction. We as a people do not appear to be concerned about whence we have come and whither we are going. We seem to be milling about aimlessly in the manner of a herd of cattle, making short moves from one bunch of grass to another. Though we have forgotten or do not keep in mind the political theory which is woven into our system of free government and personal liberty, we have not devised another political theory which can be infused into our present political system and can take its place as foundation and guide.

Our mortal enemies are aware of the vital role of political theory. Never for one moment do the Communists lose sight of the theory

on which they are rapidly basing a world-wide system. For over a
hundred years an ever-increasing number of shrewd, fanatical, and
vicious men have kept to the forefront of their thoughts and actions
the doctrines of Karl Marx. Communists regard the Lenin-Marxian
theory of scientific dialectic materialism—the Communist theory—as
the science of human society and the law of history from which there
may be temporary avoidance but never final escape. Stalin, in his
Problems of Leninism, gave the vital role of theory in the development and maintenance of government and society based upon
theory. Stalin, of course, is speaking of the Communist theory, but
the same principle holds true for the role of theory in any form of
government. "Practice gropes in the dark," says Stalin, "unless theory
throws light on the past. But theory becomes the greatest force in the
working-class movement when it is inseparably linked with revolutionary practice; for [theory] and [theory] alone can give the movement confidence, guidance, and understanding of the inner links between events; it alone can enable those engaged in the practical
struggle to understand the whence and the whither of the working-
class movement." Note the words, "guidance," "the whence and the
whither." These are the very essence of the meaning of a political
theory in a government based upon this theory. These intellectual
spiders of the Kremlin know whence they have come and whither
they are going. All important actions must be kept in line with the
guideposts of Communist theory.

The Communist theoreticians—those intellectuals who can inter-
pret and elaborate Marx without violating his principles—are held
in awesome esteem. The theoreticians hold the secrets of life and
death and they watch their comrades always for signs of deviation
from the fundamentals of Marxism. To them a deviationist is the
most dangerous public enemy, for he has lost his way or has never
known it and hence he misleads the people. Deviation is, consequently, the greatest of all crimes, and the leaders of importance
who stray from the path of Marx and Lenin are doomed to liquida-
tion. Thus the Communists hold to their political theory as the price
of their individual lives and the life of their system.

Political theory on which a system is based is as vital to the perpetuation of that system as a theology is to the perpetuation of a
religion. Had we been as vigilant and constant in our devotion to
the theory of natural rights on which our government was founded
as the Communists have been to the Marxian theory on which they

are founding their proposed world-embracing system, we would have
much stronger inner defenses against our mortal foes abroad and the
unintentional enemies of free government at home. But in failing to
take constant reckoning of the whence we have come and the
whither we are going, by not keeping in view always the guideposts
of our political theory, we have greatly weakened our system of constitutional government. We have, because of this, too rapidly permitted our government to make detours around the roadblocks
placed in our Constitution to restrain ourselves from violating the
rights of individuals, of minorities, and eventually of ourselves, the
majority.

A few examples are offered at this point of the manner in which
the national government has made detours around or overleaped the
constitutional roadblocks, or self-imposed restraints. The one outstanding trend in our entire constitutional history has been the
never-ending effort at the ultimate extinction of the federal structure
of our political system. Most of the constitutional amendments
adopted since the Civil War have transferred powers to the national
government and have been aimed at weakening the federal structure. Constitutional amendment is, of course, the only legal and
moral way by which such changes can be made. The only objections
that can be offered to these centralizing amendments are: first, the
doubtful and even illegal methods by which some of them were
adopted; and, second, the fact that they seem to conflict with other
portions of the Constitution and certainly with the general intent of
that document. But after all, perhaps it is the Supreme Court's interpretations of these amendments rather than their original purpose
that have gnawed at the federal principle and conflict with the spirit
and letter of the main Constitution. One of the most fantastic
examples of Supreme Court interpretation is the circuitous and zig-
zag process of reasoning by which the First and Fourteenth Amendments have been combined or fused. The Fourteenth Amendment is
a restriction upon the actions of a state; the First Amendment is a
restriction upon the United States government. But by interpretation the Supreme Court has made the First Amendment a restriction
upon the state also. In this way the teaching of the Bible in public
schools has been prohibited in Chicago and can be in a similar fashion forbidden in any public school.

Congress has likewise constantly, and of late years rapidly, enacted laws that eat away the foundations of the federal structure of

government. This has been especially noteworthy in the field of social and economic legislation, much of which pertained to matters predominantly local in character. But social legislation will be commented on again in connection with the desirability of drastic amendments to the Constitution.

The executive branch of the government has also for a long time had a tendency to ignore the structural design and to disregard other constitutional limitations—all under the dire necessity, so it has always contended, of prompt action in the never-ending national and international crises. Since Theodore Roosevelt and Woodrow Wilson used the executive agreement as a short circuit of senatorial approval of treaties, this kind of procedure in foreign affairs has become standard. But under our Constitution as it now stands, the executive agreement is a violation of the structural character of the Constitution. By ignoring the Senate, the President violates the two-thirds requirement for the ratification of a treaty. Phrasing it another way, the President usurps the treaty-making function of the Senate, and to that extent he subordinates a coordinate branch of the federal government. In another way he overrides the federal principle in as much as the United States Senate thus overreached is historically and legally the representative of the states as well as the people of the country as a whole.

Other alarming features of the executive agreement are that it is made in secret and that it reveals a lack of faith in the democratic process—and a lack of faith on the part of those who have so often assumed to be the voice of the people. Another serious deviation from constitutional procedure—another detour around the road-blocks of the Constitution—is the growth of administrative law, so called. In many cases law-making is, in fact, delegated to commissions and bureaus that have no responsibility to the people and no practical responsibility to either Congress or the President.

Much of these and other such violations of our constitutional restraints have been and are justified on the grounds that we are facing a great crisis and must have prompt and adequate action; but that because the Constitution is an eighteenth-century document and out-of-date, it must be liberally interpreted—otherwise we cannot take adequate and prompt action. The answer to this argument—usually by some mighty small voices—is as follows: Since the crisis is an old one and will continue, the Constitution should be thoroughly overhauled; otherwise we are and will be operating under no tangible, provable constitution. The impatient ones glibly reply that the amending process is too slow, and that the enlightened Supreme Court is fully qualified by the process of interpretation to keep the Constitution up-to-date and in conformity with our great emergency at home and abroad. What we really must have, they say, is an elastic constitution. Of course the Supreme Court wholeheartedly shares this philosophy and has assumed more and more the power of remodeling the Constitution by interpretation. In short, our high court has taken upon itself the character of a permanent constitutional convention with powers to add to, subtract from, and repeal whole sections of the constitutions of the United States and the states. While thus assuming to act as a sovereign constitutional convention, the Supreme Court has entered on a broad front the field of social legislation. In this field it has, apparently and without opposition, set itself up also as the supreme legislative body of the United States. But the Supreme Court is responsible to no one for its actions.

There has been considerable doubt in the minds of our historians whether or not the makers of the Constitution and certainly the states that ratified it intended to allocate to the court the power of passing upon the constitutionality of a state or federal law. Certainly our founding fathers had no intention of violating the theory of the sovereignty of the people and the separation of powers by bestowing legislative powers upon the judiciary. The very genius of the American concept of free government is that the law-making body must be chosen by the people and made responsible to the people through frequent elections.

The argument that constitutional amendment is too slow is pure sophistry. If the leaders of the country, with understanding and courage, could explain to the people the mortal necessity of having a tangible and provable constitution, a national constitutional convention could be easily held. Certainly, with the proper leadership any sensible amendments covering the new field of social legislation and related matter would be quickly adopted. It does not seem that the impatient champions of humanity want amendments; and, above all, the present Supreme Court wants no amendments and no constitutional convention.

The question may now be asked: Why have we forgotten or opposed the political theory which lies behind our constitutional system of government and in turn why do we ignore or oppose the limitations of the Constitution? Several explanations come to mind if one reflects on the matter: first, our loss of zeal for free government; second, the acceptance of freedom as a universal and free commodity; third, the recurring and ever-lengthening national and world crises; fourth, the impatient humanitarian friends of the people; and finally, the closely related cult of unlimited rights of mass will—or democracy unlimited. These will be taken up in order.

Our zeal for the doctrine of natural rights and constitutional government, born of oppression and revolution nearly two hundred years ago, has grown cool as revolutionary zeal eventually cools. But our zeal has abated with unusual rapidity, so it seems. This is probably the result of our failure to keep ever before us the principles of a free society and especially our acceptance of freedom as a matter of course.

We Americans have long taken freedom for granted. We have had it so long that we cannot imagine ourselves not possessing it; nor can we picture our children—who must succeed us—either as the slaves of a totalitarian state or as composing the little clique of oppressors who would hold the present children of other parents in slave pens. We do not seem to realize that freedom is a new and relatively restricted experience of mankind. Never in the million or more years since man has been an intelligent being has more than a very small fraction of the species enjoyed even partial freedom. In ancient times the peoples bordering the Mediterranean—Greeks, Romans, Jews, and a few others had some conception of individual liberty and government responsible to the people. In modern times a fringe of Western Europe and North America have had some understanding of the principles of a free society. The other billion and a half or more of mankind do not have and never have had freedom or any conception of the elements that constitute a free society. Only a very small fraction of the human race at the present time may be considered to be living under a government of their choice and one based upon enduring principles. And we, the largest fraction of this small fraction of humanity, are growing ignorant of these principles or treat them with indifference or with downright belligerency because they stand in the way of the swift accomplishment of an immediate and short-range objective.

The recurring and often long-drawn-out crises in our history have given justification or excuse for overriding the barriers that stood in the way of certain courses of action. The era of the Civil War and Reconstruction witnessed many and far-reaching violations by both executive and Congress of individual and minority rights guaranteed by the Constitution. The crises of the First World War, the Great Depression, and the Second World War were almost continuous. The present crisis, the mortal struggle with world Communism, if we survive as a people, will probably outlast the present century. Most of the important legislation and governmental policies as related both to domestic and foreign affairs for years have been primarily of an emergency character. They have been adopted in haste, are often contradictory, and frequently are of doubtful constitutionality. They usually have two features in common: they move away from the federal principle of the division of powers between state and national government and toward centralization and total authority. Our leaders both political and intellectual have offered very little criticism of the trend of crisis legislation. Many understand the drift, but do not possess the moral courage to express their opinions. Others either do not fully comprehend whither we are ultimately bound or do not care, if the immediate objective may be reached.

Those who comprehend but stand idly or helplessly by while we drift from our moorings are caught between two complementary forces: the impassioned champions of unbridled democracy, on the one hand, and the press of mass democracy on the other. These belligerent leaders of mass rule object most strenuously and with no little sophistry to the doctrine of natural rights and the restraints of the federal Constitution. Yet they frequently and with emotion use the word *democracy,* and they sincerely regard themselves as the special defenders of a free society. Certainly they are the champions of the Bill of Rights in the federal Constitution. Such champions of unlimited democracy and civil rights usually have a most worthy program for the social and economic improvement of the people, and they are in a mighty hurry to advance their program through federal legislation. Naturally they can not accept the theory of the limited sovereignty and the limitations of government by the Constitution. There must be no limit upon the United States government, they most zealously contend. Not for one moment would I suggest that those who pursue this train of thought and action are bent upon doing injury to free society and free government. Many are humanitarian, sensitive to suffering and personal injustices, and soft-hearted, but they are soft-headed friends of the freedom of man. How often must we call on the Almighty to save our nation from the hands of such friends.

The last important cause of the rapid weakening of the restraints of our theoretical principles and those of our national Constitution is the rise of the cult of the mass will or democracy unlimited. This is a manifestation of the anti-intellectualism of the twentieth century which in Germany produced Hitler and made Russia and China easy prizes for Communism. With blazing eyes, in the sacred name of democracy or the right of the majority to have its unchallenged way in all matters, we cry down as being outmoded and discredited those hardy souls who even mention the possibility that any proposed measure or act may be unconstitutional or unwise. In fact the mention of the word Constitution often induces a puzzled and vacant stare or a look of angry suspicion. To attempt to halt, slow down, or divert the onrushing masses, led by their humanitarian friends and by designing demagogues, is to be denounced as an enemy of democracy.

But when we, the majority, operate without constitutional restraints, whether it be those of the present Constitution or one that has been modernized, we, in the name of democracy, overrun the rights and crush the aspirations of those with whom we differ but whom we outnumber. In this headlong course we, the majority, deprive ourselves of our own rights also; for after all, majorities are composed of individuals. Furthermore, if one scans the political history of the last few decades he will realize that majorities are composed of a mosaic of minority groups, so that it will eventually transpire that the majority has trampled upon its own rights when it overruns individual and minority rights. We seem to have forgotten what the founders of our nation knew so well—that the unrestrained majority, under the sway of short-sighted, ignorant, or designing leaders, will do themselves and their country mortal injury. We are thus undermining our freedom when we throw off in the name of democracy those self-imposed theoretical and constitutional limitations designed for the security of the individual, for the protection of those whom we outnumber, and for the perpetuation of free government.

V

The Making of Andrew Jackson

Lucius Quintus Cincinnatus Lamar

A Rebel War Clerk
   and His Diary

A Southerner's View
   of Abraham Lincoln

The Soldier Who Walked
   with God

The Making of Andrew Jackson*

The re-creation of the portrait of one from a past age, about whom storms have raged, against whom invectives have been hurled, to whom bad motives and high praises have been accorded, offers obstacles which perhaps omniscience alone can leap. Great labor must be performed in mastering the history of the period in which the subject lived, the imagination must be strong enough to restore the period of the times and to grasp the sweep of complex forces which motivated the collective mind. This is only preliminary to a greater labor, it is merely setting up the stage and preparing the properties and lighting effects for the actor. This accomplished, the writer is ready to begin his real work. He must now spend years perhaps in search for personal information, and must weigh and test the evidence of both friends and foes of his protagonist. When this collection of fragments is completed he is ready to begin piecing together a human being with the chances all against his being successful. Among many obstacles which still confront him the greatest, perhaps, will be the problem of proportion between historical narrative or background and pure biography or personal narrative—the same problem which confronts the historical novelist. In steering away from the Charybdis of too much historical narrative lest he submerge his characters as have Beveridge and Nevins in their lives of Lincoln and Cleveland, the author crashes against the Scylla of the historical vacuum so characteristic of modern biography.

Marquis James in his first volume of the life of Andrew Jackson has probably found himself confronted with as many difficulties as it is possible to have and he has met them splendidly, on the whole. His narrative is stirring, dramatic, beautifully balanced between pure biography and history, in its form an artistic triumph. His portrait of Jackson is, I believe, the most authentic one thus far presented—and many have been presented. In my own lifetime I have been quite conscious of two contrasting pictures of Jackson. The older was a man who embodied the frontier in its crudeness, fierceness and unreasonableness, a man whose unbridled temper and insuperable will and spirit crushed all opposition, a lawless, head-

*Andrew Jackson: The Border Captain by Marquis James. New York: Bobbs-Merrill Company, 1933.

strong champion of the West and democracy, whose personal integrity and moral character and passionate love of country raised him above mediocrity. He was blunt, frank, and without guile. His political career was largely the work of close and astute friends such as Major Lewis and Senator Eaton. The more recent picture of Jackson corresponded with the above portrait in the period covered by James's first volume; but he was transformed in his middle age into a Southern gentleman with fine manners, much guile and profound political insight. This is the generally accepted Jackson.

James has made considerable alteration in the portrait of the younger Jackson. Jackson was never the crude, lawless democrat of lowly origin; he was a high-spirited and ambitious boy of excellent family, always conscious of his good breeding, a gentleman in manner and in character. Jackson and his family, though they settled on the frontier in the Waxhaw country, felt themselves no ordinary backwoods people. Jackson's educational advantages in his youth were as good as those of Washington, Patrick Henry or Calhoun. That he did not, in spite of great ability, take more advantage of his opportunity is due to the fact that he proposed to carve his fortunes with other than academic tools. The indomitable will, the blasting temper, the fearlessness, the energy so characteristic of later years are all here, but one is made aware also of the presence of great shrewdness and power of calculation and self-control far beyond that of an ordinary youth. The guileless and outspoken young man of early myth is not here. A youngster of twenty who could manipulate his own appointment as attorney general for the western district of North Carolina knew his way about.

As a young man, contrary to tradition, Jackson disclosed a fine sense of justice. As a judge who served six years on the bench of the superior court he has, perhaps, surpassed any judge on the Tennessee bench in popularity. The tradition of rashness and injudicious conduct is not borne out by a careful study of his career as a judge, plantation master, or general. The American army has had few more rigid disciplinarians. But he was no martinet. The victories of Horseshoe Bend and New Orleans would have been impossible without this discipline. Nor were the proclamation of martial law in New Orleans and the refusal to honor the writs of habeas corpus the acts of a tyrant. When peace was declared and the danger over, Jackson showed his respect for law, by standing in federal Judge Hall's court and receiving a thousand-dollar fine for his refusal to obey the writ of habeas corpus. He could have easily defied Hall—in fact could have thrown him in prison with impunity—but he gracefully submitted.

Jackson's nature was not all iron and fire. His deep and lasting love for Rachael, his all-embracing affection and sympathy for her family, his tender love for his adopted children, including an Indian boy, are fundamental traits in his character which draw him closer to the heart than any public man America has had.

James, while doubtless giving the best picture thus far presented of Jackson's life from 1767 to 1821, has not written a definitive biography of this first period of his protagonist's life. In view of the fact that the author is now in the process of collecting material for his second volume, he should profit from some adverse criticism, for the ground is still hot and smoking in the second chapter of Jackson's life. With his fine equipment for writing the perfect biography— almost—the author has tripped over one of the first obstacles in his way. He has neglected to master the history of Tennessee from 1788 to 1803, the period in which Jackson entered middle Tennessee and rose to high position and found himself in conflict with John Sevier. Chapters IV and VIII inclusive deal with this part of Jackson's life and constitute a fundamental defect in the otherwise fine work. James in his lack of knowledge of this period has found himself forced to choose between the historical vacuum on the one hand and semi-fictional background on the other. He abhorred the vacuum and rendered that portion of his biography invalid to a certain extent. Had he consulted Driver's *Life of John Sevier,* William's *Lost State of Franklin,* Whitaker's *The Spanish American Frontier* and the newspapers of the region, he would have discovered that John Sevier, and not Andrew Jackson, was the colossus on the frontier at this time. He would have known that the quarrel between Jackson and Sevier had more to do with Jackson's desire to usurp Sevier's leadership than with land frauds or personal insults. He would have probably discovered, too, that old Nollychucky Jack Sevier outmaneuvered Jackson and drove the latter out of politics until the War of 1812 brought him forth again.

With the exception of the faulty historical background of these few chapters, James's biography is eminently satisfactory. His narrative of the Creek War and the Pensacola-Mobile-New Orleans Campaigns of the War of 1812 is the best in the field. His account of Jackson's generalship leaves one feeling that Jackson possessed military gifts of a high order.

James shows Jackson emerging from a war whose main drama outside of the naval battles had been furnished by Old Hickory himself, the greatest hero, perhaps, that America has ever possessed outside of Washington—and certainly the most loved. In the Florida governorship one sees the crafty politicians attempting to draw the curtain of oblivion over the sick old man lest the people rise up and make him President. The clamor for Jackson was great. He could have had the presidency for the asking in 1816. But Jackson felt satiated. His ambition was dead. He was and had been for many years very ill; malaria, chronic dysentery and gunshot wounds had, he thought, brought him to the brink of the grave at the age of fifty-four. What little time was left to him would be spent with Rachael. As a matter of fact, Jackson was destined to live over a quarter of a century longer and to outlive his beloved Rachael by nearly twenty years. He considered that he had had enough honors and that he had performed enough services for his country. He thought his career was over. It had only begun. The years 1767 to 1821 covered by James's first volume might well be called the making of Andrew Jackson.

Lucius Quintus Cincinnatus Lamar*

Some critics may, no doubt, judge adversely Mr. Cate's biography of L. Q. C. Lamar. His faulty use of material, his neglect of certain manuscript collections, and his heavy reliance upon Mayes' *Life and Times of L. Q. C. Lamar* for information which he might have obtained at first hand will be sufficient, if a narrow view be taken, to obscure the merit of the work. On the other hand, if one takes a broader view of the book, seeks to separate the essential from the unessential and goes to the basic principles, he will be forcibly impressed with the insight and balance with which the author has presented the historical background; and he will be convinced of the authenticity of the portrayal of Lamar's character and of that of many of his contemporaries. Finally, he will feel that the author has, in an unobtrusive way, managed to write an extremely interesting biography. The book is fundamentally sound. In fact, Mr. Cate's book deserves a wide audience, because he has rescued from partial oblivion one of the few truly great men of American history.

Lucius Quintus Cincinnatus Lamar was born in Georgia in 1825 of a famous family. His father, of the same name, who took his life while still young, was a brilliant jurist; Mirabeau Buonaparte Lamar, one of the leaders of the Texas revolution and the second president of the Republic of Texas, was his father's brother. He was a first cousin of Howell and W. R. Cobb, nephew and cousin of Absolom Chappell; in fact he was related by blood or marriage to most of the first families of Georgia, and to many in Virginia and Maryland. He married the exquisite Virginia Longstreet whose father was A. B. Longstreet, noted jurist, preacher, writer, president and chancellor of Emory College, the University of Mississippi, and the University of South Carolina.

This high connection of L. Q. C. Lamar is an important factor in his public and private life; and it identifies him as a leading member of the slave oligarchy, upon which the study of his private and public life casts a flood of light. While Lamar was intellectual beyond most of his contemporaries, nevertheless the breadth of his education and of his interests gives some insight into the culture and

Lucius Q. C. Lamar by Wirt Armistead Cate. Chapel Hill: University of North Carolina Press, 1935.

education of the slave oligarchy and the professional classes of the South. Metaphysics, logic, psychology, ethics, law, theology, history, political economy, the classics, English and Continental literature were fields in which Lamar laboured seriously all his life. At one time or another he taught philosophy, psychology, and law at the University of Mississippi and could have taught the other subjects mentioned. An examination of the intellectual interests of other members of the slave oligarchy and professional classes will disclose in a vast number of cases a similar mental discipline.

Out of this background one might be led (it has been done) to expect arrogance and a passion for dominion over others; but, as a matter of fact, excepting his belief in the righteousness of Negro slavery, which he, like other Southerners, regarded as a God-given institution, he was modest and democratic. Lamar's devotion to constitutional republican government and human liberty was as deep as that of Thomas Jefferson. Upholding slavery and freedom was no paradox to Lamar and the South. The explanation involves no sophistry; it was based upon human realities; the Greek or Roman concept of liberty was closely kin to that of the Southerners.

Lamar immigrated to Mississippi about 1850 when his father-in-law, Judge A. B. Longstreet, became Chancellor of the State University. He farmed, taught law and metaphysics, and served in Congress in the years just preceding the Civil War. When he entered Congress at the age of thirty-two Lamar immediately attracted national attention by his oratory and masterful logic. He was one of the foremost leaders in the secession movement; he drafted the ordinance of secession for Mississippi and proposed that a Confederacy of the Southern States be set up in which the Constitution and laws of the United States be adopted *without a single change*. Lamar gained for himself —as all Southern leaders did who advocated secession—the epithet of "Fire Eater"; yet a careful scrutiny of this man's life reveals one of the sanest and most judicious minds and temperaments in American history. I can think of no public character in our history whose thoughts on affairs of state were less coloured or directed by prejudice or emotion than were the thoughts of L. Q. C. Lamar; and this does not except Washington, Jefferson, Hamilton, Marshall, the Adams's, or Lincoln. This observation should throw light upon the whole category of "Fire Eaters," who were essentially reactionary or conservative in principle; and most of whom were men of average Anglo-Saxon reserve and self-discipline. In fact a study of the speeches of the leaders and of the newspaper editorials of the North and South, respectively, during the five years preceding the Civil War (this study has been made by Northern historians) reverses the picture. Few "Fire Eaters" by temperament or principle can be found to match the uncontrolled passion of the Radical Republicans and Abolitionist leaders, or of the New York *Tribune* and the Chicago *Tribune*.

Lamar and twelve other kinsmen of his name, mostly from Georgia, served in the Confederate Army with rank not lower than lieutenant colonel. Seven—including Lamar's two brilliant young brothers—were killed; while scores of other relatives, including the able W. R. R. Cobb, died in the war—casualties typical of the oligarchy. After a year's service in the Confederate Army Lamar was sent to Europe as a diplomatic agent, with instructions to proceed to the Court of St. Petersburg at the proper moment (which never arrived). Henry Adams was so impressed with Lamar that he wrote many years later that had this brilliant young Confederate been sent to England in J. M. Mason's place, he would have carried the English people with him by his eloquence and logic and would have gained recognition for the Confederacy. While this is hardly true, it does furnish strong testimony of Lamar's transcendent ability. I am, however, willing to venture this: that had Lamar been made president of the Confederacy instead of the punctilious and irritable Davis, such military chieftains as Joe Johnston, Beauregard, and Bedford Forrest would never have been deprived of their commands and permitted to sulk in their tents; and the narrowly patriotic Joe Brown and Zeb Vance would have been conciliated and brought into greater cooperation with the Confederate Government.

When the Confederacy was overthrown, Lamar—like R. E. Lee and most other responsible leaders—counselled the Southern people to accept the situation in good faith, which they undoubtedly did. But Lamar in common with the same leaders regarded the establishment of Negro and carpet-bag governments over the South in 1867–1868, supported by federal bayonets often wielded by Negro troops, as a betrayal of the soldiers' faith plighted at Appomattox and elsewhere, and a repudiation of the principles of free government for which, the North had said, the war had been fought. Nor is there much doubt that by 1872 the majority of Southern leaders and people were fearfully balancing in their secret thoughts the consequences of another revolution fought by desperate guerilla bands as against the consequences of a continued submission to Africanization and spoliation sanctioned by the executive, legislative, judicial, and military arms of the federal government. No Southern white person —man, woman, or child—could be sure of federal protection until 1879. On the other hand the feeling was universal that the strong arm of the United States Government, controlled by the Radical Republican Party, was always ready to reach into the remotest corner of the South and crush anyone whom the whims or political needs or greed of the Radicals deemed it expedient to crush. Had not some of the upper Southern states been able to regain home rule and rid themselves of carpet-bag and Negro rule by 1872, and thereby hold out some dim hope to the lower South, it seems highly probable that one of the bloodiest and most desperate revolutions of all history would have taken place before the end of Grant's second administration.

That L. Q. C. Lamar was contemplating the raising of such a desperate revolt was the opinion of his own household at this time, who watched him fearfully and narrowly while he sat silent and impassive upon his porch at Oxford and saw Negroes, often armed, shove white women and children from the walks. Lamar and other potential leaders of a new revolution had their hopes of peaceably escaping carpet-bag-Negro rule roused by the overthrow of radical Negro governments in Virginia, Georgia, and Tennessee; and they put out of mind the resort to violence. Lamar in particular, ably seconded by J. B. Gordon and Ben Hill of Georgia, conceived of a strategy by which self-government might be won for the Southern states. They would divide the enemy in the South and recruit allies from his ranks. The North was already divided between the Democrats and Conservative Republicans on the one hand and the Radicals on the other in the matter of Southern policy. This division must be accentuated, and allies recruited from the Radical ranks.

Lamar's first step in 1872 was to run for Congress in Mississippi, which was still in the hands of the Negroes, carpet-baggers, and federal troops. He urged all white men to vote the Democratic ticket; but at the same time urged the Negroes also to support the Democratic ticket and denounced the radical policy of *drawing the color line,* by which the two races were pitted against one another. Lamar was overwhelmingly elected despite federal bayonets and carpet-bag-Negro election boards.

He had not been in Congress long when the second stage of his grand strategy was reached. On March 28th, 1874, the aged Charles

Sumner died, politically discredited and isolated by the Grant administration. Lamar had great respect for Sumner's culture and learning; he believed in his genuine devotion to free government; and in his sincerity in his crusade against the South and slavery. In short, while Lamar agreed with much of Sumner's principles and disagreed with more, he respected the Old Crusader's integrity, and that of thousands of his followers. It must not be forgotten that Lamar was, like Lee, a man without vindictiveness and practically without prejudice, so when he rose in the house on April 27th and delivered an oration in honour of the recently deceased Sumner he spoke with complete sincerity. It was one of the most powerful perorations ever delivered in House or Senate, comparable to Webster's 7th of March speech which postponed the Civil War ten years. The theme was sectional reconciliation. "Know one another and you will love one another," resounded through the land. Congressmen and Senators broke down and wept; even the hard-boiled and unscrupulous Blaine wept. The country wept. Unrepentant secessionist, life-long champion of Jefferson Davis and the Confederacy though he was, few questioned Lamar's sincerity—few ever questioned the rightness of this man of complete integrity. Yet it was the most deadly blow thus far struck against the Radical Republican control of the federal and state governments. It was the blast of the trumpet which caused the walls of Jericho to crack. The Radical Southern policy had been tolerated because a majority of Northern people had been convinced by their political leaders that the South had never accepted the decision of the war; that they were cruel and oppressive and were prevented from the wholesale slaughter and re-enslavement of the Negroes only by the ruthless preventive measures of the federal government. In brief, the North had been led by propaganda to regard the members of the late slave oligarchy as monsters of treachery and cruelty. Lamar's eulogy of Charles Sumner undoubtedly shook the faith of millions of people in the truthfulness of this picture.

Lamar's great speech, some years later, against the payment of the war debt in "depreciated" silver or in greenbacks, went far toward laying the ghost of "Southern repudiation" of the Civil War debt, which had been constantly raised by the Radicals and marked another step in his grand strategy of convincing the Northern people of the sincerity of the South in accepting the results of the war. When Lamar and J. B. Gordon supported the electoral commission in 1879 to settle the Hayes-Tilden election dispute another stride was taken toward ending the Radical grip upon the Federal government and the South. These two ex-Confederates prevented another civil war which this time would not have been sectional, for the followers of Tilden in the North were ready to settle the dispute with violence; they were certain that the Radical Republican Party, which had become almost insensitive to public decency, had by fraud and the use of federal troops in Florida, Louisiana, and South Carolina robbed Tilden of the election. History upholds this conclusion. Lamar ably seconded by Gordon proposed that the matter be settled by a Congressional committee. The Radical Republicans refused to consider any of the evidence of fraud or violence, but by a party vote seated Hayes. Lamar urged the public to abide by the decision. This gained wide applause and confidence for him and it made it easy for him and General Gordon to exact a promise of Hayes that he would withdraw federal troops from the South and bring to an end the rule of the carpet-bag-Negro governments.

This promise was carried out—though with reluctance—and reconstruction technically ended in the South. Lamar felt that his work had been accomplished. Partial reconciliation of the sections and self-government for the Southern States had been brought about.

But Lamar was soon to learn that the sword of Damocles had not been removed. Only by unremitting caution and self-discipline were Lamar and other Southern leaders enabled to push back and hold in leash the tide of passion so constantly stirred in the North by Blaine and the old Radical leaders. Another reconstruction threatened the South until the election and inauguration of Grover Cleveland in 1884 by the Democratic Party, which, despite the opprobrious epithets of "copperhead" and "rebel" applied to it by the Radical Republicans, was the only national party in America.

Cleveland thoroughly appreciated the great service of Lamar in the reconciliation of the sections. He regarded him as the ablest man in America and a person of complete integrity. He made him secretary of the interior and thereby ended the proscription which had been placed upon the South, for Lamar was the first Southerner to hold a cabinet position since the administration of Buchanan. Lamar was one of the most successful administrators the department has had; he put an end—during his term of office—to the Indian frauds, land stealing, and pension graft which had been so much oil for the Radical Republican machine.

As a fitting end for the career of a man, who had he not been born a Southerner would probably have been president, Cleveland nominated Lamar for associate justice of the Supreme Court. Though Republicans screamed that the Union was endangered in 1889 by the appointment of a Southerner to the supreme bench, three or four liberal Republican senators voted for the ratification of Lamar's appointment, and for the first time in thirty or more years a Southerner became a justice of the United States Supreme Court. In this capacity he served till his death in 1893.

As great a secessionist as Yancy or Rhett, as great a unionist as Daniel Webster, as magnanimous as Lincoln or Lee, as ready to fight on proper cause as Bedford Forrest and as judicious and poised as George Washington, Lucius Quintus Cincinnatus Lamar appears to us in the pages of Mr. Cate's fine biography as one of the most intriguing and distinguished figures in American history.

A Rebel War Clerk and His Diary*

Mr. Swiggett, author of *The Rebel Raider* and *War Out of Niagara* has, through the Old Hickory Book Shop, presented the students of Confederate history with a new edition of J. B. Jones's *A Rebel War Clerk's Diary*. Readers of Southern history will consider this a great book, for the *Diary*, published in 1866, was so scarce that few people have had access to it during late years. Mr. Swiggett's editing has been keen and penetrating. He brings a thorough knowledge of the period to bear upon his work.

Jones's *Diary* is the most valuable diary of the Confederacy—though not the most beautiful or the most charming. The little man Jones was the Boswell of the Confederacy. He came to Montgomery in the spring of 1861—from New Jersey, where he had been running a secessionist paper—and announced his desire for an appointment in the war office and his purpose to write and publish a diary of events. He obtained the place and made an entry for every day of the Civil War. So important did his diary seem to him that he appears to have felt completely justified in having both of his sons exempted from military service and placed in government employ for the sole purpose of aiding in the support of the family—support which would enable Jones to write his diary. This probably marks the diarist as an eccentric, and certainly as a man with a single-track mind; yet the student of Civil War history can easily overlook this fact.

Jones was violently prejudiced against Jews; he would have doubtless approved of Hitler. He believed that Judah P. Benjamin was a traitor, or was, to say the least, indifferent to the fate of the Confederacy. The fact that Benjamin was one of the most implacable enemies of the United States and became a British subject rather than live under the Federal flag, does not alter the value of Jones's *Diary*, for this diarist was giving expression to public opinion; and here one immediately puts his hands upon one of the weak spots of the Confederate government: the retention in office of men whom the people—and therefore the barometer, Jones—distrusted. Jones, in common with the people of the South, hated and distrusted As-

A Rebel War Clerk's Diary at the Confederate States Capital by J. B. Jones, ed. Howard Swiggett. 2 vols. New York: Old Hickory Book Shop, 1935.

sistant Secretary of War Campbell, Quarter Master General Myers, and Commissary General Northrop. His hatred for Yankees runs throughout the book. He believed them capable of any atrocity or any cunning and deceitful trick. He turns his wrath upon the Confederate-Yankee Generals Pemberton, Gustavus Smith, Lovell, and Cooper. Invariably when he mentions the name of one of the Northern men who had gone with the Confederacy he puts "Yankee" in parenthesis. He was sure that every Yankee in the Confederate service was a traitor. The fact that he was completely wrong does not weaken the value of the diary, for he was again expressing the general opinion of the Southern people.

But Jones's *Diary* is not merely valuable because it is a barometer of contemporary public opinion and feeling: The main importance, as Mr. Swiggett points out, is that the diary is the only contemporary synthesis of public events in the South. From his central position in the Confederate War Office, Jones obtained an amazing perspective upon the affairs of the Confederacy. Mr. Swiggett does not seem to think Jones understood fully what he saw, that he was in reality only a superb reporter. Understanding is a relative matter, of course: but I get the impression that this pathetic, undernourished, irritable clerk in the Confederate War Office had a keen historical sense. In rereading the *Diary* after many years, I am greatly impressed with Jones's selection of facts. Nothing of importance in the remotest parts of the Confederacy entirely escaped his notice, and the result is that any definitive history of the Confederacy will find most of its lines of development already marked out by this indefatigable recorder of events. There is noted much of the clash between the state governments and the Confederacy over conscription, over the right of appointment to office in the Confederate army, over the suspension of the privilege of the writ of *habeas corpus,* blocade-running, impressment of supplies, Negroes, and railroad equipment for military use, and the tithe or tax in kind. Jones, unlike most of his fellow Southerners, put less faith in the power of cotton to force England and France into intervention than he did in the desire of those two countries to weaken the United States and gain a stronger foothold in the Western Hemisphere. He saw very clearly that Napoleon III must either ally himself with the South or fail to establish his Mexican puppet empire. He realized with indignation that England and France were too strongly impressed by the war threats of William H. Seward; that, in fact, they were kept from a more active sympathy with the Confederacy by the implacable language of Seward and the American ministers, Charles Francis Adams and William Dayton at the Court of Saint James and the Court of Napoleon III of France. The *Diary* is one of the few unofficial records which take note of the seizure by the American Navy of British commerce on the high seas; and Jones gauged this situation accurately when he surmised that such an extension of belligerent rights on the seas was near to plunging the two countries into war.

Not in detail, of course, but in broad outline, Jones traces the bitter feuds between Davis and Beauregard, and Davis and Joseph E. Johnston; and the favoritism which Davis showed toward Bragg, Northrop, Myers, and Benjamin—all in the face of public opinion. Jones was one of the few persons who liked Davis. Few, if any, times does he directly criticize the Confederate President; yet the pages of the *Diary*, as they slowly unfold the feud between the executive and the two generals who ranked close to Lee in military prowess, disclose Davis as one of the pettiest men who ever held high place. Here was a man whose vanity and sensitiveness were so great that he kept two of the ablest of his generals inactive during the greater part of the war. A martinet for red tape and military punctilio where his own authority was concerned, the President was constantly meddling, and undermining the authority of Johnston and Beauregard and other leaders whom he disliked. When Beauregard was defending Charleston against a terrific siege and bombardment in 1863, Davis withdrew 10,000 men from him—that is, about one-half of his men—and sent them to the incompetent Pemberton at Vicksburg. Beauregard pleaded in vain for reinforcements. He stated that the militia and the small number of enlisted men under his command were inadequate to hold Charleston should the enemy decide to land a force. Instead of considering the situation on its merits, and either reinforcing Beauregard or explaining that the men were needed even more elsewhere, Davis had the staff in the War Office—including Jones—search for several days through all of Beauregard's reports so that the general might be caught in a discrepancy—a matter which should have been exceedingly easy to do even in the case of the conservative and accurate Lee. The discrepancy was found—several, perhaps—and, instead of sending Beauregard troops, says Jones, the President gleefully endorsed upon that general's urgent plea for more troops, the comment that the statement did not agree in numbers with a previous one, and asked the secretary to note the discrepancy.

At a later stage of the Federal bombardment with long-range rifled artillery, Beauregard in desperation called for heavy guns to defend the beleaguered city. Porcher Miles, Congressman from South Carolina, obtained a promise, so he thought, from Davis that certain long-range guns, then in Richmond and lying idle, would be sent to defend Charleston, which was being pounded to bits by the powerful Federal guns. The President did not send the guns. Finally, Miles wrote a letter to the secretary of war urging that the long-range Brooks guns stored in Richmond be sent at once to Beauregard. He reminded the secretary that President Davis had promised these guns. The secretary referred the paper to the President, who, in turn, obtained a statement that there were no Brooks guns nor had there been any in Richmond.

> Mr. Miles [Jones wrote] has been *caught* by the President, after the lapse of twenty days. It is not denied even by the Secretary of the Navy, that long range guns were on hand—but there were no Brooks guns, simply. Thus, while Charleston's fate hangs trembling in the balance, and the guns are idle here, twenty days are fruitlessly spent. Mr. Miles appears to be a friend of Beauregard. Every letter that general sends to the department is sure to put twenty clerks at work in the effort to pick flaws in his accuracy of statement.

Jones gives numerous accounts of this type of sophistry by which Davis tripped up Beauregard and Johnston and other personal enemies. One would have had to go to Vance of North Carolina or Brown of Georgia to find such a petty and vindictive spirit. As a matter of fact, the reader is convinced that President Davis was not the Davis of either pre-war or of post-war days. Personally, I am convinced that the Confederate president was mentally unbalanced by the physical suffering through which he was going and by the sorrow at the loss of his little boy who was killed in a fall from the front porch of the White House. One cannot read this diary without feeling that there was considerable truth in Jones's bitter exclamation that "never before did such little men rule such a great people."

In this careful record of events preserved by the sour but conscientious Jones one can trace the decline of public morale and the growth of war weariness. Oh! for peace, where he could cultivate his little garden in the evening of his life, with his family safely about him! Oh! for the ending of the slaughter, on both sides, of the flower of the nation's manhood. One feels this weariness of soul and body creeping into the diary and taking the place of the passionate hatred for Yankees of the earlier pages. Not that Jones lowers his flag. He, like the bulk of Southern people, sank exhausted and benumbed. He died on February 4, 1866, less than ten months after the fall of the Confederacy—probably as a result of chronic malnutrition—without seeing his diary published.

A Southerner's View
of Abraham Lincoln*

A Southern historian is, I suppose, as objective and impartial
as a Northern historian. Every good historian tries to tell the
truth. But historians are human, and, Northern or Southern, they are
bound to have emotional reactions to every human situation, no matter how much they try to exercise self-restraint. When emotion is too
much in the ascendancy, the historian may be accused of bias, sometimes more elegantly spoken of as "point of view." Facts are supposed
to be facts, but they have a queer way of arranging themselves so that
one historian may see them one way, another historian another way.
Some facts which seem obscure and dim to one may shine clear and
bright to another. No one sees them all in their true, clear light.

I am looking at a portrait of Lincoln in a room with a Southern
exposure. The Northerner has the light coming from a Northern
window. Neither of us sees Lincoln as he really was. Lincoln looks
different to the descendant of a Civil War Republican from the way
he looks to the descendant of a Civil War State Rights Democrat. In
the light from my window I also see what seems to me a Lincoln cult
bordering on pagan deification which is taking place in the popular
mind of the North; and this has been unconsciously inspired by serious scholars, who have allowed their emotions and bias to over-
emphasize certain elements and minimize others. In the long run
this has had and will have harmful effects. In the first place, it has
made more and more difficult a sane evaluation of the events leading
up to and including the Civil War. And in the second place, sooner
or later it will obscure the real Lincoln. At the least, he will suffer
the fate of Washington at the hand of Parson Weems; at the most—
your guess is as good as mine. But you may recall the fate of Aris-
tides the Just, who was finally ostracized partly because the Athen-
ians became wearied with hearing about his many great virtues. Any
such reaction against a deified Lincoln will probably come from the
North, not the South. The Southern historians as a rule occupy a
middle ground from which they will not have to retreat.

Most Southerners who have studied the Lincoln sources like the
man; they enjoy his wit and his humorous stories and recognize

*This essay was originally an address delivered at the May 1946 meeting of the
Illinois Historical Association in Harrisonburg.

them as belonging to the same school of humor as those of Mark Twain, Sut Lovingood, and A. B. Longstreet. They rightly or wrongly recognize him as a familiar legal figure of rural Southern towns, so often seen sitting on courthouse porches reading newspapers, talking, and, when court is in session, shrewdly winning jury trials. They are inclined to regard his political career, from the passage of the Kansas-Nebraska Act in 1854, through the election of 1860, and until after the secession of the lower South as primarily the standard and familiar procedure of a shrewd and ambitious politician making concessions to political expediency for the sake of personal and party victory. During the next period—from the assumption of office until the First Battle of Bull Run—Lincoln, according to this view, continued to resort to measures whose primary objective was to keep the Republican Party together. It is believed, however, that many of Lincoln's major decisions during this early war period were also conditioned upon or resulted from errors in judgment as to the true meaning of the situation. Lincoln clearly did not understand at this time the popular support of secession in the lower South nor the psychology of the border states.

In other words, it is believed that many of Lincoln's policies during this period were based upon a complete miscalculation of the magnitude that a war to put down secession would assume and how the border states would react in any attempt to force the lower South back into the Union. Had he foreseen the titanic character of the war and the reaction of Virginia, North Carolina, Arkansas, and Tennessee to his call for troops to use against the Confederacy, surely he would have adopted, to begin with, broad, long-ranged and vigorous war measures, or an entirely different approach to the secession movement, a peaceful approach, which might have saved all the border states and would have probably disintegrated the Southern Confederacy within a few years at the most. If Lincoln was a man never motivated by malice, hate, and the spirit of revenge, as I conceive him, it seems probable that he would have adopted a policy of peaceful persuasion rather than war—had he foreseen the loss of the four border states and the *ferocity and magnitude of the Civil War* and its long-time disruption of national unity.

Once enmeshed in the most destructive and deadly war since the legendary wars of ancient times, and bowed down under personal bereavement and domestic sorrows, Lincoln's personal ambition vanished. Although he had always been a man of personal integrity and morality, one usually spoken of as a "good man," it is doubtful whether he had been a religious man. But as the war ground on in what seemed interminable slaughter and destruction, and Lincoln's personal sorrows increased, he turned more and more to religion and dependence upon God. Though in his political conduct he often resorted to expediency, it was probably an expediency which, rightly or wrongly, he regarded as necessary to shortening and winning the war.

More and more Lincoln thought in terms of ultimate values—peace and a restoration of the Union on terms of brotherhood—the only enduring basis of a national state. And it is as peace statesman rather than warrior statesman wherein, according to many Southern historians, Lincoln reveals his greatest qualities.

In broad outline, the above sketch is, perhaps, a common view of Southern historians who have studied Lincoln's career with considerable care. Except in dealing with Lincoln as a peace statesman, it differs sharply with the Northern view in interpretation of details and whole situations. Lincoln, unlike Minerva, who sprang full-grown from the brow of Jove, is regarded as one who grew in stature until his death—from that of a shrewd, likeable, rural lawyer and politician to that of a great statesman.

I shall elaborate somewhat on this outline. First let me discuss Lincoln's attitude toward the Crittenden Compromise introduced in Congress December 18, 1860, and give an evaluation of his opinion. It will be recalled that the extension or non-extension of slavery into the Western territories had been an issue since the Mexican War. The Southerners insisted on the right to carry slaves into the territories as the price of Union, and the Republicans had incorporated as the chief plank in the platforms of 1856 and 1860 a demand that no further extension of slavery into the territories should be permitted. Yet well-informed leaders everywhere generally agreed that neither the great plains nor the semi-arid territories of the Southwest could sustain agricultural slavery. Webster in his famous speech of March 7, 1850, had told his audience that slavery could not exist there, "Why re-enact the ordinances of God?" he had asked. Clay, Douglas, John C. Calhoun, and Lewis Cass held similar views. To show how correct this view was, the census returns of 1860 revealed that there were only two slaves in Kansas, and in all the organized territories of the United States there were less than sixty.

In 1860, despite the knowledge that the issue of further extension of agricultural slavery into the territories was an abstraction, the political leaders of both the North and the lower South were uncompromising. After the election, however, the Southern border states attempted to settle the issue by compromise. Several compromises were offered in Congress, and in the peace convention held in Washington in February 1861 under the leadership of Virginia. The most important of these was the compromise which Senator John J. Crittenden of Kentucky proposed on December 18, 1860. There were several provisions incorporated in this compromise; but the one vital provision proposed to restore the Missouri Compromise line by constitutional amendment. This would have left most of the Indian territory and the semi-arid territory of New Mexico theoretically open to slavery. In all the remaining territory slavery would have been prohibited. Crittenden's compromise proposal was submitted to a senatorial committee of thirteen. This committee was composed of five Republicans including William H. Seward, three Northern Democrats including Stephen A. Douglas, three representatives from the upper South including Crittenden, and two from the lower South—Robert Toombs and Jefferson Davis. Had the committee adopted the compromise and Congress approved at that time, there is strong evidence that all the lower South except South Carolina would have accepted it, with the result that secession would have been checked. Had South Carolina then been left alone, secession would have probably been ended. The committee's adoption of the compromise depended entirely upon the action of the five Republican members, for the three members from the upper South and the three Northern Democrats pledged themselves to support the compromise. The two men from the lower Southern states, where secession conventions were about to meet, pledged themselves in advance to support the compromise if the Republicans would support it. This agreement of Davis and Toombs was made in the presence of Stephen A. Douglas. But the action of the Republican committeemen, with the apparent exception of Bluff Ben Wade, was dependent upon that of President-elect Lincoln. Lincoln, however, had already made it clear to friends in Congress that he was strongly opposed to any compromise measure sanctioning or seeming to sanction the extension of slavery into the territories. He had, for example, a few days before the formation of the Crittenden committee, written Congressman William Kellogg of Illinois to "entertain no proposition for a compromise in regard to the extension of slavery"; and he had urged his friend Congressman E. B. Washburne of Illinois "to hold as firm as a chain of steel" against any concessions on the extension of slavery into the territories. Give way on this point, he enjoined, and they will have us under again, and in a year or two will be demanding Mexico and other Latin American possessions as the price of union.

Seward, who favored such a compromise, persuaded Thurlow Weed, the old Whig Party boss of Albany, New York, who was going out to Springfield on political business, to urge the President-elect to support the compromise; but Weed was unable to move Lincoln from his stand on the territorial question. His position was stated again that if such a concession were made, the South in a year or two would be demanding the annexation of Mexico and Cuba as the price of union. He also reminded Weed that the acceptance of the compromise would be a repudiation of the chief plank of the Republican platform of 1860 on which Mr. Lincoln had been elected. It would mean an end to the Party. Of course the Republican members of the committee voted against the compromise, and, as agreed, Davis and Toombs voted with the Republicans. Thus ended the first and greatest effort at compromise. Later this and other similar measures were brought up in the House and Senate; but the attitude of the President-elect and that of the leading Republicans remained unchanged, and soon it was too late to arrest the secession of the lower South.

The refusal of Mr. Lincoln to accept the restoration of the Missouri Compromise line, when such a gesture might have been effective, seems ironic when, in February of 1861, after the lower South had seceded, he showed no concern at all that Colorado and Nevada were organized, without prohibiting slavery, from part of the very territory which had been the bone of contention.

It is my belief that Mr. Lincoln shared Webster's, Douglas's, and Clay's opinion that slavery could never exist in this territory, or he would have raised the same objection as he had to the Crittenden Compromise.

Why did he reject the Crittenden Compromise? Did he really believe that the South would demand Mexico and Cuba as the price of remaining in the Union? And that the tug of war had better be settled now than later? This idea that the South would demand that Mexico and Cuba be annexed as the price of union was the chief justification that Lincoln and the Republican Party spokesmen gave for refusing to approve the Crittenden Compromise. It has for many decades been accepted by many historians as sound reason for refusing such a compromise. Actually, there is very little evidence to support such a contention. And that brings me to what may be a shocking assertion. This is that in 1860 Mexico and other Latin American countries were in graver danger from the Republican administration than from the South. Seward, Charles Sumner, and many other leaders were imperialists who wanted the Western Hemisphere from pole to pole. It may be startling to discover that in return for a proposed loan of eleven million dollars to Mexico in 1861, Seward and Thomas Corwin, United States minister to Mexico, negotiated a loan treaty by which Juarez pledged as security "the several Mexican states of Lower California, Chihuahua, Sonora and Sinoloa" with the condition that "the property so pledged [is] to become absolute in the United States at the expiration of the term of six years." Corwin assured Seward that "this would probably end in the cession of the sovereignty to us. It would be certain to end there, if the money were not promptly paid as agreed on." The long drawn-out correspondence on the subject of the loan of eleven million and the annexation of Mexican territory is to be found in the United States Department of State, Despatches, Mexico, Vol. 28, 29; Instructions, Mexico, Vol. 17; Instructions, France, Vol. 16, and Despatches, France, Vol. 50. It is a chapter in the diplomatic history of the United States which has never been adequately written. Mr. Lincoln, of course, was fully aware of the Corwin-Seward deal, and approved of it. I am therefore convinced that the President's justification for not approving the Crittenden Compromise was not based on moral scruples against acquiring Mexican territory. Rather it was a political and partisan decision. At this time he believed that, with the exception of South Carolina and a few men like Rhett and Yancey, the lower South was bluffing. This being so, to concede anything to such bullying and bluffing would be cowardly, and would wreck the Republican Party. This is what I meant when I said that during this period, Lincoln made many concessions to political expediency. He obviously did so in the belief that such concessions to expediency would have no very harmful effect. In other words, the tug of war would not be much of a tug. The late William E. Dodd, one of the great admirers of Lincoln both as a politician and as a democratic statesman, maintained that Lincoln, once the desperate and ruinous nature of the war was revealed, deeply regretted his failure to accept the Crittenden Compromise.

Let us glance at the period from Lincoln's assumption of office through the First Battle of Bull Run. What impresses a Southern student of the Civil War is the failure of Mr. Lincoln during this period to adopt either a conciliatory policy toward the seceded states or vigorous war measures. His peace measures and his war measures seem half-hearted. It appears that the President did not comprehend the possibilities of a vigorous peace offensive.

Let me repeat: President Lincoln seemed to have believed during these months that the mass of Southerners were at heart loyal unionists, and that a relatively small group of unconditional secessionists were simply misleading the masses. He misread the situation, and his peace policy was halting and lame. According to his conception of the situation, if the mass of Southerners were loyal unionists, he would not have to make any great concessions to regain them, nor any great effort to put down the secession leaders. Where Lincoln failed to judge correctly was that the mass of Southerners had three strong patriotic loyalties. Before the election of 1860, and probably up to the failure of the Crittenden Compromise, the ascending order of these loyalties in terms of their strength was state, sectional, and Union. From January 1861 to the fall of Sumter they were reversed, and the ascending order in terms of strength was Union, state, sectional. But the old loyalty to the Union was, unquestionably, reasserting itself in the period before Sumter. Many leaders of the lower South and the majority of the rank and file, I believe, would have welcomed eventual reunion on the basis of the proposed Crittenden Compromise. Mrs. Davis in her memoirs of her husband says frankly that President Davis himself really hoped for an amicable settlement and reunion until after the fall of Fort Sumter. Certainly the loyalty to the Union was in the ascendancy over the loyalty to state and section in the upper border states, and they would never have seceded had not the Sumter issue forced them to choose sides. The few unconditional secessionists such as R. B. Rhett, Edmund Ruffin, and Wigfall were in a desperate state of mind until Sumter fell, lest the Confederacy disintegrate, and the states straggle one by one back into the Union. It is my considered opinion that, had Mr. Lincoln shown more patience in the Fort Sumter matter, an eventual settlement and reunion would have been possible without war. But, according to Mr. Kenneth Stampp's brilliant study of Northern opinion in his book *And the War Came,* the hard core of the Republican Party, composed of the Radicals, demanded war, and Lincoln himself became convinced that war would be necessary to restore the Union.

Another miscalculation, it appears to me, was Mr. Lincoln's belief concerning the reaction of the border states to his call for volunteers. President Lincoln once again failed to grasp the fact of the triple loyalties—state, sectional, and Union—and counted on Union sentiment to determine the action of the border states. But, as is illustrated by the conduct of R. E. Lee, when forced to choose sides, four border states found state and sectional loyalties prevailed over Union loyalty. In Kentucky, Maryland, Missouri, and Delaware, the people were badly divided on the same lines.

Lincoln's war measures until after Bull Run, were, as I said, not any more vigorous than his peace measures. This failure to make strong preparations for war during this early period grew out of the President's persistent belief that the mass of people in the South whom he believed to be loyal would not vigorously support a war to separate from the old Union. In short, that the war should be a very small struggle. Let me explain what I mean by weak or halfway measures in preparation for war. To begin with, Mr. Lincoln did not convene Congress until July 4, nearly three months after the issue of war had been determined by the Fort Sumter affair. This, of course, meant that long-range and large-scale financial and military measures necessary for the prosecution of a large-scale war were subject to serious delay. There was, in short, no real organization for war; and to show further that the President at this time was thinking in terms of a small war, probably not more than large-scale riots, he called for only 75,000 three-month volunteers, most of whom were from the state militia, and added a few thousand recruits to the regular army and prepared for a small force of three-year volunteers. Furthermore, arms and munitions production and procurement from abroad were not seriously undertaken until after Bull Run. This Union disaster convinced the President that the war was developing into greater proportions than he had anticipated. Real armies were now recruited, equipped, and trained. Yet, just as the spring campaigns of 1862 opened up, Mr. Lincoln permitted Secretary of War Stanton to put an end to further recruiting and enlistments. It was not until after the strategic failure of the Peninsular Campaign in June 1862, and the rout of Pope's army at Second Bull Run in August, that the President fully grasped the magnitude of the war.

After this year and a half of inadequate preparations and hand-to-mouth operation, Mr. Lincoln sponsored drastic military measures and prosecuted the war with unrelenting vigor. Let me call attention to some of these vigorous measures: the Emancipation Proclamations of September 1862 and January 1863, which contained potential encitement to servile revolt behind the Southern lines; conscription; the establishment of the national banking system; the levying of excise and income taxes; the imprisonment of thousands of unhappy Democrats; the launching of total war in 1863, in which both public and private property in the South were destroyed or seized by the Federal armies; and the recruiting of European soldiers—estimated at from 150,000 to 300,000.

At the very time, however, that Mr. Lincoln was prosecuting the war with every means and resource available, he was skillfully and wisely planning for a peace that would heal the wounds of the spirit and restore the Union upon the basis of mutual affection and respect of the Northern and Southern people. The same attitude that had caused Mr. Lincoln to underestimate the support of the Confederacy in the South was partly responsible for his peace measures. This, as it will be recalled, was his unshaken belief in the fundamental loyalty of the great body of Southern people. Of great import also were Lincoln's innate magnanimity and charity, greatly increased by his personal sorrows and his now profoundly-developed religious opinions. It has seemed to Southerners who have studied Lincoln that there was also another matter troubling the conscience of a conscientious man. This was Lincoln's violation of the very bed-rock of that Declaration of Independence—the consent of the governed or the right of a people to choose their own government. It seems ironic to Southerners that the United States, a nation based upon the right of a people to live under a government of their choice, should make war to prevent a people—the South—from living under a government of their choice. There seems to me only one rational explanation of Mr. Lincoln's refusal to face the fact that in making war against the Confederacy he was violating the basic principle of the Declaration of Independence, the equalitarian aspect of which he so often dwelt upon. This explanation is that the President finally came to understand more clearly the existence in the Southern mind of the three patriotic loyalties referred to earlier. These were, before 1860, let me repeat, in ascending order, state, sectional, Union; but during the struggle they had been reversed and were Union, state, sectional or Southern nationalism. Mr. Lincoln must have believed that by just and kindly treatment of the South, he could win the South back to primary loyalty to the Union—a devotion submerged but never dead. He was a man of a great understanding of human nature, and he knew that it was impossible to subjugate a people, destroy their loyalty to their own country, and win them to the country of their conqueror. He knew history well enough to know that one nationalism could not be destroyed and another substituted in its place. Hence, his peace efforts would be aimed, not at killing the Southerner's loyalty to his state and section—the only way to do that would be to kill the Southerner—but at cherishing and encouraging the Southerner's old love of the Union, so that once more it would be in the ascendancy.

In the light of this explanation Mr. Lincoln's war aims and peace aims had only one objective: winning the South back to a position in the Union where all alike, North and South, would live in brotherly affection.

Though preliminary steps had been taken toward such restoration earlier, it was only in December 1863—after Vicksburg and Gettysburg—that Mr. Lincoln set forth his official peace policy. In his Proclamation of December 8, 1863, he offered unconditional amnesty to the great body of Southerners merely on condition of taking the oath of allegiance. The exceptions to this general amnesty were the higher military officers in the army and the navy, and certain officials of the state and Confederate governments. These, of course, could receive amnesty by personal application.

The Radicals bitterly opposed Lincoln's Plan of Reconstruction. They desired vengeance on the one hand, and on the other they planned to gain and maintain control of the Southern states and use them as pocket boroughs to keep their party in control of the national government. This was finally done by the disfranchisement of the bulk of whites and enfranchisement of the recently freed slaves, who naturally voted for the Radicals. Lincoln fully realized that the Radicals would do incalculable harm to his dream of cherishing and restoring the Southerners' love of the Union.

The struggle between Lincoln and the Radicals, led by the implacable Stanton, Ben Wade, Sumner, and Thad Stevens, finds Lincoln not giving way to them as peace approached, but rather showing an increasing awareness of the vital necessity of a generous peace that would heal the wounds of the spirit, and a growing determination to establish such a peace even at the expense of a break in his party—a different attitude from that of 1860–1861.

Lincoln in refusing to accept the Radical Wade-Davis Reconstruction Bill passed by Congress on July 2, 1864, was throwing all political expediency to the wind; for he was breaking with the hard Radical core of the Republican Party who had so often since 1860 caused him in the interest of party harmony to adopt measures and policies which otherwise he would not have adopted.

As the war drew toward a close, President Lincoln gave strong evidence of desiring a more generous peace settlement with the South than the terms set forth in his Proclamation of December 8, 1863. For example, he gave his consent for the Confederate Virginia Legislature to meet and withdraw the Virginia troops; and it seems that he was considering the idea of letting other Southern legislatures meet in an extra-legal capacity to give their aid and influence in the preliminary stages of reorganization at the end of the war. The terms of surrender that Sherman first offered Johnston, including the recognition of the state government of North Carolina, were unquestionably based upon his conception of Lincoln's future reconstruction policy. But Radical opposition and Lincoln's own cautious temperament finally brought an end to this budding idea.

In the closing days of the war when there was no longer any doubt as to Northern victory, the entire trend of Lincoln's thoughts seemed toward generosity and friendship for the South, for a peace settlement that would be just and merciful, one that would recognize Southerners as fellow citizens and not prisoners of war, and above all, one that would go far toward reuniting the Northern and Southern people into a genuine Union. His second inaugural address, March 4, 1865, foreshadowed the kind of peace that Lincoln had in mind. "With malice toward none; with charity for all; with firmness in the right, as God gives us to see the right, let us strive on to finish the work we are in; to bind up the nation's wounds;...to do all which may achieve and cherish a just and lasting peace among ourselves and all nations."

On April 11, two days after Appomattox, the President spoke to the public for the last time. In keeping with the wisdom and charity of the second inaugural his voice was raised in earnest pleading against the harsh and vengeful attitude toward the South of Radicals like Thad Stevens and Ben Wade, an attitude so destructive of the spirit of mutual affection, North and South. Already Stevens, as leader of the Radicals, was demanding that the South be treated as a conquered province—without mercy. In his speech of April 11, Lincoln appealed to the people and especially to the Radicals to remember that the sole object of the war—the sole justification—had been to restore the "seceded states—so-called—to their proper practical relations with the Union." All, he urged, should join in helping to do this, and no one should attempt to settle the question "whether these states have been out of the Union." "Finding themselves safely at home, it would be utterly immaterial whether they had ever been abroad."

In his last cabinet meeting, held on the day of his assassination, Lincoln spoke with deep regret at the dire spirit of hatred and revenge that seemed to animate the Radical leaders, and he warned them that he would have none of such business.

"I hope there will be no persecutions," he said, "no bloody work after the war is over. No one need expect me to take any part in hanging or killing these men, even the worst of them. Enough lives have been sacrificed. We must extinguish our resentment if we expect harmony and union. There is too much desire on the part of some of our very good friends to be masters, to interfere and dictate to those states, to treat people not as fellow citizens; there is too little respect for their rights. I do not sympathize in these." This was spoken in the presence of the implacable Radical, Secretary of War Stanton, and it was intended as a plain and unequivocating statement to the Radical wing of his party of the wise and lofty principles on which the President proposed to act in the restoration of the Southern States. As it happened, however, this statement proved not a chart for future action, but a last will and testament soon to be ignored; for the next morning Abraham Lincoln was dead from the bullet of a madman. The course of history was thus changed for many years. With his great skill at shaping public opinion and in dealing with men, including those who opposed him, Lincoln, had he lived, would have blunted or broken the sharp and merciless blades of the Radical zealots such as Stevens, Wade, and Sumner.

When one views the malice and savagery of the Radicals who succeeded Lincoln, or contemplates the fathomless hatred and savagery of the world in which we now lead a day to day existence, Lincoln as a peace statesman, assumes great stature, greater, perhaps, to a Southerner than to a Northerner.

The Soldier Who Walked With God*

At an early age Robert Lee felt that a cloud of ancestral witnesses surrounded him and weighed his every act. He could never forget that he was the son of Light Horse Harry, the brilliant revolutionary soldier and intimate friend of Washington; he admired Washington above all men, and when he married Martha Washington's great-granddaughter and moved to Arlington to live, his admiration grew akin to worship. With great traditions and great inheritance, Lee felt that he must preserve without stain the family altar and household gods. Doubtless he inherited his great military genius and his courage, but his traditions sustained him and preserved his spirit unbroken when other men of fine qualities but no such traditions went down in the ordeal of civil war and reconstruction. Robert E. Lee, seen at this distance, is the most convincing evidence in support of an agrarian aristocracy. No other environment or ancestry could have produced such a man.

II

When one weighs the question whether Lee, who was graduated second in his class at West Point, should have chosen the engineers or become an officer of the line, it is difficult to give an answer. As an engineer, Lee learned the science of fortification, which he was to use more than any general until 1914; he learned the best placement of artillery; and, in Mexico as a member of Scott's staff (his appointment being due to his brilliant record as an engineer) he learned to see the army as a whole, had some great lessons in strategy as a result, learned the importance of accurate reconnaissance, and became, in fact, Scott's chief reconnaissance officer. To offset the practi-

*This essay was based on Douglas Southall Freeman's *R. E. Lee* (4 vols.; New York: Charles Scribner's Sons, 1934–1935) which Mr. Owsley considered the "almost perfect biography of a public character: the intimate, personal life...well balanced and interwoven with the professional career of Lee." On January 19, 1935, Freeman wrote to Owsley: "The publishers of the American Review have been good enough to let me see a proof of your article on my 'Lee.' I think I really should phrase it a proof of your article on Lee, because you have made the book the basis of what is the most discerning brief study of General Lee that has appeared in many, many years. I congratulate you on it at the same time that I thank you for it." [Ed.]

cal experience in fortifications, reconnaissance, and strategy is the startling fact that Lee had no experience in commanding troops— except two years in Texas as lieutenant-colonel of the Second Cavalry—between the time of his graduation at West Point and the Seven Days Battle in May and June 1862. That is, Robert E. Lee had had virtually no experience in handling even small bodies of troops until he was fifty-five years of age, when in accordance with human experience he should have been set in his ways, and, according to canine experience, too old to learn new tricks. Yet the War of Secession taught him new tricks every hour. The prematurely grey-bearded patriarchal leader grew more brilliant, more cunning, more daring, and more dangerous until the very ground fell out from under his boots in the winter of 1864–1865. Nevertheless, Lee's lack of experience in commanding and drilling troops must be taken into serious consideration by any military critic of his generalship in the War between the States. Up to the battle of Fair Oaks when he became heir to Johnston's army, he had been engaged in fortifying the Atlantic seaports and coast of the Confederacy or in acting as Davis's military advisor. Perhaps this will help explain in part how Lee was unable to co-ordinate his divisions and brigades and time their attacks in the Peninsular Campaign. He did not know how fast troops could march or how to calculate all the delays which mischance or natural obstacles might cause. It might help explain his deference to combat-commanders like Jackson, Longstreet, and the two Hills.

Lee has been often pictured as struggling for months to reach a decision whether to go with Virginia or stay with the Union. The correspondence of Lee during the period immediately preceding the war disposes of this misconception. During the winter of 1861 Lee expressed himself frankly as opposed to secession. "I can anticipate no greater calamity for the country than a dissolution of the Union," he wrote his son Custis. The South had many just grievances against the North, thought Lee, but he believed at this time, at least, that they could be settled without breaking up the Union. "Still," he continued to Custis, "a union that can only be maintained by swords and bayonets, and in which strife and civil war are to take the place of brotherly love and kindness, has no charm for me. If the Union is dissolved and the Government disrupted, I shall return to my native state and share the miseries of my people, and save in self-defence will draw my sword on none." This was in substance what he wrote many people in the months before the secession of Virginia. Finally, when his state withdrew, he went with it. Lee was born or predestined to make the answer which he made to Scott in April 1861 when Scott offered him the command of the Union armies: that if he must make the choice between his own people and those who were not, he must go with his. He could not make war upon Virginia. Lee was also presented with another decision before Virginia seceded: he could not fight against the South. That is something which has been overlooked. The oversight of the decision that Lee could not fight against the South has been the basis of the belief rather widespread that Lee as a general never looked beyond Virginia. Once the choice between North and South became a necessity, in sadness but without wavering Lee did the simple, straightforward thing which was characteristic of him. It was a simple problem to a serene and simple soul. There were three loyalties involved: Virginia, the South, the North (not the Union because it no longer existed according to Lee's belief). There could be no hesitancy for Lee. Loyalties being relative and of the emotions, he chose the stronger loyalties: allegiance to Virginia and the South, and his action was the epitome of that of almost all of the Southern people.

Lee, in his humility, seemed to have actually believed that he would not be called upon by his state, but that he would be allowed to remain in private life or carry a musket and fight in the ranks! Incredible but true! Lee found it almost impossible to believe himself great. Even at the height of his glory, one suspects that Lee still thought of himself only as Captain Lee.

But he was soon called upon to become commander of Virginia troops and became major-general at one stroke. This is one phase of Lee's life which has been little known. It is an amazing phase. Within a few weeks Lee had forty thousand troops in the field, armed and drilling though not under his personal supervision. He fortified the York and James rivers so that Federal steamers did not attempt to invade the state. It illustrates Lee's great ability as an organizer and disciplinarian—many critics to the contrary notwithstanding. It made the victory of First Manassas possible. When Virginia joined the Confederacy, Lee was given the rank of brigadier-general in the Confederate armies, while the forty thousand state troops were made part of the Southern army. Not only so, but Lee was put in charge of all military operations in that area. Yet he was not given any definite command. The result was that the Confederate forces were commanded by Beauregard at Manassas; Joe Johnston in the Valley; Loring, Floyd, and Wise in western Virginia. Lee's position as commander of the armies in Virginia was extremely embarrassing. It carried no power; any of the generals could ignore his orders. He was in the same position in which Joseph E. Johnston found himself in 1862–1863 when made commander of the armies of the West. Davis was unconsciously responsible for the situation. He took his position as commander-in-chief of the armies literally. And who can gainsay the fact that he was in many ways the most experienced officer in the Confederacy. He had been a combat-commander of troops in the Mexican War and had fought brilliantly. Under the Pierce administration he had proved himself one of the three ablest secretaries of war the United States has had. The result of Davis's active participation in directing troop movements in Virginia was that Lee became a mere military advisor to Davis and the war department, and occupied the position that Halleck was soon to occupy under Lincoln: a general held responsible by the public for the conduct of the war, but having no power to enforce his authority. The result of this was the abortive West Virginia campaign which placed Lee under a cloud.

Under stinging public abuse he was sent to fortify the coast of the Carolinas and Georgia. His work here was met by all kinds of insubordination because he had no real power other than his own ceaseless and calm persistence. At length, however, Lee the engineer and diplomat triumphed greatly. The defenses were so well prepared that they held out against bombardment and siege until most of them were finally taken in the winter of 1865 by land in Sherman's march.

When this work was done Davis called Lee back to Richmond as chief military advisor. By this time Joseph E. Johnston had assumed command over all the troops in the Virginia area, and was preparing to fight it out with McClellan. Lee under Davis imposed a considerable part of the general strategy of this campaign upon the self-willed and secretive Johnston, whose personal dislike for Davis explained much of his attitude. Finally, on May 31, 1862, Johnston, who passively defied Davis and Lee, fell in the battle of Fair Oaks, seriously wounded. Lee, whom Davis admired and loved more than any other officer of the Confederacy, but whom he had almost ruined by giving him responsibility without power, was now put in active command of the army which Lee named "the Army of Northern Virginia." Attention has already been called to the fact that Lee had had only a few months' experience in commanding troops before 1862. Now on May 31 he took command of an army of seventy or eighty thousand in the midst of a desperate battle. The effect was electric. One Northern correspondent said that for the North, "the shell...which wounded...General Johnston, although it confused the Rebels, was the saddest shot fired during the war. It changed the entire Rebel tactics. It took away incompetence, indecision, and dissatisfaction and gave skillful generalship, excellent plans, and good discipline."

Lee's great powers of organization and administration made an army out of men who were inadequate only in numbers, and out of material incredibly worn, antiquated, and insufficient. The Confederate artillery was, to a large extent, still the old light smooth-bore, and was ineffective against the heavier rifled artillery of the Federal Army. The Confederate infantry was still armed principally with the old smooth-bore cap-and-ball musket as against the high-powered rifles of the Federals. Finally, the only people who knew anything of the terrain, roads, swamps, and streams of the Peninsula were the Federal generals, McClellan and his staff. This is explicable on three grounds: the United States War Department had all the topographical maps in its possession; Joseph E. Johnston, a topographical engineer who could have easily prepared maps of this region, had from the beginning determined to fight a defensive battle at Richmond, where he had concentrated most of his troops; that is, he did not intend to manoeuvre, but to fight from behind breastworks and trenches which Lee as chief of staff had already partly constructed. He would need no map of the Peninsula. He had no intention, apparently, of attempting to pursue McClellan in case the latter were worsted in the struggle. Finally, the maps which the Confederate War Department had had improvised were completely inaccurate —roads, streams, hills, fords, all lay in the wrong place when Lee and, especially, Stonewall Jackson attempted to dispose their troops according to these maps.

These were the tools with which Lee had to work. Later Confederate artillery was rifled and heavy, though not as plentiful as the Federal equipment; modern, up-to-date Enfield rifles from England and from the hands of the enemy replaced the old smooth-bore musket; and shining bayonets were to gleam from the barrel of each rifle. It was obvious to Lee when he assumed command that with such tools only strategy could win a battle or campaign and strategy involved manoeuvre.

Without retelling the tragic story of the bloody Seven Days Battle, the strategy can be summed up briefly. Within the department of Virginia, there were at this time about 85,000 or perhaps 90,000 Confederate troops disposed as follows: about 65,000 near Richmond directly under Lee's command; about 15,000 in the Shenandoah under Stonewall Jackson; and a few thousand disposed in a semicircle from the Shenandoah to Fredericksburg. In the same area but on the outside of the curve were about 200,000 Federal troops converging upon Richmond: 105,000 under McClellan were only five miles from Richmond. Lee's problem was to keep the enemy dispersed while concentrating his whole force upon his weakest point, overwhelming and confusing him. The first step—already partly guided by Lee before he succeeded Johnston—in the execution of the problem was the incredible Valley Campaign under Stonewall Jackson which defeated the armies of Milroy, Frémont, Banks, and Shields; paralyzed the army of McDowell just ordered to join McClellan at Richmond; and terrified Washington. In short, around 100,000 Federal soldiers were either defeated or rendered inactive by the inscrutable Stonewall with a small army of 16,000 to 20,000. McClellan, who had depended upon the army of McDowell, numbering about 40,000, to reinforce him, and who had thrown his right wing of about 30,000 across the Chickahominy to make contact with McDowell, was now greatly shaken by the sudden turn of events. In the meanwhile Lee began the execution of his next step: to fall with the major portion of his army upon this weak right wing north of the Chickahominy and roll it up.

In order to do this he had almost to uncover Richmond. However, the main feature of the assault on the Federal right was to consist of a surprise attack by Jackson from the right rear. The story of how Jackson got there a day or more late is well known, as is also the story of how he rendered very little service in the whole campaign of the next seven days. Its explanation has never been totally satisfactory. Stonewall's troops had completed one of the most daring and brilliant campaigns since the days of Napoleon's Italian campaigns. His men were utterly exhausted from the endless and fast marches and fighting; and then without rest they had been forced to march a good part of the distance from the Valley to Richmond on foot and go into battle. As for Jackson, he had been in the saddle without rest or sleep for endless days. He seemed dazed and in a trance during the entire campaign. Finally, the accurate and exacting Jackson who calculated every foot of his manoeuvres, whose tim-

ing and placing of troops had mathematical precision, was handed a
bundle of maps which bore the same resemblance to the Peninsula as
the medieval maps did to the earth.

But this second step was not a failure, despite Jackson's tardiness.
Although it did not disorganize the fine army of McClellan as expected, nevertheless it did confuse them, and struck something akin
to terror into the heart of the commanding general which caused
him to begin a hasty retreat. Again and again Lee practically had
the Federal army in the bag, but again and again Lee's divisions
failed to synchronize, and Jackson's least of all. McClellan was
finally able to withdraw his army under the protection of the Federal gun-boats where he was safe from Lee's manoeuvres. Without
discrediting in any way the fine generalship of McClellan on this
retreat, there hardly remains a doubt that had the parts of Lee's
army worked as planned, he would have captured the Federal army.
This failure of Lee's subordinates to bring up their men where and
when ordered has been attributed to Lee's lack of tactical ability
and his inability to control subordinate commanders. However, when
Lee's almost complete lack of experience in commanding even a
small body of troops and his lack of accurate maps—for which he
was not responsible—are considered, one wonders that his tactics
were successful at all. As it was he had practically lost the battles by
tactical weaknesses but had won the campaign by strategy.

As to Lee's inability to control his subordinates there is much to
be said, which is in no way special pleading. Lee time and again was
known to have been excessively amiable or patient with unwilling or
stubborn subordinates. Yet it was really Longstreet alone who per-
sistently refused Lee unquestioning obedience. After one year of
fighting Lee had overcome this excessive consideration for subordinates; in fact, while always tactful, he was indomitable in his purpose. Nothing could shake him, and if he found a subordinate
inefficient and inclined to disregard orders, Lee gently and tactfully
sent this officer on some safe and unimportant front in another part
of the Confederacy where he could do no harm. Only Longstreet
challenged Lee's supremacy, and Lee permitted this because, next to
Jackson, he considered Longstreet the ablest general in his army, and
for a while after the Seven Days he thought he was superior to Jackson. He spoke of Longstreet as his war-horse and loved him personally. Moreover, except at the battle of Gettysburg, Longstreet's conduct really never offered Lee any real cause for severe discipline.

Anything short of arrest and some penalty would have done no good; yet had Lee disciplined the vain and sensitive Longstreet and disgraced him before his army, he would have resigned; and Lee did not believe that he could be replaced. The probability that the policy of coercive discipline among general officers would have been practically impossible in the Confederacy is not given careful consideration by some critics—especially the English.

Insurrectionary armies cannot be dealt with as armies .of well-established governments—not even so far as the private soldier is concerned, unless the government is a dictatorship. Discipline has to be attained by winning the confidence, respect, and even the love of the army. Lee was able to do this and create an army well-disciplined and with morale equal to Napoleon's veterans. One of the best tests of discipline is the invasion of the enemy's country. In both of Lee's invasions of the North little plundering occurred: in fact Lee had a hungry soldier shot for stealing a pig! Sherman contended that plundering of private property was forbidden in his famous march to the sea and into the Carolinas, but nearly all private property for fifty miles on each side of the army was burnt or stolen— and Sherman was not leading an insurrectionary army.

While McClellan was trying to decide what to do next, at Harrison's Landing, and while Lee was trying to find out what he had decided, a large Federal army began to concentrate near Manassas Junction where the first great battle of the war had taken place the year before. Jackson guessed that McClellan had had enough and Lee soon agreed and left only a small force to watch him. Lee began concentrating troops to the west of Richmond; but not too far away to meet McClellan should he come back up the Peninsula. Soon the pugnacious Jackson fell upon a portion of Pope's army operating along the line of the Orange and Alexander railway and threw it back upon its base. Meanwhile McClellan began to transfer his army of 100,000 or more to Fredericksburg on the Rappahannock on Pope's left wing. To allow the armies of Pope and McClellan to unite would bring together between 150,000 and 200,000 to oppose much less than half that number. It was the same problem which confronted Lee when he succeeded Johnston at Fair Oaks: Lee must defeat one army before the other arrived. Pope had made large boasts about seeing only the backs of his enemies. He had ordered the plundering of the occupied region, and the execution of the inhabitants on any suspicion that they had communicated with the enemy; he ordered civilians shot in retaliation for guerrilla activities in their neighborhood. Lee's reactions were that General Pope "must be suppressed." He usually spoke of "our friend, the enemy," but now he showed anger in this campaign and remarked that no civilized people had ever conducted such a war as the Federals were then waging.

The race between McClellan and Lee to reach Pope began as soon as Lee was certain that McClellan was going to transfer his army from the James. Quickly Lee moved upon Pope in the triangle made by the Rapidan and Rappahannock Rivers and the Orange and Alexander Railway. But Pope squeezed out of this hole before the Confederates could confront him. Next began a manoeuvring up the Rappahannock, Pope trying to delay, and Lee meaning to come to grips with him and destroy him before he was joined by McClellan. Suddenly the enemy disappeared, drawing back toward his base at Manassas. Then Lee evolved his strategy. First Stuart was to ride around Pope's army and find his exact position, next Jackson screened by the foothills of the Blue Ridge Mountains was to make a swift march by his left flank around Pope's right flank and to his rear, cut off his communication, and destroy his supply depot. Longstreet's corps was to remain in front of the enemy's position until Jackson had had time to get within striking distance of the enemy's rear, then Longstreet was to follow swiftly and join him in battle upon the Federal rear and right wing. Thus again Lee divided his force in the face of the enemy, but it worked almost perfectly, and Pope was surprised and overwhelmed and fell back within the Washington fortifications.

Soon Lee made his famous march into Maryland, and once again divided his army into several parts, the primary purpose being to clear the Shenandoah Valley, capture Harper's Ferry, and thereby secure his line of communication. The order dispersing the troops fell into the hands of McClellan and that usually cautious general began to show activities which astounded Lee. Lee found it necessary to fight a heavy rear-guard action at South Mountain in order to hold McClellan back while concentrating his army at Sharpsburg. While this was happening Jackson was mopping up the Valley, taking Harper's Ferry with 13,000 new rifles, 11,000 men, and 73 much-needed pieces of artillery and other stores. Before more than 25,000 could be concentrated at Sharpsburg the battle began. The battle was in appearance a slugging match at close quarters with the Federal heavy guns far superior to the Confederates. But the Federals made the mistake of attacking successively the three sectors of the Confederate forces rather than the whole front simultaneously with their great numbers and powerful artillery. As it was, by use of the inside lines, Lee was able to thin out the parts of the line not under heavy fire and rush fresh troops to the point under greatest pressure. When the Federals finally attacked the right sector, the last of Lee's detached divisions arrived on the field—the division of A. P. Hill. Hill's 3000 men charged the attacking lines of the enemy and pushed them across Antietam Creek. That was the end of the battle. The next day Lee waited in vain for an attack, and then decided to deliver one himself if feasible. He would try a turning movement, but Jackson had already, in the company of Stephen D. Lee, famous artillerist, found the enemy's guns so heavily massed that any such move would be suicide. McClellan, while he waited for reinforcements, sat there holding Lee in an iron grip so that manoeuvring was impossible. Lee slipped quietly across the river and the Maryland campaign came to an end.

Lee's purpose in invading Maryland had been sound: to clear Virginia of Federal troops and find fresh pastures and food for horses and men, and to give Maryland an opportunity to join the Confederacy. Finally a victory on Northern soil would have a great moral effect; and, while Lee did not know it, such a victory would have brought English and French recognition, probably, to the Confederacy. The lost despatch which disclosed to McClellan the dispersed condition of Lee's army frustrated all possibilities of gaining these objectives.

We may pass over Fredericksburg in December 1862 as having little value in showing Lee as a general. It was essentially a massacre of the Federal troops led by the incompetent Burnside—a bravely but foolishly fought battle.

The winter of 1862–1863 carried warning of impending disaster to the Confederacy: and here is where the English critics lose contact with reality. Fuller treats the army as if it were a nice warm vacuum. The railways, not built for military purposes, were inadequate to transport food and clothing to the soldiers. Commissary-General Northrop was not only incompetent, but spiteful; and, as far as is known, the only man in the world who hated Robert Lee. Instead of sending what food and blankets were available this strange person sent arguments and discourteous letters. There was much distress among the poor up-country people who had so fully responded to the call for troops. Their women and children were starving, and, wherever the enemy invaded, were frequently abused and labored under great fear. By this time, peace societies destined to grow larger and larger were forming among those who had reached the limit of physical and mental suffering. State governors were frequently obstructing the operations of the Confederate government. Attempts to send any of the numerous state troops from Georgia or North Carolina or Texas were met by abrupt and discourteous refusal from the state governors. The same attitude toward conscription existed among these state rights officials. The blockade was becoming more stringent, and people, despite Lee's brilliant victories, were in deep distress. No doubt there was sufficient food for people and army, but the transportation system could not supply both adequately. Horses and mules were mere shadows in the army, and there were scarcely enough to plow the lands and cultivate the crops; without sufficient horses to pull wagon trains or artillery, men and horses must eventually starve; and in the meanwhile, the army which fights and moves on its belly must become paralyzed. From the winter of 1862–1863 until the end of the war this situation grew worse, and more and more limited the movements of Lee's army and determined his strategy. It made it impossible to follow up any victory.

During the winter of 1862–1863 we have the pathetic spectacle of Lee sending Longstreet with the greater portion of his corps to North Carolina partly to watch the enemy but chiefly to find food for horses and men, and other parts of his army in other directions to procure food and clothing. Lee divided his army again in the face of the enemy, now under the command of fighting Joe Hooker whom Lee rated highly. This time, however, he was making a flanking movement not against the enemy but against starvation. To add to the difficult situation Lee became seriously ill.

With his army reduced to almost half, barefooted, hungry, and many without blankets, Lee emerged from this long, cold winter with the powerful enemy just across the river from Fredericksburg. Soon Hooker became active. Lee was alarmed at the scattered condition of his own army. He began concentrating smaller fragments but he left the matter to Longstreet's judgment whether it was better to attack the enemy on the coast, or continue his collection of food-stuffs, or come back and rejoin the depleted army of northern Virginia. While leaving this to Longstreet's judgment, Lee actually planned to meet the enemy without his sure but slow-moving general. This meant that Lee would have to fight the best equipped army in the world numbering about 140,000 men, with an army of 62,000 tatterdemalions gaunt and hungry and harried by letters from home filled with tales of suffering and despair and sometimes of brutalities committed by the invaders. There was a difference, however, in the two armies which did not appear to the casual observer. Every man in the Confederate army felt that "Marse Robert" was his personal friend and the grand patriarch and father of his "boys." They instinctively felt that God was close to Marse Robert, for they had seen him during their years with him kneeling in prayers which God would not ignore; they had seen him reading the burial services over their fallen comrades and, after each victory, his proclamations and orders thanked God for the victory. These naive and religious boys—many were barely eighteen—felt that Marse Robert who walked with God could never suffer defeat under any conditions. Then there was stern unsmiling Stonewall Jackson who was kind and who cared for his men: he prayed all night before battles, and breathed a constant prayer for the guidance and success of the army while the guns were smoking in battle. Stonewall Jackson and Marse Robert and God were with the army: they were invincible. Nor does it seem that Stonewall or Robert E. Lee regarded it in any other aspect. Lee a Low Churchman and Jackson a Presbyterian were equally confident of the presence of God in their armies and humbly believed that He would lead them to victory. But these two fatalists left nothing to chance: they and their troops, like the Mohammedan Arabs of the Middle Ages, took to heart the proverb that God helps those who help themselves.

Hooker's army, though well trained and equipped, had no such confidence in their commander, though he was an excellent soldier. They frankly admired Lee, many of them, and, unfortunately for their success, believed that he and Jackson could not be defeated. Then there was another element which cannot be overlooked: the Army of the Potomac was coming to be made up more and more of foreign mercenaries brought into America in the guise of laborers secretly pledged to enter the army for the large bounties offered. Before the war ended nearly 500,000 such troops were employed, not to mention 250,000 Negroes. This was in addition to those foreigners who had emigrated to America during the fifties. Whole brigades could not speak English, and pillaging and spoils were their chief concern. Such an army could hardly have the morale of an army composed of a homogeneous race, which had an almost religious reverence for their commander and a belief that a very real and personal God was in their camps.

In April and May 1863 Hooker's magnificently-equipped army was strung out for many miles along the Rappahannock. It looked as if he might cross at Fredericksburg on the Confederate right flank or as if he might cross miles up the river. He finally did both, but at the wrong time. Hooker's main army crossed the Rappahannock and was exactly in the position occupied by Pope the year before when Lee had attempted to catch him in the triangle formed by the confluence of the Rapidan and Rappahannock, and the Orange and Alexander Railway. Lee, however, now felt that his men were too badly shod, and his horses and mules too weak for large-scale manoeuvring, so he allowed Hooker to get out of the triangle by crossing the Rapidan just above Chancellorsville. This put the bulk of the Federal army on the side of the river with Lee, while the remainder of the Federal army under General Sedgwick was showing signs of crossing at Fredericksburg, attacking Lee from the rear, getting between him and Richmond and cutting his line of communication. This was good strategy, but Lee's and Stonewall's was better. They did not wait for the Federals to attack. After feeling out the enemy they knew that a frontal attack would be suicide. Then the strategy which Lee had so often employed in one way or another was agreed upon: a movement by the left flank so deep as to be completely concealed from the enemy; followed by an attack from the rear of his exposed right flank. Jackson's contribution to the strategy was one of emphasis rather than principle. He and Lee were perfectly agreed that surprise flanking movements were the only chance of defeating an enemy superior in numbers and artillery. In the words of Freeman:

> Lee had left the execution of the movement to Jackson and had not prescribed a definite route or designed how many troops were to follow. He now turned to "Stonewall" who was still studying the map. "General Jackson," said he, "what do you propose to do?"
>
> "Go around here," Jackson said, and traced the route that Hotchkiss had marked.
>
> "What do you propose to make this movement with?"
>
> "With my whole corps," Jackson answered.
>
> That was Jackson's own conception, his major contribution to the plan. He would not attempt a simple turning movement that would merely confuse the enemy and give an opening for a general assault. In moving to the enemy's rear, as Lee had planned, he would march with all

his 28,000 men and would attack in such force as to crumple the enemy and throw the whole right wing back against the fords. It was a proposal Lee had not expected, and it floored him. "What will you leave me?" he said in some surprise.

"The divisions of Andrews and McLaws," Jackson answered unabashed.

This meant perhaps a mere screen of not over 10,000 and possibly not more than 6,000 men to oppose the Federal front of not less than 50,000. But Lee's fighting blood was stirred to its depths by such colossal boldness. If never before, surely now he must have recognized in Jackson the supreme strategist and military executive. Jackson rode away slightly flushed:

> He disappeared like a Norse god into the forest. As Lee looked, it must have been with confidence, with personal affection and with admiration. "Such an executive officer," he said not many days thereafter, "the sun never shone on."

Crossing from the right flank behind the left flank into the wilderness Jackson swiftly executed his deep circuit around the enemy's right flank and into the rear. Falling upon the Federal General Howard, while the men were cooking supper, Jackson rolled up the division and threw it back upon Hooker's center where great confusion was created. Had Jackson not been shot down, mortally wounded, it seems hardly possible that Hooker could have escaped from the battlefield. The next day Stuart, in command of Jackson's corps, continued to drive back Hooker's line; and at the same time the division of McLaws and Andrews, reinforced by some of the Confederate forces near Fredericksburg, commenced a frontal attack, sliding always to the left until contact was finally made with Jackson's second corps. Hooker was about to be driven in the river, when Sedgwick crossed below and occupied the fortifications at Fredericksburg and threatened Lee's army from the rear. But such a movement was too late: it was quickly met by sending Early back to support Andrews and McLaws who had been detached from Lee's right to hold off Sedgwick while Hooker was being driven back. Like the other commanders, McClellan and Pope, Hooker had found Lee invincible with half his army grazing horses and gathering supplies in North Carolina.

The wounding of Stonewall Jackson saddened Lee deeply. When he was reported ill with pneumonia and beyond hope Lee would not give him up. There was one thing he could do for Jackson after all human aid failed, that was to pray for him.

> On Saturday night as the doctors shook their heads and expressed their fear that the outlook was hopeless Lee went down spiritually to the brook of Jacob and like Jacob, wrestled with the angel. Never in his life had he prayed with so much agony of spirit. While the army slept and Jackson in his stupor fought his battles over, Lee on his knees implored Heaven to grant to his country the mercy of the deliverance of Jackson from death.

But the doctors had given Jackson up. He was in a coma. "A. P. Hill," he was saying, "prepare for action"; and again: "I must find out whether there is high ground between Chancellorsville and the river...push up the columns, hasten the columns." But Lee could not believe that God would permit Stonewall to leave him. "Surely, General Jackson must recover," he said in a shaken voice to the chaplain. "God will not take him from us now that we need him so much. Surely he will be spared to us, in answer to the many prayers which are offered for him." When the chaplain who had brought the news of Jackson's impending death was ready to return to the dying man's side, Lee said, "When you return, I trust you will find him better. When a suitable occasion offers, give him my love, and tell him that I wrestled in prayer for him last night, as I never prayed, I believe, for myself." And he had to turn away abruptly to hide his emotions. As Lee sat waiting, a chain of memories of his great lieutenant must have been awakened in his mind, and the great achievements of the dauntless Stonewall passed in review. If Jackson could recover, they would assume the offensive and Harper's Ferry would not stop them again. The fear of Jackson's name would cause the enemy to evacuate it, they could march into Maryland and Pennsylvania and carry the war into the enemy's territory.

> There was a stir outside the tent, a moment of hesitation, then some one brought in a bit of folded paper. It contained the dreadful news. In the little cottage at Guiney's Station Jackson had aroused from his restless sleep and had struggled to speak. His mind had been wandering far—who knows how far—but with an effort, in his even low voice, he had said: "Let us pass over the river, and rest under the shade of the trees." And then, as so often on marches into the unknown, he had led the way.

Had Jackson lived, even with the Confederacy falling into ruins in his rear it seems impossible for Lee to have lost the battle of Gettysburg. Later, when a Presbyterian preacher referred to the overthrow of the South, he said, in substance: "When O God, in thy inscrutable way, Thou didst will that the Confederacy must be overthrown, it was first necessary to remove thy servant Stonewall Jackson." For the moment, with the tragic death of Stonewall who had, according to the generous Lee, made the victory of Chancellorsville possible, "Marse Robert" almost retires from the stage.

III

After the death of Jackson it became necessary for Lee to reorganize his army from top to bottom. Jackson's corps was put under the command of Ewell, who was so weak and debilitated from the loss of a leg and from dyspepsia that Lee doubted his ability to keep the field; A. P. Hill, a good fighter, but a poor tactician and strategist, was given command of the new Third Corps of Jackson and Longstreet. Similar changes and promotions were made below because of casualties among the lower grades. The army, as an organization, was, in fact, about as new as it had been at the beginning of the Peninsular Campaign the year before. Lee could not predict the conduct in battle of any corps commander, including Longstreet, or of many of his major or brigadier generals. It was with such an organization that he commenced his second invasion of the North to find food for horses and men, to encourage the peace movement, and to win, perhaps, a decisive victory upon the enemy's soil. If Lee could not predict the conduct of his generals, he was supremely confident of his ragged army. The private soldiers were seasoned, their morale was high, their discipline perfect and their endurance almost unbelievable. Full rations were luxuries which his soldiers had seldom known. Frequently they marched two or three days without any food at all; other times they fought a campaign on a few ears of parched corn.

The invasion of Pennsylvania was accompanied by what proved to be a fatal error, though at the time there was nothing to indicate that it was such. Lee ordered Stuart to ride around Hooker's army by crossing the Rappahannock below his left flank. Stuart was then to place himself on the right flank of the Confederate army and shield its movements from the Federals. There was, however, a condition attached: in case Stuart found the enemy in strength on the left flank, he was to reverse his march and cross above the enemy and thereby maintain contact with the Confederate forces all the time. Stuart did not find the enemy in force on the lower Rappahannock, but when he crossed the Potomac near Washington he discovered that the Federal army had not remained on the Rapidan but had also crossed the Potomac. It was too late to turn back in time to act as screen for the Confederates who were well over in Pennsylvania. It was more economical to cut his way through and join Lee. However, as it developed, Stuart was unable to reach Lee in time to aid in the battle of Gettysburg.

Lee always gave Stuart orders contingent upon a changing situation—for it seems hardly possible that a cavalry officer could successfully operate under any other kind in a large area. Usually Stuart's rides were successful, so much so that Lee said of Stuart, after the latter's death, that he had never failed to bring him correct information. Lee trusted only Stonewall and Stuart in obtaining accurate information. (After the death of those two men, he discovered that General Gordon possessed high qualities as a reconnaissance officer, but Lee was forced more and more to make his own investigations of enemy positions and strength.) Under the almost uniform success of Stuart when acting on such orders, it is not sound criticism to state categorically, as some critics have, that one of Lee's weaknesses as a general was the conditional orders which he gave to his generals. In a battle-field too large to be supervised personally, and where proper telegraphic communications were lacking, it would seem that common sense would demand that discretion should be given the general in command at any remote point. Such was Lee's theory, and it succeeded much more often than it failed.

The battle of Gettysburg would not have occurred at that point had Stuart been with Lee's army; nor is it probable that it would have been a drawn battle had Longstreet obeyed orders on the second of July when he was ordered to take little Round Top before the Federals had taken it in force. From this point, if the Confederates had taken it, the Federal forces could have been enfiladed with artillery at the same time that Ewell delivered an enfilading fire from Culp Hill on the Federal right. Again had Longstreet delivered his attack at daybreak of July 3, as he had been ordered, instead of waiting until afternoon when the enemy had thoroughly strengthened the center of the line, it is difficult to see how he could have failed; this is emphasized by the fact that even the charge under Pickett, which comprised only a portion of Longstreet's corps, succeeded in penetrating the Federal lines a quarter of a mile. But Longstreet deliberately disobeyed Lee and tried until the very moment of Pickett's charge to impose upon the Confederate commander his plan to turn the enemy's left flank. Lee, who had always favored flanking movements, was unwilling to make this one in absence of any knowledge of the disposition of the enemy behind the ridge; and it later proved to be a correct judgment as the enemy was in great force behind the left flank.

The disobedience of Longstreet brought no reprimand. Lee was still convinced that this general was the best corps commander he had, and history will uphold that judgment. Hill and Ewell were neither as good strategists nor as good tacticians as Longstreet, nor were they as steady under fire. Longstreet's rebellious temperament was all that stood in the way of his being a great general.

When the spring of 1864 opened, it found the Confederate army, man and beast, ragged and ill-fed. Thousands of the army horses and mules had died of starvation or were unable to draw the wagon trains and artillery. This situation almost destroyed the mobility of Lee's army until crops could be grown behind the lines to feed men and horses. Lee repeated the strategy which he had employed against Hooker the year before in the battle of Chancellorsville, and practically on the same spot, when he permitted Grant to cross both the Rappahannock and Rapidan without molestation. Grant was obviously overconfident, for he crossed the river and marched into the wilderness without sufficient flank and rear guard protection. The result was that Lee with an army of 60,000 marched into the tangled wilderness and fell upon the Federal army numbering about 120,000 men. He struck them from the rear and on the right flank, and it was Longstreet who carried out the flanking movement as Jackson had the year before at the same spot. Like Jackson, Longstreet was shot down and disabled for the rest of the campaign. The Federal loss was 17,800 men. However, the army did not retreat across the Rappahannock.

Lee was aware that Grant was a stubborn fighter. Grant's own army, too, realized it, for instead of marching back to the river he marched by the left flank at night in a swift effort to place his army between Lee's army and Richmond. Lee expected him to do this and rushed the First Corps, now commanded by Anderson, to Spottsylvania Court House while he withdrew his other troops from the battlefield to reinforce Anderson. Anderson's troops on reaching Spottsylvania ahead of Grant raised the shrill, quavering, rebel yell which passed down the line of Hill's marching corps back to Ewell's

Second Corps still in the Wilderness, and back to Anderson's, where it started back again to the Wilderness. In the dark depressing gloom just before the break of day of May 7, this weird demonstration must have awakened dark thoughts in the minds of Grant's soldiers who were marching to take their place before the entrenched position of the Confederate army. The position taken by Lee was a strongly entrenched semicircle, with a salient at the center. Grant threw his army against the Confederate breastworks and attempted flanking movements only to find a strongly entrenched force in his path, then returned to the battering of the breastworks until he had lost over 30,000 men. The battle lasted from May 8 through May 21. Yet Grant determined, as he said, "to fight it out along this line if it takes all summer," and, he might have added, "the whole Federal army." He had lost about 47,000 men in three weeks, Lee about 15,000.

Grant's next move was another attempt to slide around Lee's right flank and get in between the Confederate army and Richmond, at Hanover Junction. But again he was foiled. Lee retreated to the south bank of the North Anna and entrenched. Grant threw his left and his right wings across the river, but in the midst of this double flanking movement, Lee seized the high banks of the North Anna opposite Grant's center, and thus divided Grant's army in two. The position of Lee's army was that of an inverted V. It made it impossible for Grant to use either wing to reinforce the other. On the other hand Lee was in a position to reinforce either wing of his own army with the greatest speed. It was a unique strategic movement carried out without premeditation, but as an opportunist stroke to checkmate Grant's shortsighted manoeuvre. Grant was not too stubborn to withdraw as soon as possible under the cover of night. This was the only piece of strategy which Grant attempted during this hammer-and-tongs campaign and it was so bad that he realized that a battle fought in such a position would be more disastrous than that of Spottsylvania.

From this point Grant marched rapidly to the position around Gaines' Mill and Cold Harbor which McClellan had occupied two years before. But Lee was waiting for him behind breastworks. The Federal commander was so exasperated and maddened by Lee's swift marches and constant entrenchment that he lost his head and ordered a frontal attack. It is said that he sent in storm-troops in ranks fourteen men deep, only to have them mowed down by artillery and rifles at point-blank range. Again and again Grant ordered his troops to storm the Confederate works. It was sure death and the men pinned their names and addresses on their backs and bravely went to their certain doom. Finally the army refused to charge, very much as it had under Burnside at Fredericksburg. It was another massacre. This was on June 3, 1864, less than a month since Grant had crossed the Rapidan. He had lost 54,000 men, or nearly half of his original army. (Of course his army was being recruited rapidly so that it remained above 100,000. But the troops filling the ranks were always inferior. Negroes and mercenaries were taking the place of native sons who had not been fighting for money.) During this time Lee had lost 19,000 troops.

Grant now executed a swift change of base to the James River such as McClellan had made in 1862. He crossed to Petersburg, but found Beauregard and most of Lee's army waiting for him behind the breastworks. Another frontal attack and the famous battle of the Crater ended on July 27 the campaign which Grant had boasted would continue along this line if it took all the summer. Yet there were months in which manoeuvring and campaigning were possible. But Grant's loss had now risen to 64,000 and even he realized that further fighting was impossible for the time being.

What made further fighting such as he had been carrying on impossible was the state of mind in the North. They were denouncing Grant as a butcher and asking for his removal; besides, General Early was operating in the Valley and was soon to march up to the outworks of Washington and force Grant to send detachments from his army in front of Petersburg. According to Rhodes, Grant settled down to gloomy despair and hard drinking, while Meade carried on the siege. Public opinion in the North was such that Lincoln fully believed that the Democratic party would win, and the platform of the Democratic party demanded peace. Independence was in sight when Grant, by settling down before Petersburg in the middle of the summer, admitted defeat at the hands of Lee.

But Jefferson Davis, with his strong prejudices and often unsound judgment of men and military affairs, intervened at this time and did two things to bring down ruin upon the Confederacy. He chained Lee to the defense of Petersburg and Richmond at the very moment when Lee's army could have lived off the country and manoeuvred for position, a game in which Grant was not a good player (in fact Grant boasted that he never manoeuvred, but just fought) and one in which Lee was master. Lee had, since 1863, wanted to abandon the capital and retire to the Valley where he could operate upon the rear of any army which might invade Virginia, or upon Washington, and finally upon the rear of Sherman's army. By chaining Lee down, Davis was instrumental in rendering the army immobile. The horses were so weak by winter that it was obvious that they could not haul the artillery and wagon trains, and the men were so badly clad and fed that they were hardly capable of sustaining a long march. Lee's only chance of success, after the winter rains set in, was for Grant to repeat those suicidal frontal attacks of the Spottsylvania Court House and Cold Harbor. Grant, however, had no taste for such murderous work any more. Besides, he had without doubt been cautioned by Lincoln that the North could not stand another such performance. So Lee's confidence in Confederate success dwindled as spring approached and he considered the possibility of a withdrawal and a junction with Johnston, who had been restored to his command after Hood had practically destroyed it by his poor military judgment.

The second act of Davis which hastened and made almost certain the doom of the Confederacy was his summary dismissal of Joseph E. Johnston from the command of the Army of Tennessee. Johnston was leading Sherman as far from his base as possible with the ultimate aim of turning his flanks and cutting off his line of supplies, or of constantly fighting him from a defensive position just as Lee was fighting Grant at the same time. The dismissal of Johnston, as suggested, destroyed the Army of Tennessee and made Sherman's ravaging of Georgia and the Carolinas possible; and this war upon noncombatants disheartened the families of those who composed much of Lee's army, and contributed greatly to the desertion from the Army of Northern Virginia.

When Lee notified Davis that he would be compelled to evacuate Petersburg, the President refused to believe such a contingency possible and delayed Lee so long that the Confederate general, had there ever been a chance of withdrawal after the fall of 1864, found no avenue of escape when he marched his men out from behind the breastworks. If Lee had been able to escape even in the spring of 1865 there were strong probabilities of success. By joining his army with that of Johnston's, and picking up the scattered forces such as those of Forrest on this side of the Mississippi, and moving to the Trans-Mississippi where numerous forces under the general command of Kirby Smith were stationed, Lee could have assembled an army of 150,000 already under arms. The cavalry could have been remounted and the armies better fed in this region. It was Lee's plan to assemble the Confederate armies in this region and wear down the patience of the Northern public, which was hardly able to stand another great battle. However, Davis's stubborn unwillingness to let General Lee or any other man tell him the truth defeated his plan. The surrender of Lee's army cut the heart out of all those who were willing to fight on under his leadership, and brought the collapse of the Confederate military power and the fall of that government.

Lee after Appomattox, the president of Washington College, according to tradition, was the spiritual exemplar for the South. To the Southern people he was not only the greatest soldier but the greatest gentleman and the greatest saint of the ages. Robert E. Lee was still commander-in-chief of the South during the remainder of his life and his spirit hovered over the South after his body had decayed. His patient, uncomplaining attitude in the face of petty persecution at the hands of the federal government and the radicals of the North, who demanded his head and spread rumors of Lee's duplicity and cruelty, poured oil upon the troubled waters and restrained many a hothead who would have sprung to arms at the first sign from Lee. This was most particularly true after the Radical Republicans had gained control of the federal government and had disfranchised or debarred from public office the leaders of the South, including Lee, and had set over the Southern states governments the enfranchised slaves.

Lee's administration of Washington College was successful beyond all expectations. The endowment was increased, the student body soon ranked fourth or fifth among American universities, and the curriculum became, without doubt, the most liberal and modern. While holding on to the old classical education, Lee added departments or schools of engineering, chemistry, physics, agriculture, and horticulture. His ideas were always practical either as a soldier or as a college president and he saw clearly, and so admonished the South, that its salvation lay in hard work and most particularly hard work with the hands. The use of chemistry and of scientific agriculture in rehabilitating the neglected and eroded fields of the South was, perhaps, the uppermost thought in planning the new curriculum. His experience in the war made him more conscious than any other Southerner of the industrial deficiencies of his section. Somewhat in the spirit of Thomas Jefferson and Calhoun after the war of 1812, Lee urged the study of mechanical, mining, and civil engineering. Unlike the "New South Champions" such as Henry Grady, L. Q. C. Lamar, and Walter Hines Page, Lee always regarded agriculture as the most pleasant occupation as well as the most dignified. He would have deplored, undoubtedly, the "New South" doctrines soon to become so widely disseminated, namely that the true destiny of the South was to become a great industrial community in which agriculture played a menial role.

In war or peace, Lee proved himself a great man. Always serene, simple, and straightforward in manner, yet reserved and dignified, there is much similarity of character between George Washington and Robert Lee. Washington, though possessed of great integrity, self-control, and generosity, was lacking in the profoundly religious nature which sustained Lee in his hours of triumph and defeat. However, Lee became interested in religion only in middle life, when his children were being confirmed in the Episcopalian Church. His conduct before his confirmation had been guided by the code of a gentleman which was practically identical with Christian ethics, so that Lee's bearing was unchanged by his religious conversion.

But whether Lee was a simple soul or whether he, like Washington, was a man of many complex impulses and hidden battles always gained in the end, so that his conduct was simple and straightforward, cannot be answered categorically. Lee was a man of many human impulses not all of which were approved by his Christian code or by the code of a gentleman; yet however much wild thoughts, like crows, might fly over his head, they never found nesting place within. But Lee's few expressions about the war, to Lord Acton for instance; his reprimand of the young student who complained that he had wasted four years in the Confederate army, and to whom Lee said: *"However long you live and whatever you accomplish, you will find that the time you spent in the Confederate Army was the most profitably spent portion of your life";* and his dying words: *"Tell Hill he must come up"* and *"Strike the tents,"* indicate that he brooded over what might have been and over what might be if he had said the word.

Frank Lawrence Owsley: A Bibliography 1925-1962

EDITORIAL NOTE: This bibliography of Frank Lawrence Owsley's published work is divided into five sections: books, textbooks, articles (including miscellaneous pieces), essay-reviews, and reviews. Each section is arranged chronologically.

I. Books

1925

State Rights in the Confederacy. Chicago: University of Chicago Press, 1925. Reprinted by Peter Smith in 1961 and 1966.

1931

King Cotton Diplomacy: Foreign Relations of the Confederate States of America. Chicago: University of Chicago Press, 1931.

1949

Plain Folk of the Old South. Baton Rouge: Louisiana State University Press, 1949. Reprinted by Quadrangle Paperbacks, Chicago, 1965.

1959

King Cotton Diplomacy: Foreign Relations of the Confederate States of America. Revised by Harriet Chappell Owsley. With a Memorial Foreword by William C. Binkley. Chicago: University of Chicago Press, 1959. Reprinted by the American History Book Club as the book-of-the-month in 1959.

II. Textbooks

1945

A Short History of the American People. Vol. I. New York and Princeton: D. Van Nostrand Company, Inc. (With Oliver Perry Chitwood, co-author.) First published, May 1945 (twelve reprintings); second edition, January 1955 (two reprintings); third edition, June 1962. (With Oliver Perry Chitwood and Rembert Patrick).

1948

A Short History of the American People. Vol. II. New York and Princeton, New Jersey: D. Van Nostrand Company, Inc. (With Oliver Perry Chitwood and H. C. Nixon, co-authors.) First published, January 1948 (four reprintings); second edition, July 1952 (three reprintings); third edition, August 1962. (With Oliver Perry Chitwood, H. C. Nixon, and Rembert Patrick, co-authors.)

1949

The United States From Colony to World Power. New York and Princeton: D. Van Nostrand Company, Inc. (With Oliver Perry Chitwood and H. C. Nixon, co-authors.) First published, August 1949 (four reprintings); second edition, January 1954.

1957

Know Alabama: An Elementary History, 1890–1956. Birmingham: Colonial Press, 1957. (With John Craig Stewart and Gordon Thomas Chappell, co-authors.) Revised by Frances Roberts and Viola Ayer, and reprinted by the Colonial Press in 1961.

III. Articles

1925

"Local Defense and the Downfall of the Confederacy," *Mississippi Valley Historical Review,* XI (March 1925), 492–525.

1926

"Defeatism in the Confederacy," *North Carolina Historical Review,* III (July 1926), 446–456.

1928

"Joseph Anderson," *Dictionary of American Biography,* I, 267–268.

1929

"The Confederacy and King Cotton: A Study in Economic Coercion," *North Carolina Historical Review,* VI (October 1929), 371–397.
"Aaron Venable Brown," *Dictionary of American Biography,* III, 98–99.

1930

"The Irrepressible Conflict," *I'll Take My Stand.* New York: Harper & Brothers, 1930, pp. 61–91; (reprinted in paperback as a Harper Torchbook in The Academy Library, 1962, with an Introduction by Louis D. Rubin, Jr., and Biographical Essays by Virginia Rock). Reprinted in *The Causes of the American Civil War,* ed. Edwin C. Rozwenc. Boston: D. C. Heath and Company, 1961, pp. 119–133.

1932

"William Selby Harney," *Dictionary of American Biography,* VIII, 280–281.
"Isham Green Harris," *Dictionary of American Biography,* VIII, 310–311.
"John Larue Helm," *Dictionary of American Biography,* VIII, 513–514.
"Leonidas Campbell Houk," *Dictionary of American Biography,* IX, 256–257.

1933

"Scottsboro, the Third Crusade: The Sequel to Abolition and Reconstruction," *American Review*, I (Summer 1933), 257–285.
"James Murray Mason," *Dictionary of American Biography*, XII, 364–365.
"Ambrose Dudley Mann," *Dictionary of American Biography*, XII, 239–240.

1935

"America and the Freedom of the Seas," *Essays in Honor of William E. Dodd*, ed. Avery Craven. Chicago: University of Chicago Press, 1935, pp. 194–256.
"The Pillars of Agrarianism," *American Review*, IV (March 1935), 529–547.

1936

"Foundations of Democracy," *Southern Review*, o.s., I (Spring 1936), 708–720. Also published in *Who Owns America? A Declaration of Independence.* Boston: Houghton-Mifflin, 1936, pp. 52–67.
"James Williams," *Dictionary of American Biography*, XX, 267.

1938

"The Third Annual Meeting of the Southern Historical Association," *Journal of Southern History*, IV (February 1938), 55–67.
Foreword, *Secession and Restoration of Louisiana* by Willie Malvin Caskey. University, Louisiana: Louisiana State University Press, 1938, pp. xi-xii.

1939

Foreword, *Joseph E. Brown and the Confederacy* by Louise Biles Hill, Chapel Hill: University of North Carolina Press, 1939, pp. vii-viii.

1940

"The Economic Basis of Society in the Late Ante-Bellum South," *Journal of Southern History*, VI (February 1940), 24–25. (With Harriet C. Owsley, co-author). Reprinted in the Bobbs-Merrill Reprint Series in History [1964].

1941

"The Fundamental Cause of the Civil War: Egocentric Sectionalism," *Journal of Southern History*, VII (February 1941), 3–18. Reprinted in *Vanderbilt Miscellany*, Nashville: Vanderbilt University Press, 1944, pp. 232–247; *The Literature of the South*, ed. R. C. Beatty *et al.* (Chicago: Scott, Foresman and Company, 1952), pp. 659–668, and in the revised edition (1968), pp. 645–654; *The Pursuit of Southern History*, ed. G. B. Tindall (Baton Rouge: Louisiana State University Press, 1964), pp. 77–89, and in the Bobbs-Merrill Reprint Series in History [1964].
Foreword, *The Tennessee Yeomen*, 1840–1860 by Blanche Henry Clark. Nashville: Vanderbilt University Press, 1942.

1942

"The Economic Structure of Rural Tennessee, 1850–1860," *Journal of Southern History*, VIII (May 1942), 161–182. (With Harriet C. Owsley, co-author.)

1945

"The Pattern of Migration and Settlement on the Southern Frontier," *Journal of Southern History*, XI (May 1945), 147–176. Reprinted in the Bobbs-Merrill Reprint Series in History [1964].

Foreword, *Mississippi Farmers, 1850–1860* by Herbert Weaver. Nashville: Vanderbilt University Press, 1945, pp. 11–12.

1949

"The Clays in Early Alabama History," *Alabama Review*, II (October 1949), 243–268.

1952

"The Agrarians Today," *Shenandoah*, III (Summer 1952), 22–28.

1953–1954

"The Education of a Southern Frontier Girl," *Alabama Review*, VI (October 1953), 268–288; VII (January 1954), 66–73.

"The Writing of Local History, *Alabama Review*, VII (April 1954), 113–126.

1956

"John Williams Walker," *Alabama Review*, IX (April 1956), 100–119.

1957

Foreword, *Slavery in Tennessee* by Chase C. Mooney. Bloomington: Indiana State University, 1957, pp. vii–viii.

1958

"A Southerner's View of Abraham Lincoln," *Georgia Review*, XII (Spring 1958), 5–17.

1961

"Democracy Unlimited," *Georgia Review*, XV (Summer 1961), 129–143.

IV. Essay–Reviews

1932

"Two Agrarian Philosophers: Jefferson and DuPont de Nemours" (*The Correspondence of Jefferson and DuPont de Nemours* by Gilbert Chinard, *Correspondence Between Thomas Jefferson and Pierre Samuel DuPont de Nemours,* ed. Dumas Malone, and *The Educational Work of Thomas Jefferson* by Roy J. Honeywell), *Hound and Horn,* VI (October-December 1932), 166–172.

1933

"The Making of Andrew Jackson" (*Andrew Jackson* by Marquis James), *American Review,* I (May 1933), 220–225.

1934

"The War of the Sections" (*The Secession of the Southern States* by Gerald Johnson and *The Irrepressible Conflict* by Arthur Charles Cole), *Virginia Quarterly Review,* X (October 1934), 630–635.

1935

"The American Triangle" (*America's Tragedy* by James Truslow Adams and *The Eve of Conflict: Stephen A. Douglas and the Needless War* by George Fort Milton), *Virginia Quarterly Review,* XI (January 1935), 113–119.

"The Soldier Who Walked with God" (*R. E. Lee* by Douglas Southwell Freeman, 4 vols.), *American Review,* IV, (February 1935), 435–459, and V (April 1935), 62–74.

"Slavery and the Struggle of the Sections" (*America's Tragedy* by James Truslow Adams), *Yale Review,* XXIV (Spring 1935), 643–644.

"Abolition and Secession" (*The Antislavery Impulse, 1830–1844* by Gilbert Hobbs Barnes and *The Secession Movement in Virginia* by Henry T. Shanks), *Virginia Quarterly Review,* XI (Summer 1935), 461–466.

"The Historical Philosophy of Frederick Jackson Turner" (*The United States, 1830–1850* by Frederick Jackson Turner), *American Review,* V (Summer 1935), 368–375.

"Lucius Quintus Cincinnatus Lamar" (*Lucius Q. C. Lamar* by Wirt Armistead Cate), *American Review,* V (September 1935), 502–512.

1936

"A Rebel War Clerk and His Diary" (*A Rebel War Clerk's Diary at the Confederate States Capital* by J. B. Jones, ed. Howard Swiggett, 2 vols.), *Southern Review,* o. s., I (Winter 1936), 680–685.

"The Old South and the New" (*The South Looks at Its Past* by Ben B. Kendrick and A. M. Arnett), *American Review,* VI (February 1936), 475–485.

1937

"A Key to Southern Liberalism" (*It's a Far Cry* by Robert W. Winston), *Southern Review*, o. s., III (Summer 1937), 28–38.

"Reconciliation and Reunion" (*The Road to Reunion 1865–1900* by Paul H. Buck), *Yale Review*, XXVII (Autumn 1937), 171–173.

1938

"Paths of Glory" (*Andrew Jackson: Portrait of a President* by Marquis James, *Henry Clay: Spokesman of the New West* by Bernard Mayo, *The Life of Henry Clay* by Glyndon G. Van Deusen, *Winfield Scott: The Soldier and the Man* by Charles Winslow Elliott, *Old Fuss and Feathers: The Life and Exploits of Winfield Scott* by Arthur D. Howden Smith, *Jefferson Davis* by Robert McElroy, and *The American Civil War* by Carl Russell Fish, ed. William Ernest Smith), *Virginia Quarterly Review*, XIV (Winter 1938), 136–144.

"Jefferson Davis" (*Jefferson Davis* by Robert McElroy, 2 vols.), *Southern Review*, o.s., III (Spring 1938), 762–768.

1939

"Mr. Daniels Discovers the South" (*A Southerner Discovers the South* by Jonathan Daniels), *Southern Review*, o.s., IV (Spring 1939), 665–675.

1940

"Origins of the American Civil War" (*The Antislavery Origins of the Civil War in the United States* by Dwight Lowell Dumond), *Southern Review*, o.s., V (Spring 1940), 609–626.

"History of the Old South" (*The South to Posterity* by Douglas Southall Freeman and *Freedom of Thought in the Old South* by Clement Eaton), *Yale Review*, XXIX (Summer 1940), 849–853.

1941

"Confederate Justice" (*Justice in Grey, A History of the Judicial System of the Confederate States of America* by William M. Robinson, Jr.), *Virginia Quarterly Review*, XVII (Autumn 1941), 630–632.

1943

"Civil War on Two Fronts" (*Lee's Lieutenants: A Study in Command, Manassas to Malvern Hill* by Douglas Southall Freeman and *The Hidden Civil War: The Story of the Copperheads* by Wood Gray), *Virginia Quarterly Review*, XIX (Winter 1943), 124–129.

"The Anatomy of Military Command" (*Lee's Lieutenants: Cedar Mountain to Chancellorsville* by Douglas Southall Freeman), *Virginia Quarterly Review*, XIX (Summer 1943), 436–439.

1945

"A House Divided" (*Divided We Stand: The Crisis of a Frontierless Democracy* by Walter Prescott Webb, rev. ed.), *Sewanee Review*, LIII (Summer 1945), 500–503.

1946

"President Lincoln" (*Lincoln, The President* by J. G. Randall, 2 vols.), *Virginia Quarterly Review*, XXII (Spring 1946), 300–304.

1947

"Fear May Come Too Late" (*The Shore Dimly Seen* by Ellis Gibbs Arnall), *Sewanee Review*, LV (Summer 1947), 514–517.

1948

"Prelude to Conflict" (*The Ordeal of the Union* by Allan Nevins, 2 vols.), *Virginia Quarterly Review*, XXIV (Spring 1948), 297–300.
"The Everlasting South" (*The Dixie Frontier* by Everett Dick and *The South Old and New* by Francis Butler Simpkins), *Sewanee Review*, LVI (Autumn 1948), 716–720.

1950

"The Life and Death of the Confederacy" (*A Diary From Dixie* by Mary Boykin Chesnut, ed. Ben Ames Williams), *Virginia Quarterly Review*, XXVI (Spring 1950), 280–284.

V. Reviews

1924

David Wilmot: Free Soiler by Charles Buxton Going, *Nashville Tennessean*, November 30, 1924.

1925

Reconstruction in Arkansas, 1862–1874 by Thomas S. Staples, *Mississippi Valley Historical Review*, XI (March 1925), 591–593.
Czecho-Slovakia by Josef Gruber, *Nashville Tennessean*, July 26, 1925.

1926

A Short History of the American People by Robert Granville Caldwell, *Nashville Tennessean*, January 3, 1926.
The Life of Thomas Jefferson by Francis W. Hirst, *Nashville Tennessean*, March 21, 1926.

Six Years With the Texas Rangers, 1875 to 1881 by James B. Gillett, ed. M. M. Quaife, *Mississippi Valley Historical Review,* XII (March 1926), 608–610.

1927
George Rogers Clark: His Life and Public Services by Temple Bodley, *Nashville Tennessean,* March 27, 1927.
The Memoirs of Lieutenant Henry Timberlake, 1756–1765, ed. Samuel Cole Williams, *Nashville Tennessean,* May 8, 1927.

1928
Simon Girty: The White Savage by Thomas Boyd, *Nashville Tennessean,* October 21, 1928.

1929
Jefferson Davis: His Rise and Fall by Allen Tate, *Nashville Tennessean,* October 20, 1929.

1930
The War of Independence by Claud H. Van Tyne, *Nashville Tennessean,* January 26, 1930.
Jefferson Davis: His Rise and Fall by Allen Tate, *Mississippi Valley Historical Review,* XVI (March 1930), 570–572.
Beginnings of West Tennessee in the Land of the Chickasaws, 1541–1841 by Samuel Cole Williams, *Mississippi Valley Historical Review,* XVII (September 1930), 320–322.

1935
Lee: West Point and Lexington by Walter Creigh Preston, *Journal of Southern History,* I (May 1935), 237–239.
Wilsonian Diplomacy: The Versailles Peace and French Public Opinion by Bernard Noble, *Nashville Banner,* June 2, 1935.
A Rebel War Clerk's Diary at the Confederate States Capital by J. B. Jones, ed. Howard Swiggett, *Journal of Southern History,* I (August 1935), 402–404.
Government in Business by Stuart Chase, *Nashville Banner,* September 29, 1935.
War Memoirs of Robert Lansing, Nashville Banner, October 6, 1935.

1936
The Living Jefferson by James Truslow Adams, *Nashville Banner,* April 26, 1936.
Jefferson in Power by Claude G. Bowers, *Nashville Banner,* September 6, 1936.

The Aaron Burr Conspiracy by Walter Flavius McCaleb, *Nashville Banner,* November 29, 1936.
Mainland by Gilbert Seldes, *Nashville Banner,* December 13, 1936.

1937

French Opinion on the United States and Mexico, 1860–1867: Extracts from the Reports of the Procureurs Generaux, ed. Lynn M. Case, *American Historical Review,* XLII (April 1937), 566–568.
Andrew Jackson: Portrait of a President by Marquis James, *Nashville Banner,* October 3, 1937.
William G. Brownlow, Fighting Parson of the Southern Highlands by E. Merton Coulter, *Mississippi Valley Historical Review,* XXIV (December 1937), 403–405.

1938

The Confederate Ironclad "Virginia" ("Merrimac") by Harrison A. Trexler, *Journal of Southern History,* IV (August 1938), 401–402.
Two Soldiers: The Campaign Diaries of Thomas J. Key, C.S.A., December 7, 1863–May 17, 1865, and Robert J. Campbell, U.S.A., January 1, 1864–July 21, 1864, ed. Wirt Armistead Cate, *Nashville Banner,* March 19, 1938, and *Journal of Southern History,* IV (August 1938), 394–396.
Tom Watson, Agrarian Rebel by C. Vann Woodward, *Mississippi Valley Historical Review,* XXV (December 1938), 431–432.

1939

Letters of James Gillespie Birney, 1831–1857, ed. Dwight L. Dumond, *Journal of Southern History,* V (May 1939), 263–264.

1940

Origins of Class Struggle in Louisiana: A Social History of White Farmers and Laborers During Slavery and After, 1840–1875 by Roger W. Shugg, *Journal of Southern History,* VI (February 1940), 116–117.
The Southern Poor-White from Lubberland to Tobacco Road by Shields McIlwaine, *Mississippi Valley Historical Review,* XXVI (March 1940), 616–617.
Freedom of Thought in the Old South by Clement Eaton, *Journal of Southern History,* VI (November 1940), 558–559.

1941

Sectionalism and Internal Improvements in Tennessee, 1796–1845 by Stanley John Folmsbee, *American Historical Review,* XLVI (January 1941), 425–426.

1942

The Army of Tennessee: A Military History by Stanley F. Horn, *Tennessee*

Historical Quarterly, I (June 1942), 181–183.
Everyday Things in American Life by William C. Langdon, *Mississippi Valley Historical Review,* XXIX (September 1942), 276–278.

1943

A Decade of Sectional Controversy, 1851–1861, by Henry H. Simms, *Journal of Southern History,* IX (February 1943), 119–120.
The Arkansas Plantation, 1920–1942 by Donald Crichton Alexander, *Mississippi Valley Historical Review,* XXX (December 1943), 466.
Gideon Welles, Lincoln's Navy Department by Richard S. West, Jr., *Nashville Tennessean,* October 31, 1943.

1944

The Soul of a Nation: The Founding of Virginia and the Projection of New England by Matthew P. Andrews, *Journal of Southern History,* X (February 1944), 95–96.
Judah P. Benjamin, Confederate Statesman by Robert Douthat Meade, *American Historical Review,* XLIX (April 1944), 506–507.

1946

War Years With Jeb Stuart by William W. Blackford, *Journal of Southern History,* XII (May 1946), 285–286.

1947

An Introduction to the Papers of the New York Prize Court, 1861–1865 by Madeline Russell Robinton, *American Historical Review,* LII (April 1947), 524–525.

1948

The Dixie Frontier: A Social History of the Southern Frontier from the First Transmontane Beginnings to the Civil War by Everett Dick, *Journal of Southern History,* XIV (August 1948), 413–415.

1949

The Development of Southern Sectionalism, 1819–1848 by Charles S. Sydnor, *Journal of Southern History,* XV (February 1949), 108–110.

1950

Mobile: History of a Seaport Town by Charles G. Summersell, *Alabama Review,* III (January 1950), 77–78.
The Journal of Benjamin Moran, 1857–1865, ed. Sarah Agnes Wallace and Frances Emma Gillespie, *Journal of Southern History,* XVI (May 1950), 236–238.

A Diary from Dixie by Mary Boykin Chesnut, ed. Ben Ames Williams, *Alabama Review*, III (July 1950), 234–236.

Andrew Stevenson, Democrat and Diplomat, 1785–1857 by Frances Fry Wayland, *American Historical Review*, LVI (October 1950), 133–134.

1951

The Gallant Hood by John Percy Dyer, *Alabama Review*, IV (April 1951), 152–154.

Confederate Leaders in the New South by William B. Hesseltine, *Alabama Review*, IV (April 1951), 150–152.

The Blue and the Gray: The Story of the Civil War as Told by Participants, ed. Henry Steele Commager, *Journal of Southern History*, XVIII (November 1951), 559–561.

1952

Ploughshares Into Swords by Frank E. Vandiver, *Alabama Review*, V (October 1952), 291–293.

A Two-Party South? by Alexander Heard, *Mississippi Valley Historical Review*, XXXIX (December 1952), 587–588.

1953

The Texas Revolution by William C. Binkley, *Tennessee Historical Quarterly*, XII (June 1953), 185–186.

Atlantic Impact, 1861 by Evan John, *Journal of Southern History*, XIX (November 1953), 540–541.

1954

Confederate Georgia by T. Conn Bryan, *Mississippi Valley Historical Review*, XL (March 1954), 741–742.

The Growth of Southern Nationalism 1818–1861 by Avery O. Craven, *Annals of American Political Science*, XCI (January 1954), 165–166.

1957

Auburn: Loveliest Village of the Plain by Mollie Hollifield, *Alabama Review*, X (April 1957), 155–156.

Index

Abolitionists: attack of, 62, 213

Acton, Lord: on Lee, 257

Adams, Charles Francis, 220; on wheat famine, 113; black list of, 135, 137, 153, 157–160; on seizures, 145, 146; on British crews, 166, 167

Adams, Henry: on Lamar, 213

Adams, John, 212; on natural rights, 191

Adams, Samuel: on natural rights, 191

Adela: case of, 154, 160

Agrarianism: opinions on, 177; definition of, 178; five pillars of, 188, 189

Agrarian program: for farming population, 180–184; for South, 186; regional governments, 186–188

Agricultural population: migration of, 4, 5, 6, 15, 16–19; migration pattern of, 18–24; herdsmen forced west by, 6, 7. *See also* Farm population

Alabama: livestock grazing in, 6, 11, 12; piney woods in, 11, 12; factors in immigration to, 20; family groups settle in, 22–24; secession vote in, 42; cost of education in, 46; arms held by, 65, 66; state troops retained by, 72; conscription in, 75, 84; opposition to secession in, 98; disloyalty in, 102, 104; Jay treaty proposals for, 196

Alabama, Confederate cruiser, 119, 126, 146, 152

Alliance, British steamer: crew held prisoners, 166

American merchant marine: destruction of, 118, 119

American navy: size of, 127

American Review, 177

Anderson, Richard Heron, C.S.A. general, 252, 253

Archer, Hugh, C.S.A. general: on Florida troops, 85

Arizona: Indian tribes in, 64

Arkansas: livestock grazing in, 6; emigrants seek familiar lands in, 15; arms held by, 65, 68; state troops retained by, 72; opposition to secession by, 98; troops sent out of, 100; peace societies in, 102; reaction of, 224

Army of Northern Virginia: Lee in command, 238, 239; desertion in, 255

Army of Tennessee, destruction of, 255

Arnold, R. Arthur: on cotton profits, 114, 115

Articles of Confederation: weakness of, 59

Austria: Napoleon's fear of, 109

Bagley, governor of Bahamas: on unneutral use of ports, 143

Baltimore, Maryland: market for livestock, 38, 39

Banks, Nathaniel Prentiss, Union general, 240

Banshee, British steamer: crew held prisoners, 165, 166

Baracouta, H.M.S., 134, 135

Barnard, E.H.: on blockade of neutral ports, 136

Beauregard, Pierre Gustave Toutant, C.S.A. general, 213, 220, 221, 239, 254

Begbie, T.S., shipowner, 162

Benjamin, Judah Philip, C.S.A. secretary of war and state: on Confederate arms, 67, 68, 70; on volunteers for army, 71; on local